D0978988

MANAGING
Government
Employees

MANAGING

Government

Employees

How to Motivate Your People,
Deal with Difficult Issues, and
Achieve Tangible Results

Stewart Liff

AMACOM

American Management Association

New York • Brussels • Chicago • Mexico City • San Francisco
Shanghai • Tokyo • Washington, D.C.

Special discounts on bulk quantities of AMACOM books are
available to corporations, professional associations, and other
organizations. For details, contact Special Sales Department,
AMACOM, a division of American Management Association,
1601 Broadway, New York, NY 10019.
Tel.: 212-903-8316. Fax: 212-903-8083.
E-mail: specialsls@amanet.org
Website: www.amacombooks.org/go/specialsales
To view all AMACOM titles go to: www.amacombooks.org

This publication is designed to provide accurate and authoritative
information in regard to the subject matter covered. It is sold with
the understanding that the publisher is not engaged in rendering
legal, accounting, or other professional service. If legal advice or other
expert assistance is required, the services of a competent professional
person should be sought.

Library of Congress Cataloging-in-Publication Data

Liff, Stewart.
        Managing government employees : how to motivate your people, deal with
    difficult issues, and achieve tangible results / Stewart Liff.
            p.   cm.
        Includes index.
        ISBN-13: 978-0-8144-0887-2
        ISBN-10: 0-8144-0887-7
        1. Civil service—Personnel management.   I. Title.

JF1601.M29   2007
352.6'8—dc22

                                                                    2006035489

© 2007 Stewart Liff.
All rights reserved.
Printed in the United States of America.

This publication may not be reproduced,
stored in a retrieval system,
or transmitted in whole or in part,
in any form or by any means, electronic,
mechanical, photocopying, recording, or otherwise,
without the prior written permission of AMACOM,
a division of American Management Association,
1601 Broadway, New York, NY 10019.

Printing number

10   9

*This book is dedicated to my wife, Pat,
the bravest person I know.*

—Stewart Liff

Contents

Contents

Acknowledgments

This book was written under unusually difficult circumstances and would not have been completed without the love and support of a wide variety of people.

First of all, I would like to thank my editor, Adrienne Hickey, for her knowledge, encouragement, flexibility, and commitment to this project. She has been a tremendous help to me. Also, I would like to thank both Barry Richardson and Jim Bessent from AMACOM for their able assistance. They certainly made my job easier. Lastly, I would like to thank Pamela A. Posey, D.B.A., for her continued guidance and perspective. Pam, you have taught me more than you could possibly know.

I've had many excellent mentors in the field of human resources management, including Herman Greenspan, Dan Bisgrove, Dan Kowalski, John Coghlan, and Barry Jackson. Thank you all for sharing your knowledge and experience with me.

I've also been lucky to have many terrific mentors, both inside and outside of government, who have influenced my thinking with respect to managing people. Within government, I would like to thank Tom Lastowka, Rick Nappi, and Joe Thompson. Outside the government, I would like to thank Paul Gustavson, Bill Snyder, Alan Checketts, and Paul Draper. Each and every one of you has made me a better leader and a better person.

As I mentioned earlier, this book was difficult to write because both my wife and I were ill during the time I was writing this book. Fortunately, during our ordeal we have learned about the generosity of the human spirit and how many people truly care about us. While I cannot possibly mention everyone who has helped us, I would like to acknowledge my parents, Pearl and Hal Liff; my mother-in-law, Jaffa Schlusselberg; my children, Rob, Jen, and Marc; my brothers, Jeff and

Mike; my uncle Jerry Goldman; and my cousins Ricki, Lori, Harold, and Lenore. I love you all dearly and appreciate your support and inspiration.

I also want to thank the hundreds of friends who contacted us during the past year to lend us support. Believe me, we have soaked up your positive energy and are deeply appreciative of your friendship and concern.

MANAGING
Government
Employees

CHAPTER 1

Overview

Introduction

I came to work for the federal government in the summer of 1974. I did not want to work there, but it felt as though I had nowhere else to turn. I had graduated from college with a degree in fine arts and quickly learned that there was little demand for someone with my limited business skills.

Prior to entering government service, I floated among a variety of unsatisfying jobs, ranging from a private investigator to a taxi driver to a stereo salesman. Finally, at the urging of my wife, I took several civil service exams and eventually secured a civilian job with the United States Army as a personnel intern.

I kept looking for better jobs in the private sector, but my education and background always seemed to get in the way. Over time, I began to see the benefits of working for the government, as I enjoyed the mission, career opportunities, pay, job security, and other benefits. Eventually, I decided to make it a career.

During my 32-year career, I worked for a number of different agencies, including the Department of Defense, the General Services Administration, the Federal Energy Administration, the Veterans Health Administration, and the Veterans Benefits Administration. I also worked in multiple locations, including Brooklyn, Manhattan, and the Bronx, New York, as well as Roanoke, Virginia, Los Angeles, California, Washington, D.C., and Atlanta, Georgia.

I spent my entire government career working in human resources and/or management. Three of these years were devoted to representing the government before third parties on such diverse issues as removals, grievances, discrimination complaints, and unfair labor practice (ULP) charges. I've worked both in the field and in headquarters, and in a staff and a line management capacity. During my last 12 years, I served as a senior executive.

I've been fortunate enough to receive numerous awards, ranging from the Presidential Rank Award for Meritorious Service to the President's Council on Management Improvement Award. More importantly, I've had the opportunity to work with and learn from a wide variety of first-rate people, both within and outside of government. I've also been lucky enough to spend half my life serving my heroes—America's veterans.

As a fine artist by nature and by training, I tend to see the world a bit less rigidly than most government employees. I learned early on that while the government has many rules, regulations, and procedures, they are generally there both to provide a governing framework and to avoid the abuses of the past. These rules can and should be interpreted and applied flexibly, so we can carry out the mission of government while managing and treating our employees in a fair and equitable manner.

There is no doubt that working for the government is different from working for the private sector. Although they both have their challenges, the government's challenges are clearly exacerbated by the systems that are in place for hiring and managing its people. That being said, it is my firm belief that once you understand how and why things work the way they do in government, and recognize all of the forces that are at play, you will begin to see that you do not have to choose the status quo and follow a course of inaction. This book will teach you that if you have the right mindset and skill sets, you can successfully manage the government's employees and accomplish great things.

In order to understand this even more clearly, I am providing a series of Examples and Cases in Point. The Examples are general scenarios, and the Cases in Point are situations in which I was personally involved or of which I had direct knowledge.

Let's explore the key issues in more detail so we can learn how to better address the enormous challenges that face government managers.

What Is Different About Working for the Government?

There are many reasons why working for the government is different from working for the private sector. We will take a detailed look at seven of these reasons:

1. The private sector is in business to make a profit, while government exists to serve and protect its citizens.

2. Government organizations are typically run at the highest levels by elected officials, meaning the agenda and direction of the organization are subject to change every few years.

3. Government organizations, especially at the federal level, are generally larger than most private companies and, as such, require a higher degree of bureaucracy, rules, and regulations.

4. Government organizations typically receive more scrutiny than the private sector because of oversight by Congress, the Inspector General, the media, consumer advocates, and others, which means that the organization will probably move more slowly and be less innovative than the private sector.

5. Government employees are often paid at a different rate from their counterparts in the private sector.

6. Government employees usually have better job security than private-sector employees because they have more legal protections and do not have to worry about their organization being taken over by another company.

7. In the federal government and in most state and local governments, employees do not have the right to strike.

For all of the reasons stated above, working for the government is clearly different from working in the private sector. Let's look at each reason in more detail and see how it affects government employment.

The Private Sector Is in Business to Make a Profit

Companies are in business to make money. Everyone knows that if a company does not make a profit, it will eventually go out of business. That is why organizations are always competing for the largest possible share of their market—the larger the market share, the greater their profit. The employees all know that a sudden change in the organization's financial situation can result in many people losing their jobs. They also know that a new product can greatly alter the market, so innovation is highly valued in the private sector.

This ongoing pressure to survive typically creates a sense of urgency that does not exist to the same extent in government. In a sense, working for the private sector can be riskier and sometimes more exciting than working for the government.

By the same token, while government employees do not have to focus on making a profit, they have incredible opportunities to make a difference in the lives of this country's citizens. Government employees are charged with protecting America from its enemies, taking care of its veterans, providing social security payments to the elderly and infirmed, administering its immigration program, collecting taxes, and protecting the environment, among other things. Government employees also educate our children, police our streets, fight fires, and collect our garbage. Perhaps the best thing about working for the government is the ability to have an impact on the lives of our fellow Americans.

Thus, the first and most pronounced difference between working for the government and for the private sector is the very nature of their missions. The missions themselves drive the way people think and act within these two very different environments.

Government Organizations Are Run by Elected Officials

Transfer of power at the federal, state, and local levels is part of the American system of government. Elections are held every few years, which often triggers a dramatic change in the leadership, philosophy, and approach within a particular government entity. While private-sector companies also experience leadership changes, such changes are not as predictably cyclical as they are in government. This means that government employees, particularly the supervisors, need to be prepared for constant ongoing change, and in many cases a 180-degree change when one political party takes over from another. While private-sector employees also have to deal with frequent change, such change is driven more by the profit margin, whereas in government, change is driven more by ideology.

Some Political Generalizations. In my experience, when Republicans take over, they tend to focus more on business-oriented issues such as productivity, efficiency, oversight, accountability, and consolidation. They seem to be less interested in working with unions and less concerned about employee issues. They generally look to shrink the size of government by transferring work to the private sector. At the federal level, they normally try to increase the percentage of the government's budget that will be devoted to national defense.

Conversely, Democrats seem to be less focused on applying bottom-line business principles and more focused on service delivery, emphasizing areas like customer and employee satisfaction. They look to partner with government unions and tend to focus on employee concerns. They may also look to allocate a greater portion of the budget to social issues such as health care, welfare, or the environment.

Government Organizations Generally Require a Higher Degree of Bureaucracy

The federal government employs almost 2 million people. while state; city, and county governments employ millions more. Although some corporations are very large and also have a fair amount of bureaucracy, most companies are much smaller than the government. Moreover, they are usually not covered by the overwhelming number of laws, rules, regulations, and labor agreements that government organizations are, meaning they have more flexibility and more room to maneuver when dealing with their employees.

To put this in perspective, according to Vice President Al Gore, the reinventing government initiative ". . . forced agencies to cut 16,000 pages of needless regulation, and 640,000 pages of internal rules . . . those rules and regulations make government services slower and more expensive."[1] Despite his efforts, imagine how many pages still remain in the federal government!

Private-sector companies have much more leeway than their government counterparts when it comes to hiring, promoting, and rewarding their employees. Although they cannot discriminate against anyone based on race, creed, or national origin, it is much easier for them to hire the person of their choice because they do not have to deal with the multitude of rules and regulations that the government faces.

Veterans' Preferences. Most government organizations are required to give veterans' preference to prospective applicants. This means that a veteran may get as many as five or ten extra points when being rated and ranked for a government job. Moreover, in many cases, government organizations are precluded from passing over a veteran in order to select a nonveteran. The rationale for this is that veterans have made an enormous sacrifice for our country and therefore deserve priority when competing for government jobs. While few people would argue with this rationale, the principle of veterans' preference does limit a government selecting official's options when trying to select the best possible candidate for a government job.

Rule of Three. In the federal government, selecting officials not only have to apply veterans' preference; they also have to follow "the rule of three." This rule means that when they hire someone from outside government, selecting officials have to choose one of the three highest-ranked candidates. Although that seems to make sense at first blush, the rule of three often constrains government officials from selecting a far better candidate who may be ranked lower on paper.

Government Organizations Typically Receive More Scrutiny

Pick up any newspaper and you will find that it contains many articles about the government. Most of these articles seem to be negative, since exposés about the government always sell more newspapers than stories detailing how well the government is operating. These articles invariably cover mismanagement, inefficiencies, and sometimes outright fraud.

The government is an easy target because of its size and scope, and because almost everyone is a taxpayer and expects to get a good bang for their buck. Moreover, the Freedom of Information Act[2] ensures that there is more access to information about the government than ever before, which invites even more scrutiny.

Government managers also have both Congress and their organization's Office of the Inspector General (IG) looking over their shoulders on a regular basis. Beyond this, government unions are always there to hold management accountable for any actions that they deem to be unfair or inappropriate. Lastly, employees are frequently encouraged to report incidents of fraud, waste, abuse, or corruption.

With all of these forces in play, it is difficult for government managers to take action that might be controversial without expecting a strong reaction from one or more of the above players. On top of this, the political leaders of their organizations are carefully watching how things play out, and they often reverse course when it is the politically expedient thing to do. Is it any wonder that it is so difficult to get things done in government?

For example, due to local media attention in Illinois and at the behest of certain congressmen, the United States Department of Veterans Affairs (VA) IG reviewed a large number of decisions that were made by VA in response to claims for benefits that were filed by veterans in that state. The review commenced because records indicated that veterans in Illinois were receiving a disproportionately low amount of benefits when compared to veterans in other states.

As the review advanced, the IG decided to look at how claims were decided across the country. Eventually, it concluded that while veterans may have been underpaid in Illinois and a few other states, other veterans across the country were probably overpaid for certain types of conditions at an enormous cost to the taxpayer.

In response, VA officials decided to take an even-handed approach to these findings by (1) reaching out to veterans in the states where payments appeared to be low and inviting them to file new claims for benefits; and (2) reviewing the claims decisions of veterans who were receiving benefits in those categories that the IG deemed were highly questionable.

Veterans' service organizations and advocates vigorously protested VA's decision to review decisions that could result in reducing the benefits of certain veterans. From their perspective, the government was trying to reduce the federal deficit on the backs of veterans. The media also chastised VA for this decision in a series of local and national newspaper articles. Eventually, all of the scrutiny and pressure forced VA to cancel its review of the decisions that may have resulted in too many benefits, even though its intent was to make sure veterans were receiving only the benefits that they are entitled to by law. Conversely, VA did contact the veterans who may have been underpaid, and invited them to file new claims for benefits.

Government Employees Are Often Paid at a Different Rate

According to the Congressional Budget Office (CBO),

> [There is a] wide variation in federal/private sector pay differences by occupation. For example, federal employees in selected professional and administrative occupations tended to hold jobs that paid less than comparable jobs in private sector firms . . . For about 85% of those federal employees, their pay lagged behind private sector employees by more than 20%. By contrast, about 30% of federal employees in selected technical and clerical occupations held jobs with salaries above those paid by private sector firms . . . In general, jobs in technical and clerical occupations showed much smaller differences in pay between federal and private sector workers.[3]

The challenge of paying federal employees is greatly exacerbated by the fact that geographic differences around the country result in many federal employees being greatly underpaid in high-cost areas such as New York, Los Angeles, and Washington, D.C. The Federal Employees Pay Comparability Act of 1990 (FEPCA) was intended to address this situation by providing for "locality" pay raises based on comparisons between federal and nonfederal salaries in local areas. However, the federal government never implemented the full raises required by the FEPCA because of the cost involved and because of questions regarding the methodology used to calculate the pay comparisons.

To be fair, the FEPCA focuses only on pay and not on benefits. In an earlier report on the federal personnel system, the CBO determined that the value of federal employee benefits often exceeds the value of private companies' benefits by as much as 7 percent of pay, offsetting at least to some extent the federal disadvantage in salaries.[4]

Conversely, according to several studies, the average state and local government employee collects considerably more in total compensation than the average private-sector employee. "Wages average a hefty 37 percent higher in the public sector, but the differences in benefits are even more dramatic. Local governments pay 128 percent more, on average, than private employers to finance workers' health care benefits, and 162 percent more on retirement benefits."[5]

While pay and benefits vary across governments and geographic areas relative to the private sector, few if any government organizations follow private-sector practices that include market-based and performance-oriented raises. According to U.S. Comptroller General Davis Walker, "There is widespread agreement that the basic approach to federal pay is broken . . . (but) pay increases are no longer an entitlement but should be based on employees' contributions to the organization's missions and goals."[6] Although state and local governments, for the most part, have the advantage of competitive pay and benefits, their pay systems generally lack the same flexibilities as the private sector, making Davis Walker's comments equally applicable to them.

Government Employees Usually Have Better Job Security

We all know that private-sector employees do not have the same job security as government employees. They can lose their jobs in many ways, ranging from corporate takeovers to the relocation of their activity to another city or even another country, or to a downturn in the economy. They can also lose their jobs if their corporation's stock price takes a tumble due to poor performance or loss of market share, or if their company is engaged in fraud or malfeasance, all of which will hurt the bottom line and can trigger layoffs.

One notable case involved an excellent salesman in the private sector who was laid off four times, for many of the reasons just described. Having a wife and two young children, he was very concerned about his future. He eventually went to work for the government because he knew he would have greater job security and, hopefully, more career growth.

The government is funded by one of the few things in life that are certain, taxes. While the tax base can certainly shrink if the economy falters, government will always exist. The only question is its size. Moreover, the government can and often continues to function with a deficit, although because of its sheer size, the federal government can operate with far more debt than state and local governments can. A private company simply cannot operate in this fashion for an indefinite period of time because it constantly has to compete in the marketplace in order to survive and has no tax base. Moreover, it does not have the ability to simply raise taxes like the government can.

Most private-sector employees also do not enjoy the same job protections as government employees. Unless they have a contract, which most do not, private-sector employees can be fired at a moment's notice, and for almost any reason, and they will have little recourse to challenge that action. The tenuous nature of many private-sector jobs contributes to a culture that is often edgier than that in government.

Government employees generally have far more protections than their private-sector counterparts. Once they pass probation (usually a year), it can become quite difficult to fire them without a lot of hard work, documentation, third-party intervention, and aggravation. Most government employees can contest any action taken against them, and the cumulative effect of having to discipline or actually fire a government employee can discourage supervisors from taking action. At the same time, employees quickly figure out when management is not prepared to fire many of its employees, and this helps contribute to a culture that often lacks a sense of urgency.

A government human resources specialist from Bremerton, Washington, explained the challenge:

> We have certainly removed poor performers, but supervisors are reluctant to assign meaningful work to poor performers for extended periods in order to build a case. If we wind up overcharging a customer for redoing work or missing a contracted completion date, we risk losing the customer.[7]

Most Government Employees Do Not Have the Right to Strike

The right to strike is a fundamental principle in the private sector. It serves as the basis for collective bargaining and encourages both parties to try and reach agreement. This right confers an enormous amount of power on private-sector unions and motivates them to focus on broad issues such as pay, benefits, and job security.

The same does not hold true through much of government. For example, 38 states have no-strike laws.[8] The federal government makes it a felony for its employees to strike. Even those jurisdictions that recognize a public employee's right to strike prohibit police and firefighters from striking, as well as other employees they deem essential.[9]

In my experience, since the vast majority of government unions do not have the ability to strike, they tend to focus on narrower, more mundane issues than their counterparts in the private sector do. Lacking the ability to strike, unable to negotiate pay, and not having the same job security concerns as private-sector unions, they have to find other issues to make themselves relevant and to galvanize the workforce. As a result, many will seek to negotiate on even minor changes in policy, will often "make a mountain out of a molehill" of obscure personnel issues, and will vigorously represent even the worst employees, so they can maintain a high profile with the bargaining unit.

Newer, more educated employees often do not join government unions, because they cannot negotiate on issues that are of importance to them. In addition, even though unions are legally obligated to represent all employees in the bargaining unit, motivated employees often resent them for protecting people who do not contribute to the organization.

All of these factors contribute to a different type of relationship and a different level of tension between management and government unions than you will find in the private sector.

In several of the organizations that I have worked in, union officials would frequently raise issues that, from many people's perspective, were innocuous. They would complain about the arrangement of a couple of desks, argue over a short-term assignment for one employee, criticize the phrasing of a vacancy announcement, and so on. Although I was able to resolve the vast majority of these issues, I couldn't help but wonder how much of the government's time was being wasted on nonsense. Sometimes, it almost felt like a *Seinfeld* episode. That is, a show about nothing.

Why People Come to Work for the Government

In my experience, government workers represent the full spectrum of our nation's population, in the same way that workers in the private sector do. They are young and old, male and female, black and white, Asian and Hispanic, Jewish and Gentile, veteran and nonveteran, educated and not educated. Some expect to work for the government their entire careers, while others only expect to work there for a short period of time.

People come to work for the government for many reasons, including but not limited to the following five:

1. They want to make a difference.
2. They want the total package of government pay, benefits, and retirement savings plans.

3. They want the job security offered by government.
4. They want the right job and the training that the government can offer.
5. They know the government offers many opportunities to advance.

Interestingly, in a survey done by Hart-Teeter Research of people who did not apply for jobs with the federal government, 38 percent of respondents said it was too much of a hassle to apply, 27 percent indicated that pay would be less than the private sector, and 10 percent said the jobs would be boring.[10] Let's look at the reasons why people work for the government in a bit more detail.

They Want to Make a Difference

Many people want to do something more than simply make money—they want to make a difference. For example, after 9/11 "more than 100,000 people . . . sent applications or resumes" to the Central Intelligence Agency.[11] Other people want to fight crime, work with foreign governments, protect the environment, or simply maintain our libraries. There is no better place to accomplish these goals than with government.

A few years back, we hired a young attorney from the private sector. When I asked her why she wanted to work for the government, she replied that she was very unhappy as a private family attorney. She felt as though she was constantly stuck in the middle of disputes involving unhappy families, and she wanted to do something more positive and productive with her life. Moreover, she was unhappy working up to 70 hours per week. After much soul searching, she chose to work for the government.

They Want the Total Package of Government Pay, Benefits, and Retirement

I discussed the government's pay and benefits in the last section, so I will not rehash those issues. Another major advantage of working for the government is its generous retirement package. Many people retire with 50 percent, 60 percent, 70 percent, or even 80 percent of their last few years' average pay.

Let's look at the overall issue of pay, benefits, and retirement in more human terms: A friend of mine had lost his job in the private sector, and, given his age, had a hard time finding another job in the private sector. He was very concerned about the lack of health insurance for his family and the fact that he was ill prepared for retirement. Although he knew that he would be virtually starting over at a relatively low salary, he decided to go to work for the government, knowing that he could improve his family's long-term financial health with the government's package of pay and benefits. He also realized that if he worked for the government for 15 years or more, he would be at least somewhat prepared for retirement.

They Want the Job Security Offered by Government

In the previous section, I also discussed how the government offers job security. Accordingly, there is no need to repeat that a government job is more secure than most.

A real-life example of someone who was looking for such security would be a close relative of mine who lost his business and eventually took a job in the private sector. After moving from job to job, he was let go because his company was experiencing financial difficulties. Recognizing that he was living from paycheck to paycheck and had no solid long-term prospects, he decided that he needed a job with more security. As a result, he submitted his application to work for the government.

The Government Can Offer the Right Job and Training

Most government employers look for the same set of knowledge, skills, and abilities that private-sector employers look for. Many, if not most, government jobs are filled at the entry level, which means that in most cases, the government is simply looking to hire good people and then train them to become journeymen.

This approach provides a wonderful opportunity for recent graduates, as well as people looking for a job change, to work for and develop a career within government.

One young man I know left the military after spending several years in Vietnam. He went to college through the GI Bill, and then began looking for a steady job in order to support his family. He found an entry-level position with the government and slowly worked his way up, taking advantage of the government's many training opportunities and being promoted to a variety of increasingly responsible positions. Eventually, the President of the United States appointed this man to be the undersecretary of that same government organization.

The Government Offers Many Opportunities to Advance

The sheer size of the government means that good people can get ahead relatively quickly. Perhaps the most difficult part of the process is getting into the government, since the application process can be both daunting and discouraging. Fortunately, for those people who are persistent, once you get into the government, you can move both up and around pretty quickly.[12]

Many entry-level positions start at a fairly low salary. However, for those positions that offer promotion potential along with a significant training period, you can move up pretty quickly as long as you do a decent job.

One case involved an individual who was hired as a trainee claims examiner making about $33,000 per year. It was tough for her to make ends meet because the salary was so low. However, she knew that if she worked hard, her salary would steadily rise. Over the next few years, she received four promotions. Five years later, she had more than doubled her salary.

Why Do Government Personnel Systems Make Things So Difficult?

We've established that there are clear differences between government and private-sector employment. We've also established that, in general, people are people, and that they choose to work for the government for a wide variety of reasons. Once they come to work for the government, they work within a personnel system that has evolved over several hundred years and is quite different from the wide variety of systems used in the private sector.

In my view, it is the system that usually creates the challenges that government managers face in trying to manage the government's employees. The more they understand how these systems have developed, and understand how to successfully navigate these systems, the more effective they will be in managing the government's workforce.

Let's take a brief look at the history of the civil service, so we can have a better understanding about its evolution.

History of the Civil Service

At the beginning of our country, successful career civil servants were usually able to retain their jobs during a change in administration. That all changed during the administration of Andrew Jackson, who removed countless civil servants from the opposition party and filled these positions with his own supporters. Jackson felt that "No man has any more intrinsic right to official station than another . . . The duties of all public officers, are, or at least admit of being made, so plain and simple that men of intelligence may readily qualify themselves for their performance."[13]

The following decades were filled with corruption, and civil service jobs became highly politicized. Machine politics became a fact of government life, and federal employees were expected to devote their time and money in support of elected officials. Moreover, the constant turnover of government employees left the government with virtually no institutional memory.

The problem was compounded by the continuing growth of the federal government. The federal government employed about 20,000 people during Jackson's presidency. By the end of the Civil War, 53,000 were employed, and that number rose to 131,000 by 1884.[13] Meanwhile, elected officials were continually besieged by supporters seeking positions within the federal government.

The problem continued well past the Civil War, and despite public support in some circles for reform, no action was taken. However, when Charles Guiteau was not selected for a position he believed had been promised to him, he assassinated President James Garfield. This shocking event struck a nerve, and the public demanded change. The political spoils system suddenly grabbed the national spotlight, and Congress eventually passed the Pendleton Act of 1883.

In general, the Pendleton Act required that applicants for classified government jobs take a competitive examination under the auspices of the newly formed Civil Service Commission. Almost 15,000 jobs were classified in this manner so that the United States would have a professional and continuing bureaucracy. That number eventually rose to 86,000 jobs in 1897, which was almost half of the entire federal government.[14]

The act was designed to screen out unqualified applicants and require government managers to select only from the people receiving the highest scores on the civil service exam. In this way, public officials would no longer be able to guarantee jobs to their cronies. At the same time, it would ensure that highly qualified candidates, including immigrants and blacks, could get ahead even if they were not connected to a political candidate.

Interestingly, the Pendleton Act did not protect civil servants from removal, even though that was one of the major flaws of the spoils system. The rationale was that since people could now be hired only under a competitive civil service examination, politicians would have no incentive to remove these individuals, as they would be unable to hire their supporters.

By the turn of the century, however, Congress had precluded removal of federal employees without "good cause." Subsequent to that, the Taft Administration required that agencies desiring to fire a federal employee first give the employee a notice of removal, written reasons for the removal, and a reasonable time in which to respond.

During and after World War II, other rights were given to federal employees, including the right to an in-person hearing and the right to appeal. Later on, as pressure developed to protect federal whistleblowers, President Nixon granted employees the right to appeal their dismissal to an outside organization (the Civil Service Commission).

Employee protections became even stronger with the establishment of federal unions. Initially President Kennedy issued Executive Order 10988, which officially recognized federal unions. In 1978, Congress, at the urging of President Carter, passed the Civil Service Reform Act (CSRA), which for the first time enacted into law the rights and obligations of the parties to collective bargaining—employees, agencies, and labor organizations. The CSRA encompassed a wide variety of management reforms, including the establishment of the Federal Labor Relations Authority (FLRA), which oversees the federal government's labor relations program; and the creation of the Merit Systems Protection Board (MSPB), the new authority charged with adjudicating employee appeals of removal.

The CSRA was not a complete success, as Carter was unable to achieve the flexibility he sought for federal managers to fire incompetent employees and it failed to weaken the hiring rules involving veterans' preference. However, he was able to lower the standard for removing poor performers from a preponderance of evidence to substantial evidence.

Other administrations attempted to improve federal personnel management with varying degrees of success. Of note was the fact that separate systems were eventually set up for the Postal Service, the Federal Aviation Administration, and the intelligence agencies.

Perhaps the most significant effort came when President Clinton established his Reinventing Government initiative under the leadership of Vice President Gore. They eliminated the Federal Personnel Manual (FPM), which contained thousands of pages of personnel rules and regulations. However, Title 5 of the U.S. Code, which covers government organization and employees, still remained, as did most of each agency's internal rules and regulations. Moreover, the actual processes and approaches with respect to recruitment, discipline, retention, and labor relations remained essentially unchanged.

As is often the case, state and local governments followed the lead of the federal government, and over the years began granting similar protections to their employees. While there are certainly variances on a state-by-state and city-by-city basis, it is fair to say that governments at all levels have had similar histories and the same types of challenges as the federal government.

According to Governing.com,

> In virtually every state, however, the demand for reform currently out-weighs the risk. . . . Pay for performance, although still controversial, is a hot topic. Improved performance appraisal is a common goal. And aggressive use of probationary periods has helped some states to hire more freely, with less fear of saddling themselves with incompetents. (Of course, there can be hitches. In both New Jersey and California, it is very difficult to terminate anyone during probation.)[15]

Perception

As you can see, the government's personnel systems have clearly hampered its managers from doing their jobs as effectively as they would like. Listen to the challenge, as described by David Osborne and Peter Plastrik:

> Imagine working in an organization that makes it so hard to fire nonperformers that managers have quit trying. . . . Imagine hiring from a list of the three top scorers on a written test that has little to do with future performance on the job. Imagine routinely losing your best employees because you can't pay them what they're worth. And imagine enduring layoffs in which those with seniority "bump" other employees—so when 100 people lose their jobs, 400 more play musical chairs, winding up in jobs they aren't trained for and don't want.[16]

Throughout my career, I've heard that it's virtually impossible to get anything done in government. People who have never worked for the government certainly believe that, as many seem to have heard horror stories from government employees and have been anxious to pass those stories on to me. I, for one, certainly have experienced these challenges.

We were hiring a large group of trainees. When we received the list of applicants for consideration, the first two names on the list were disabled veterans. After interviewing both of them, we did not think that either one of them would be a good fit with our organization. However, because they were at the top of the list and civil service rules precluded us from selecting any of the strong candidates below them without also selecting the disabled veterans, we reluctantly selected both of them.

Very quickly, they proved to us that our instincts were right. We eventually terminated both of them while wasting a lot of time, energy, and money.

In another instance, we demoted a supervisor for lying and for retaliating against an employee who had exercised her right to file a complaint. From my perspective, it was an open-and-shut case, especially since she confessed. The employee appealed to MSPB. At a prehearing conference, the MSPB Administrative Law Judge (ALJ) told me that since this was a first offense and because the employee apologized for her actions, he would almost certainly find for her if the case went to hearing, and we would also incur additional attorney's fees.

The actions of this ALJ ultimately forced me to rescind this employee's demotion (although she did not return to a supervisory position).

Government employees seem to have the same perceptions about the difficulties of managing within government. In a recent survey of 1,051 federal employees, almost 80 percent indicated that the hiring process was slow. Moreover, on average, they felt that about 24 percent of their co-workers were not doing their job very well and a full 67 percent believed that the disciplinary system was not too good or not good at all.[17]

According to one federal worker "I have witnessed people who are GS-10 through GS-12 who spend their entire day doing their own personal business. I have also witnessed GS-5s who do nothing but goof off for at least an entire day each week."[18] This individual's perceptions are hardly unique.

As I see it, the government's complex personnel systems, coupled with the perception that it is extremely difficult to implement them, have led to a collective sense of inaction when it comes to managing people. Government managers have heard the stories and experienced problems of their own, and over time have often concluded that the best approach is the path of least resistance—that is, taking no action. The bottom line is that inaction has become a self-fulfilling prophecy; people have convinced themselves that it is just too difficult to take action.

What Can Be Done?

First of all, I need to be clear that this book is not designed to address the staffing challenges caused by the government's hiring systems. My goal is to teach people how to manage their employees *once the government has hired them*. My only advice in this area is to follow the rules and regulations that cover hiring, but where appropriate, to also take maximum advantage of the flexibilities that are often available.

Options for Flexible Hiring. The federal government does not require its agencies to fill all of their positions through the traditional civil service examination. Agencies can hire outstanding scholars, certain Vietnam veterans, individuals with disabilities, and so on without being forced to make selections off of a civil service register. Under those circumstances, agencies have much more flexibility in making selections than they would if they followed the normal procedures.

Staffing issues aside, I strongly believe that it is much easier to manage and deal with government employees than you might think. Although it is certainly true that the personnel systems are somewhat constraining, they have evolved into their current form for a reason—to prevent the abuses of the past and to make sure that the government treats both job applicants and its employees in a fair and equitable manner.

In my experience, you can recognize an excellent employee(s) for outstanding performance, you can discipline a government employee for misconduct, you can remove an employee for poor performance, you can work with unions, and you can successfully deal with all kinds of issues. I've also learned that government employees will respond to the right kind of leadership, can and do work very hard, and are more than willing to do the right thing.

The reason why that doesn't happen as often as everyone would like is not primarily the fault of the government's personnel system, although it certainly makes things more difficult. The real reason is that far too many government supervisors and managers either are unable or unwilling to get things done in government, and as a result take no action. This may happen for a number of reasons:

- They have seen other managers get ahead despite taking no action and may decide that this is the way to get ahead. They follow the principle of "Don't rock the boat."
- They may have tried to take action once before and had a bad experience.
- They may be afraid of the flak they will receive if they take action (from the union, from upper management, etc.).
- They may constantly receive personnel advice that stifles them from taking action.
- They may be unwilling to devote the time required to take an action.
- They may simply not know a better way to proceed.

MSPB confirmed this problem in its study *Federal Supervisors and Strategic Human Resources Management.* The board determined that ". . . most federal supervisors do a commendable job of performing the technical work of their units, but have a much harder time with the human resource management tasks that are necessary to the ongoing effectiveness of the organization."[19]

For example, MSPB noted that one of the biggest problems that supervisors have is in the area of performance management. From the supervisors' perspective, the problem lies in areas that are out of their control (the employees' attitude, lack of confidence in the system, limited support from higher levels, etc.). However, MSPB also stated ". . . some problems with handling poor performers also stem from the supervisors' own difficulties in dealing with problem employees."[20]

Regardless of the reason(s) for inaction, it is my firm view that if you follow the philosophies, strategies, and tactics described in this book, you will conclude that you can successfully manage government employees. You will learn that "there are plenty of ways to skin a cat," and that there are multiple opportunities and more than enough flexibility to take action, both positive and negative.

The approach that I describe in the following chapters is not revolutionary, nor will it sound foreign to most readers. It is a common-sense approach to managing government employees that (1) is based on a strong set of core values; (2) emphasizes treating people fairly and on a consistent basis within the framework of an integrated set of personnel systems; and (3) is predicated on the fact that where personnel action is necessary, you can and should take appropriate action.

In fact, the lessons from this book are equally applicable to the private sector, with the main difference being that private-sector managers do not have to deal with the same constraints that public-sector managers do. That being said, wherever you work, we all face the same challenges when managing people. These challenges are the same because people are people and will respond well to good management and poorly to bad management, regardless of whom they work for.

Key Points to Remember

- Working for the government is different from working for the private sector; the civil service personnel systems make it harder to manage the government's employees.
- If you have the will and the skill, you can successfully manage government employees.
- You can and should take advantage of the flexibilities offered by the civil service personnel systems.
- The philosophies, strategies, and tactics described in this book will work equally well within the private sector.

CHAPTER 2

Guiding Principles of Managing People in Government

My overall philosophy with respect to managing government employees has developed over many years and has served me well. I have found that having such a philosophy provides both me and the employees with a sense of direction, consistency, and balance. My philosophy comprises a series of beliefs and key learnings that, when properly applied as a whole, greatly contribute to the development of a well-motivated and dedicated workforce that works together toward achieving a government organization's mission.

This is an extremely important issue that all managers—whether in government or not—must come to grips with. The bottom line is that each of us must decide what we really believe about people. You can't have it both ways because your approach is a reflection of your core values as a manager. If you have no core values, if you do not have any beliefs to guide you through difficult decisions, you will become a chameleon. That is, you will be forced to change according to the pressures of the day, with no overarching philosophy to guide you in your decision-making process. Without a clear pattern or philosophy, you are unlikely to know where you are going or get where you need to go. You will take a series of steps in a variety of directions with no apparent game plan.

Employees closely watch their managers because they are continuously looking for clues as to what they believe and for indications as to what they will do in the future. The employees all talk to each other on a regular basis and share notes, so they all form opinions about their managers' beliefs.

Consistency is very important to employees, as everyone wants to work for managers who are relatively predictable. If managers are unpredictable and seem to operate by whim, employees will not understand the rules of behavior and will worry. If they don't know what they need to do to succeed, or see others punished for minuscule infractions, they will constantly be afraid that they will not get ahead or that action will be taken against them. This kind of fear will undermine the organization because (1) people will be reluctant to share their true feelings; (2) they will become merely compliant and not engaged; and (3) they will do whatever it takes to survive. None of these unintended consequences will help the organization in the long term.

Thus, employees prefer a manager who acts according to a consistent set of core values (even if they don't agree with them) over a manager who seems to blow with the wind. The manager who does not seem to have any set of beliefs will not be respected, because he or she doesn't stand for anything. Such a manager will be seen as a caretaker, not as a leader; and once the leader loses the respect of the troops, it's almost impossible to regain it.

So what do you believe about people? Many managers feel that people cannot be trusted. They believe that people are motivated only by money or by self-preservation, and thus will always place their best interests ahead of the organization. Under this philosophy, people must be controlled in order to prevent them from gaming the system or undermining the organization. This approach is common throughout the government and the private sector and can work reasonably well within limits. It requires many rules and regulations, numerous internal controls, a high degree of oversight, and tight supervision.

The problem with this cynical view is that people don't feel valued, because they know they are being watched all the time. Under such a system, they will conform to the rules and will attempt to give management what it asks for. However, because this approach is so focused on compliance, and because the employees know they are not trusted, compliance is all that management tends to get. While compliance is important, what management does *not* get is commitment, nor does it get loyalty, both of which are essential for long-term high performance.

Overall Philosophy

Most People Want to Do a Good Job

The overwhelming majority of people that I've met during my career have wanted to do a good job. They are serious people who have come to work with energy and enthusiasm, and they desire to excel. Almost invariably, people begin their careers with excitement, a sense of great pride, and the belief that they will truly make a difference. However, as many of us have learned the hard way, time tends to transform the promise of unbridled youth into the reality of a long and often unfulfilled career. Too often, as their careers progress (or simply stagnate), we see the same people ultimately become cynical, lose their spark, and simply try to hang on.

We as managers want to try and prevent this attitude from pervading our organization. If not, we will spend more and more time trying to control our employees' hearts and minds so they will do what we want them to do. Naturally, this approach will lead us in a downward cycle, because the more we try to control our employees, the more they will resent us for it. In essence, we will wind up operating with the same philosophy toward people that we described earlier.

If you start with the premise that most people want to do a good job, you still need solid systems and controls. Good management systems are crucial to an organization's success. They provide stability and consistency and are the glue that holds an organization together and keeps it running smoothly. Internal controls ensure that you have good oversight, that problems are quickly identified and corrected, and that you are able to root out fraud. The difference between the two philosophies regarding your attitude toward people is in the *application* of the systems and controls. The former approach assumes that you need to constantly inspect what people do, because the people are generally the problem. The latter approach still requires periodic reviews of your employees' work, but assumes that people are trying to do a good job and that variances in the system(s) (training, workflow, etc.) or poor management account for many of the day-to-day problems that occur.

This book starts and finishes with the premise that most people want to do a good job. This philosophy colors everything within the book. Although the book also spends a good deal of time explaining how to deal with difficult people and the difficult decisions that government managers always seem to face, it is absolutely imperative that the reader not lose sight of the bigger picture—that is, that most people want to do a good job. If you can retain this point of view during the most stressful employee relations issues, you will keep your perspective intact, and your subordinates will recognize that you do have a consistent set of core values. More importantly, they will grow to respect you and will give you their hearts and minds, not just compliance. By contrast, if you allow the relative handful of difficult people that you deal with to make you cynical, it will color your dealings with everyone else, and you will slowly but surely lose them, one way or another.

Accepting that people want to do a good job means that your organization has the potential to strive for greater success than a rival that only wants people to comply, and then hold them accountable. People who feel valued take a much greater degree of interest in their organization's success and are willing to give much more than the minimum. Thirty-two years of experience in government has taught me that people will give you back whatever you invest in them.

I used to work with an employee who had a lot of personal problems. He was on drugs for many years and had multiple issues to deal with. Although his problems at times manifested themselves at the work, at heart I thought he was a good person who wanted to do a good job. As a result, I went out of my way to treat him well, and to make sure that he knew that I cared about him. He eventually became a very fine employee and was someone we frequently turned to for special projects. When I underwent back surgery, he sent me a card that said, "Stew, I hope this card finds you well and is not too mushy, but I wanted you to know how much you've changed my life for the better." Because I believed in this individual, he wound up paying me back tenfold.

The more you treat people as valued employees who want to do a good job, the more they will do a good job. The more you treat them as replaceable parts, the more frequently they will check out mentally and the more you will have to replace them. In essence, your philosophy regarding your employees becomes a self-fulfilling prophecy. I choose to believe that employees want to do a good job because (1) that has been my experience; and (2) that is the prophecy I want to fulfill.

Most People Want to Be Part of a Winning Organization

Hand in hand with my philosophy about employees wanting to do a good job is my belief that employees want to be part of a winner. Nobody that I know wants to go to work each day and watch an organization go down the tubes. It is simply too depressing and does not profit anyone.

People associated with poor-performing organizations have a hard time getting ahead, and the fallout can last a long time. Even for people who have worked their whole career for a successful government organization, it's the most recent assignment that seems to stick most closely. That is why so many people tend to bail out of an organization that is going downhill. If they can't leave immediately, people will do everything they can to downplay their employer. Since they dread going to work, they will not mention the name of their agency unless asked, they will try and avoid talking about work whenever possible, and they will do everything they can to avoid visitors.

By contrast, people who work for a winning organization have an overwhelming sense of pride. They look forward to going to work, let everyone know whom they work for, take pride in talking about their organization's accomplishments, and encourage people to visit their workplace. Obviously, since we all spend so much time at work, this is the type of situation we all want.

Last year, I attended a training session where I was one of the instructors. At a dinner prior to the session, I was struck by the fact that one young woman kept telling everyone that her office had achieved every goal during the prior month. It was obvious to all that she was very proud of the fact that she was part of a winning organization.

Since we know that people want to be part of a winner, why not start with that perspective and incorporate it as part of an overall strategy? That is, assume (until proven otherwise) that each person wants to play and wants to win, so give them every opportunity to help the organization become a winner. This means giving them freedom, not controlling them; including them, not excluding them; and providing them with a meaningful role in contributing to the organization's success.

It's amazing how this issue comes up time and time again. Look at how successful sports teams deal with it. In his book *The Carolina Way: Leadership Lessons From a Life in Coaching*, legendary college basketball coach Dean Smith wrote:

> Every person on the team was important. There were no exceptions. This included not only the last man on the team but also the student managers, who worked hard on our behalf. They picked up towels, washed uniforms on road trips, made sure equipment got to where it was supposed to be, set up the gym for practice. They came early and stayed late. I told many business friends that if they wanted to hire a great employee, then choose one of our student managers. They would find a hardworking, self-starting, highly organized, dependable individual.[1]

Smith recognized that every individual associated with the University of North Carolina basketball team wanted to be part of a winning team, and he made sure that each person had a role in the team's success.

Always Treat People With Respect

You would think this concept would be obvious to all, but it never seems to work out that way. Treating people with respect buys so much goodwill, and yet managers often ignore this approach. When people are not treated respectfully, the damage that occurs is hidden in the short term. However, people talk to each other and share stories about the way they've been treated. Over time, the collective stories of disrespect that have been passed from employee to employee tend to pervade the organization's culture, take on a life of their own, and undermine many of the good things that management is trying to do.

If you think about it, it doesn't take much work to treat people with respect. One of the best concepts that I've heard is to criticize ideas, not people. This means all ideas and concepts on the table are subject to intense scrutiny, but even if an idea is not ultimately accepted, the person putting forth the idea is still valued. This approach encourages new ideas and perspectives while protecting the self-esteem of all.

How often have you been in a meeting where the manager will put someone down in front of the group? Far too often, I suspect. Let's examine one real-life example.

Several years ago, a management meeting was held wherein a senior manager attempted to illustrate what he perceived to be the flaws in a new policy. During this meeting, he made a presentation wherein he cited a number of statistics to indicate how this new policy was going to adversely affect several offices across the country (he intentionally did not mention the impact on his own office). In the middle of his presentation, one particularly powerful individual, without addressing the statistics cited, remarked, "We know you're only here to protect your own office." This personal attack on him had several negative, unintended consequences: (1) The senior manager recognized that if he was going to air his views in public, he would be personally attacked, so he stopped critiquing policy issues, which means that the organization lost a valuable voice in national discussions; and (2) the individual who attacked the senior manager lost a key ally, probably for the rest of his career.

Imagine if that same powerful official had handled the situation differently. What if he first repeated his understanding of the senior manager's arguments, then explained why he did not agree with that position, citing the information he had at his disposal to support the new policy? If he took this approach, the senior manager might not have liked the final outcome, but he would have (1) at least felt that he had been heard; (2) had a deeper understanding of the rationale behind the policy; and (3) felt that his opinion counted. Moreover, in the future, he would still be inclined to come forth and offer his insight and would likely remain an ally of the powerful official.

People can and should be treated with respect, even in unusually stressful situations. One of the most difficult situations that managers—in and out of government—frequently handle involves employee discipline. These situations by their very nature are tense and can lead to hard feelings on the part of the employee being disciplined. Far too often, the manager handling this situation goes into a cold, "I'm the boss" mode wherein the employee winds up feeling humiliated and looks for passive ways to strike back at management. For example, the supervisor might say something like:

"Ms. Smith, here is a reprimand for your recent unauthorized absence. Continued instances of AWOL could lead to your removal. The reprimand gives you all of your grievance and appeal rights. I have nothing further to say on the matter. If you have any questions, speak to your union representative."

Under this approach, the employee is likely to take the message that management is the enemy and the only friend she has is the union. In addition, the employee will conclude that management doesn't want to hear what she has to say, so in the future she will probably make her communications in writing. Lastly, the employee may also decide that management doesn't care about her and she doesn't have a future with the organization, so why not become a union official and strike back at management?

What if the same manager handled the situation this way? "Shirley, here is a reprimand for your recent unauthorized absence. This is a serious matter that could eventually lead to your removal if it is not addressed immediately. I'm sure that neither of us wants to see that happen. I want you to know that I am more then willing to work with you to help you improve. Do you have questions or concerns that I could address at this point?"

With this approach, the manager let Shirley know the seriousness of her offense and the possible consequences of continued AWOL. At the same time, he treated her with respect and let her know that he would try and help her. Under this scenario, Shirley is more likely to work with management in order to try and address her shortcomings.

Respect can come (or be perceived) in many forms, ranging from the way we talk to people to the way we write to people to simply our body language. Every day management has a multitude of interactions with employees, and each interaction is an opportunity to send a positive message. If we can leverage these opportunities by sending positive messages to our employees, we will reap the benefits in a variety of ways. For example, employees will be more likely to express their concerns, more likely to share their ideas, and more likely to treat management with the same degree of respect that management treats them with. The bottom line is that by adopting this approach, everyone wins.

Apply the Golden Rule

Treat others as you want to be treated. This is a simple yet powerful concept that has been endorsed by many religions, and yet far too often, it seems to get lost in the workplace.

When I look back on my career, I realize that many people, both leaders and nonleaders, have touched my life. The ones I look back on in a favorable light have invariably been people who had strong ethics, and who treated me the way I wanted to be treated. That doesn't mean they always gave me what I wanted, or treated me better than others. It simply means they treated me like an adult, with respect, in a fair and equitable manner. Sometimes they told me I was wrong, and then explained to me why. Those lessons will stay with me forever. Other times they did the exact opposite of what I proposed, and then showed me why they chose the path they took. Sometimes I was right and they were wrong. On those occasions they acknowledged they were wrong and moved on. You see, it wasn't about ego; it was about doing the right thing, for the right reasons, for the good of the organization.

Applying the Golden Rule in government means carrying over into our careers the same principles that guide most of us in our private life. This approach means that we don't succumb to the daily pressures and strike back at people the first time we feel threatened. It also means that we always try and carry ourselves with dignity and treat other people with respect (there's that word again). It further means that when we are in difficult situations, we continue to take the moral high road, and do not sink down to the level of others who have chosen a different path.

Several years ago, I attended an employee meeting in which I was sharing information with employees, listening to their concerns, and answering their questions. Several times during that meeting, our most cynical and contentious employee at the time publicly challenged me by denigrating virtually everything I was saying. Although I often turn the other cheek when I am criticized, it was clear to me that in this instance, his actions were having a strong, adverse impact on the other employees. While my natural inclination was to verbally strike back at this employee, I knew that such an approach would stifle future debate, even if I were attacking an unreasonable employee. Moreover, I knew that if I were in a position wherein I was questioning management, I would not want to be publicly attacked and humiliated. I therefore decided to take a different approach, which yielded far better results than a direct assault might have.

With a smile on my face, I asked him the following question: "Robert (not his real name), who's the greater fool, the fool or the fool who follows the fool? If you are so unhappy here, why not find another job somewhere else? We would all understand." He turned red as soon as he heard my response. He realized that he had made a fool of himself, especially since I did not take the bait and attack him in an angry manner. As often happens when a tense situation is effectively defused, he later came back and publicly asked me a question that demonstrated his regret for the earlier outburst. Later on, a large number of employees approached me and apologized for the employee's remarks. What became clear is that by following the Golden Rule, even in a very difficult situation, I was able to both win the support of the group and make the cynic feel more isolated than ever.

Many (Not All) Problems Are Caused by Management

Too often, when things go wrong, we look to blame someone. Problems develop every day, so someone must be at fault. In today's culture of accountability, managers often look to blame someone, as if by finding a fall guy, they will somehow right the ship. In actuality, this mentality is often counterproductive because employees generally try and work with management and attempt to meet its demands. Where management builds a culture of blame, employees tend to go underground in order to stay off the radar screen and avoid committing mistakes. This response to management's actions generally results in the employees' energy and creativity going down the tubes.

So why are many problems caused by management? The answer is simple. Employees need the proper training, policy guidance, and tools to do their jobs. Moreover, they need to know their agency's code of conduct as well as its performance expectations. They also need to know how both they and the group are performing and to see that there is a clear set of consequences for exceeding expectations as well as for failing to achieve them. Lastly, communication must be crystal clear regarding changes in the organization's direction, policies, and/or procedures. Lapses in any of these categories can cause confusion, a diffusion of energy, or situations in which employees unintentionally work at cross-purposes with the organization's goals.

Problems such as those already described are the responsibility of management. Yet far too often, when they manifest themselves in an employee problem, our natural instinct is to blame the employees. Let's look at a few examples as to how this can happen.

Vague Policy Guidance. Consider an organization whose mission it is to make decisions on claims for worker's compensation benefits. Assume that the policy guidance on one type of benefit is extremely vague, resulting in confusion and a lot of erroneous decisions. On a broad scale, the net result of this will be a lower rate of quality than the organization desires. Moreover, some employees will have high error rates that are undeserved, which is likely to trigger retraining, performance-based actions, grievances, EEO complaints, and hard feelings. Many hours will be lost dealing with an issue whose root cause squarely rests in the lap of management. In fact, management should have simply taken a step back and recognized that there was a pattern to the high error rate that was caused by a poorly written policy. Had it done so, it could have avoided both the low quality rate and all of the time wasted in dealing with the performance issues that were in reality caused not by the employees but by management.

Low Leave Balance. Many government organizations have employees with low leave balances. The natural tendency is to blame the employees for taking leave. After all, if they hadn't requested leave, management would never have granted it. Continuously having many employees on leave is bad, because if employees are not at work, the jobs they are getting paid to perform are not getting done. It's as simple as that.

So, the question is this: Are low leave balances the fault of the employees or the fault of management? The answer is clearly management. While employees can request leave, in many cases, it is up to management to approve leave. Management sets the rules and it is up to the managers to enforce the same rules.

The simplest issue is annual leave (also known as vacation or personal days). These days are typically set aside for vacations, rest and relaxation, or other personal reasons. They are invariably an entitlement that employees have that is subject to management's discretion. Employees are encouraged to maintain a reasonable balance at all times because you never know when a personal emergency will occur. Since emergencies do occasionally occur, annual leave or personal leave is intended for that purpose. If the rules are applied fairly and consistently, people will understand them and abide by them. There will be no confusion, and leave will be taken in a manner that is expected and that will promote the efficiency of the government.

In most places, one individual will eventually start testing management by calling in and requesting unscheduled leave—first on an occasional basis and over time on a more frequent basis. The more management approves the leave, the more people will get the message that unscheduled leave is okay. Pretty soon, a second, third, and fourth individual will follow the same pattern. After a while, unscheduled leave will become the norm, not the exception, individual leave balances will decline, and overall attendance will drop. All of this is predictable, but it is a function of poor management, not problem employees. If management had firmly applied the rule that unanticipated absences will be held to a minimum, everyone would have gotten the message that the rule is important and would have complied accordingly.

Heavy-Handed Supervisor. You've probably seen a situation arise where a new supervisor comes onto the scene with a desire to shake things up. Typically, this supervisor sees her job as being the tough person, the one who is going to bring order and discipline to the organization by running a very tight ship and making examples of a number of individuals. Granted, there are times when discipline is clearly needed. In fact, this book advocates an approach that emphasizes appropriate responses to poor behavior.

That being said, I am very leery of the tough guy approach, because it relies on a hard-nosed, often overly emotional, egocentric supervisor to mete out punishment. Far too often, this approach demoralizes the employees in the organization because they see people unfairly punished for minor infractions, with the supervisor's apparent goal being to establish who is "the boss." Typically, instead of applying the management systems and policies in an even-handed fashion, this type of supervisor often takes action based on emotion. Once this happens, employees quickly conclude that there are no real rules, because they are being enforced selectively. Many will also believe that the supervisor is a tyrant, who is willing to beat up on someone when it's in the supervisor's best interest.

This approach may succeed in the short term, because fear can get results, at least for a while. However, in the long term, employees will not support the leader, as they will feel both used and abused. Leave usage will increase, morale will decline, and many people will look to leave the organization. As we all know, excessive leave, poor morale, and high turnover are a formula for disaster—and in this particular situation, management created the disaster.

If we start with the premise that most problems are caused by management, we will look for patterns in the behaviors of our employees that are caused by management's policies, systems, and actions. By first looking to address these issues before blaming the employees for a specific problem, we will be able to address the problems upstream rather than downstream, where they are far more costly and painful.

Look at Your Management Systems

Although most problems are caused by management's action or lack of action, sometimes problems arise because of the systems that management has put in place.

There's an old saying that declares, "If you always do what you have always done, you will always get what you always got."[2] Relating this to management systems,[3] if you continue to utilize the same management systems that are currently in place, you are likely to produce the same results that you've been getting. In many cases, the problems that management tries to deal with over and over again are a function of the management systems in place, not the employees themselves.

In a properly designed organization, all of the systems work together in a way that promotes the organization's goals and objectives. They work together and provide consistent guidance to the employees in a way that directs them and motivates them, and ultimately leads to high performance. This synthesizes all of the employee energy so that they are all working together toward the same goal, and not at cross-purposes.

Top-notch organizations feature systems that complement each other. They hire excellent employees, invest heavily in their training, and promote people based on merit. The employees work in first-class space that is designed to promote the flow of work and build morale. The organizational structure is generally lean, with relatively few layers of management. Tasks are accomplished in an effective and efficient manner that avoids rework to the maximum extent possible. Employees are given the requisite tools to do their jobs, including manuals, computers, job aids, and so on. Information flows smoothly, and decisions are made at the appropriate levels. Rewards are doled out in a fair and equitable manner and in a way that promotes the organization's goals. Lastly, the organization periodically takes a step back in order to ensure that it is continually learning and renewing itself.

When organizations have properly aligned systems, something unique starts to happen. *The systems drive the right behavior* rather than management. This means that the supervisors do not have to constantly stay on top of the employees to force them to behave the way management expects. That is because once (1) the systems are properly aligned; (2) the employees receive the necessary training, tools, and information to do their jobs; and (3) the employees see that management takes appropriate action for both outstanding and poor performance/conduct (more on that later), the employees will receive a consistent message, will know what to do, and will try and give management what it wants. Once this happens, management will find that it needs to spend less time "riding herd" over the employees and can spend more time on higher-level tasks such as benchmarking with best-in-class organizations, strategic planning, and so on.

Let's look at three barriers to effective management systems: physical barriers, ineffective rewards, and inefficiency.

Physical Barriers. We've all seen organizations proclaim that they want to have a team environment. Typically, these organizations invest a great deal of time, effort, and money in order to change the culture from one that is typically a top-down, command and control organization to one that is flatter and more team-based. The organization may spend many months utilizing the services of a consultant who will help train both management and the employees on how to function as a team. The training may involve the development of a steering committee, preparing the organization for change, multiple reading assignments, classroom work, group projects, and so on.

Once all of this prework has been completed, the organization moves forward in teams, although inevitably, problems occur because not enough attention is often paid to all of the management systems that are needed to support a team-based environment. As an example, let's say an organization suddenly converts to teams, but it has high partitions throughout its space that will send a contradictory message to the employees. High partitions allow a lot of privacy, but they tend to inhibit teamwork, as it is very difficult for people to interact when they can't see their fellow team members. Once the initial excitement of being part of a team wears off, people will spend less and less time with each other because of the artificial barriers created by the partitions, which are part of the organization's structural system.

Ineffective Rewards. Another area that typically does not receive a lot of detailed attention when an organization converts to teams is the rewards system. Far too often, when an organization converts to teams, the rewards system sends a contradictory message.

For example, if an organization desires teamwork yet rewards only individual accomplishment, what do you think is going to happen? The employees are not going to want to help each other because they recognize that individual accomplishment is what is valued and rewarded. They will focus on delivering the best possible individual performance, but will not be willing to pass on their critical knowledge to others, because the rewards system tells them that this approach is not valued by the organization. The employees who need help will stop seeking it because that is the message they are receiving from their peers. As a result, everyone will focus on his or her own best interests in the short term, at the expense of what's best for the team and the organization, *because this is the message that management's rewards system is sending.*

By the same token, management will notice the lack of teamwork and will become frustrated with the employees. The typical view will be that we supplied these people with all the training they needed to work as a team. Since they are obviously not working together, it must be the fault of the employees!

Inefficiency. I once worked in a government organization whose mission was, in part, to sell foreclosed properties to the public. The more properties that could be sold at a reasonable price, the more cost-effective it would be for the government. However, properties were being sold at a very slow pace for one primary reason: the real estate brokers who were selling these properties were not being paid until at least 120 days after close of escrow. Naturally, as word got out to the real estate community about how long it was taking to get paid, more and more brokers dropped out of this program, which sent it into a downward spiral. So what was the reaction of some members of management? It was to blame the employees, who must have been lazy, untalented, or just poor performers.

In fact, the opposite was the case. The employees were competent, hard-working people who were suffering in a poor system that management had set up. Every time a property was sold, the paperwork needed to pay the broker was so labor intensive that it had to go through many different hands before final payment was issued. The problem was an outdated technical system, not the employees.

The solution was to change the payment system from an assembly-line process to a central location and to make the payment through electronic transfer, enabling the brokers to be paid at the close of escrow. Shortly thereafter, word spread about this change. Many brokers reentered the system, resulting in far more properties being sold and the government actually making a profit on the sales. Had management taken the time much earlier in the game to examine its technical systems, as opposed to blaming the employees, it could have saved an enormous amount of time, energy, and money.

The primary point in this section is that when a human resources problem arises, make sure you are addressing the right issue. There is no doubt that at times, employee performance issues and conduct issues must be addressed firmly and directly. Much of this book is devoted to that very point. However, what I am also advocating is to continually examine both management's actions and/or its systems. The more these are scrutinized, the more often you will be able to spot trends that, if addressed up front, will prevent the need to take future personnel actions. One of the basic principles of this book is that the more management acts appropriately toward its employees, and the better aligned its systems, the easier it will be to manage the organization's employees.

Make Sure Your Systems Are Reliably Applied

Once an organization has clear and consistent management systems in place, the next step is to ensure that the systems are applied in a highly reliable manner. To do this properly, management must first ensure that the employees are given all of the tools that they need to succeed. As stated earlier, this means that they all must receive the training required to do their jobs and be provided with the resources to implement that training. In addition, they must be taught the organization's policies and procedures (both written and unwritten). Lastly, they must be given clear expectations so that they are aware of both the minimum acceptable performance standards and what they need to do to excel.

Once this is accomplished, the burden then shifts to the employees. They are responsible for behaving in a manner that is consistent with the organization's code of conduct. Moreover, they are responsible for meeting or exceeding the organization's performance standards. Once the employees are trained and possess the necessary tools, *the more reliably the systems are applied, the more reliable will be your employees' behavior.*

This is one of the absolute keys to sound management of government or nongovernment employees. People want to know the rules, and also want to know that they are being applied fairly, since we all want to play on a level playing field. If some people do not play by the rules and there are no consequences for their misbehavior, problems will invariably occur.

Look at what happened in Major League Baseball. We now know that certain players cheated by using steroids, which gave them an unfair advantage when competing against players who did not take banned substances. The records that were broken are now looked at with suspicion, reputations have been severely damaged, and the U.S. Congress has conducted investigations because it believes that Major League Baseball has been derelict in its duty to enforce the rules of America's pastime.

The same principle applies at the work site. Once the rules and expectations are set, the employees need to know that management will fairly and consistently take action against people who do not follow the rules and/or meet performance expectations. This especially includes supervisors and managers who do not follow the rules or whose performance falls below par. Conversely, they must also know that management will fairly and consistently reward those employees who go beyond the call of duty and/or exceed performance expectations. It's that simple.

Let's look at a few examples of what to do—and what not to do.

Proper Use of Performance Standards. A large government organization has a performance standard where each employee is required to make a certain number of decisions per day. For the sake of this example, we'll say that the minimum standard is 10 decisions. Three of the employees fail to achieve that standard, so each of their supervisors quickly intervenes by meeting with them. The meetings are an attempt to identify the root cause of the performance problem so they can get each employee up to snuff. In some cases, that is all that is needed to resolve the problem, while in other cases, a more formal plan is put in place to assist the employee.

Occasionally, despite the best efforts of management, an employee will still fail to meet the minimum standard, and action is reluctantly taken to remove that employee from the position. If everyone sees that management is dealing with the bottom performers in a fair and equitable manner, and that its first goal is to assist them, not to fire them, the employees will conclude that management is doing the right thing. Moreover, the employees will conclude that management is serious about the systems being reliably applied, and will act accordingly, resulting in fewer performance actions needing to be taken.

Conversely, if four employees are making 15 decisions or more (and have excellent quality), then they should have a reasonable expectation of being rewarded for their outstanding performance (especially if management has informed the employees in advance what the benchmark is to be rewarded). If management consistently rewards outstanding performance based on preestablished goals, then everyone will perceive the rewards system to be fair, and more and more people will strive to achieve that level of performance. Again, the more reliable the application of the systems, the more reliable will be the employees' behavior.

Failure to Enforce Performance Standards. A government organization's leader did not believe in taking performance-based actions against his employees. He came to this conclusion because he believed that taking action was tantamount to organizational capital punishment, and he didn't believe in capital punishment. As a result, every time a supervisor tried to take action against someone who was failing her performance standard, the leader would always find a reason why he could not sustain the proposed action.

Both the supervisors and the employees got the message that the performance standards did not have to be achieved because management was not serious about applying them on a reliable basis. The net result was that the supervisors stopped wasting their time proposing actions against poor performers, productivity slowly but surely declined over time, and some of the best employees left because they did not want to be part of an organization where poor performers were allowed to continue.

In another case, my organization ended the year with excellent performance. However, when we distributed our individual rewards, the employees went into an uproar because they did not understand the rationale for the distribution of the reward money. Rewards standards had not been published that year, so people did not have a clear sense as to how they were doing with respect to rewards. Moreover, they didn't receive much feedback, either.

In essence, the employees concluded that we were rewarding our favorites, because they could see no reliable basis for the way we distributed rewards. The result of this debacle was that management's credibility in the eyes of the employees was severely undermined and performance suffered for months. I vowed to never again use a rewards system whose results were not transparent. An example of a transparent rewards system will be discussed in Chapter 6.

In summation, reliably applying an organization's systems to its employees in a fair and equitable manner will actually prevent many personnel problems from occurring because people will quickly get the message that this is an organization that is serious about performance. Once the employees recognize that management will take appropriate action if they do not comply with the systems and meet the performance/conduct expectations, and will reward the employees if they exceed expectations, the need for day-to-day supervisory oversight will be greatly reduced, because the employees will conscientiously attempt to deliver the best possible performance.

Always Remember that Your Decisions Affect People's Lives

It's important to remember how much power management really has. Every time we make a decision, we affect the lives of countless people. For example, if we make a selection to either hire or promote someone, we affect not only the life of that person, but also the person's family, as well as the lives of the people who were not selected, and their families as well. If we have to fire someone, the effect on the family can be quite profound. As managers we wield a tremendous amount of power and influence, and it is up to us to use that power wisely. We should not use that power to promote our own agendas, to make ourselves look good, to get back at people, or to settle old scores. We must use that power for the right reason, which means to do the right thing.

Doing the right thing is easier said than done. As managers, we face all kinds of pressure from above and below. We are pressured by political appointees who come into office with a certain agenda, and with relatively little time to accomplish their goals. Our bosses pressure us to do things that make sense to them in the big picture but we may not believe are right. Special interest groups pressure us to select certain classes of individuals. The union often pressures us to do certain things because it receives pressure from its constituency. Other groups that may pressure us include the media, congressional oversight groups, and/or even the Inspector General. The bottom line is that everyone wants a piece of the pie. Unfortunately, there are not enough pieces of the pie to go around, which therefore requires us to make choices.

So how do we go about making these difficult choices? Where do we go for guidance when we know our choices are going to be scrutinized and criticized? For me, the most important thing is to have a core set of values that will guide me through the difficult times. If you truly believe in the values that you espouse, you will have a moral compass to guide you through the darkness. That is absolutely critical.

Far too often, I have seen people who have sacrificed their values for the sake of their career. These individuals made personal decisions to step on other people in order to promote themselves. Some tried to make themselves look good by making others look bad. In essence, they would intentionally paint a bad picture of others to people in power and then set themselves up as the solution. Others did what they thought their bosses wanted them to do even though they knew it was wrong. A few would even take action against people because they wanted to show senior management that they were tough. These individuals made conscious decisions that power was more important than values, and they will have to live with those decisions for the rest of their lives.

That being said, such an approach can work for a period of time. As Abraham Lincoln once said, "You can fool some of the people all of the time, and all of the people some of the time . . ." However, as most of us know, power is transitory; it does not last. Even the President of the United States will eventually lose his power. At the end of the day, all that counts are the things we did to make the world a better place. Did we make a difference? Did we help others? When we're lying on our deathbed, the amount of power we once had will be meaningless, if we did not live our lives according to a principled set of values.

I recognize that the world is not always black and white. Sometimes we have to make real-world decisions that we don't like. The way I approach that issue is as follows. If someone above me in the organization tells me to do something, I will comply, as long as it is legal. If I disagree, I will state my case, but if I am overruled, I will comply. After all, I work for an organization that needs to know that I will be a team player.

By contrast, if I am put in an uncomfortable position but have the discretion to make a decision, I will do what I believe is the right thing, even though it may personally hurt me.

I was once asked to testify in an EEO case about an issue on which I disagreed with my headquarters. I knew that my superiors would not view my testimony favorably. However, my greater obligation was to what I believed to be the truth, so I testified accordingly. Although I knew that I did not ingratiate myself with anyone above me, I could at least look at myself in the mirror and know that many people would respect me for having the courage of my convictions.

When it actually comes down to making difficult decisions, I use the deathbed approach, which goes like this: If I were looking back at the decision currently before me on my deathbed, what should I have done? Did I try to do the right thing for the right reasons, or did I make my decision based on political expediency or for another spurious reason? If I make the decision for the right reason, even if later information proves me to be wrong, then I am still doing the right thing based on the information before me. This approach, coupled with the continuous use of your core values, is an excellent method of ensuring that you are exercising your power wisely.

The Objective: Performance

In discussing how to manage government employees, it is easy to lose sight of the objective, which is outstanding performance. We tend to see the management of human resources as compliance with a bunch of complex personnel rules and regulations. Although these rules and regulations are important, they are merely a foundation upon which we manage our employees. We can meet every rule and regulation set forth in the personnel manual, we can win every case that goes before a third party, and we can cross every *t* and dot every *i*, yet lose sight of the big picture, which is performance.

Early in my career as an inexperienced personnel officer, I dealt with a new group of union officials that were determined to wreak havoc on management. They believed that they had been treated poorly and were determined to make management pay for its sins. They filed numerous grievances and unfair labor practice charges (ULPs) against management, which forced many management officials to devote their energy to rebutting these complaints. From my perspective, we were doing a good job in holding off the union, because third parties did not sustain any of its complaints.

However, this was very narrow thinking on my part, because we were unable to concentrate our energy on the day-to-day work, and our performance clearly suffered. Instead of concentrating on the underlying issue behind the officials' complaints, which was the way that they and others had been treated by management, I took it personally, developed a bit of a bunker mentality, and simply tried to resist them. In retrospect, we spent too much time fighting the union and not enough time resolving issues that would have allowed us to focus more on performance.

The lesson from this episode was that you should never lose sight of performance. Without a reasonably high level of performance, organizations will slowly lose resources, lose support, and ultimately lose credibility—and that's exactly what happened to that office.

It is interesting to note that in many organizations, the chief of human resources is left out of the decision-making process, even though every key decision made by management has personnel ramifications. Unfortunately, I think the reason for that is rather simple: Many senior managers do not believe that human resources plays a role in improving performance. Its staff are seen as the custodians of the rules, regulations and personnel records, and not as drivers of performance. Moreover, they are rarely aware of the agency's metrics and how their advice and assistance affects performance. However, if both senior management and human resources leaders change their view and approach toward people management, in a way similar to what is described in this book, then human resources will inevitably be seen as a key management player, not as merely staff advisors.

As you review and absorb the philosophies, strategies, and tactics contained in this book, recognize that they are always designed to improve performance. The goal is not to have happy employees, nor is it to have as few complaints as possible. It is to manage employees in a way that allows them to flourish, by doing the following:

- Providing them with clear training, guidance, information, expectations, and direction
- Giving them the tools they need to successfully perform their jobs
- Holding them accountable
- Rewarding the top performers
- Sharing information
- Dealing with the wide variety of employee issues that are sure to crop up, in a fair, direct, timely, and even-handed manner

If management can accomplish this in a highly skillful manner, it is on the road to excellent performance.

The Workforce

So far, we've talked a lot about my philosophy of dealing with people, as well as systems theory and how to apply it to the workforce. Let's now turn our attention to workforces in general, as well as tactics for dealing with them in the real world. To some extent, the next two sections will overlap with the earlier section on overall philosophy. However, these sections are intended to build on the broad concepts discussed earlier, with a deeper focus on day-to-day management.

Winning the Battle for the Hearts and Minds of the Middle 80 Percent

In my experience, virtually every organization has roughly the same distribution of employees. The top performers make up about 10 percent of the workforce, the middle performers make up about 80 percent, and the bottom performers make up the remaining 10 percent. The percentages may vary a bit (Jack Welch, former CEO of General Electric, says that it is 20%-70%-10%[4]), but the basic principle is the same. It always seems to work out that way, with the distribution forming a bell curve.

By far, the two most influential groups of employees within the workforce are the top 10 percent and the bottom 10 percent of the employees. As we all know, their reasons for trying to influence the remaining 80 percent of the workforce are different. In fact, they are so different that they are diametrically opposed to each other.

The top 10 percent of the workforce are your best employees. They are highly motivated and very skilled, and want to see the organization become a great success. They constantly push others to perform at a higher level, because they believe that everyone should strive to achieve his potential. These are the people who always volunteer to take on the tough assignments, because they know that someone has to do it, and they are up to the task. They want to see the organization rise to its potential, and they do everything they can to help achieve it.

By contrast, the bottom 10 percent are the organization's worst employees. Many are poorly motivated; they generally have a host of personal problems, and their performance is often barely acceptable, or worse. They are the most difficult employees to deal with because of their behavior, and because of the employee protections contained in the government's rules, regulations, and union contracts.

Some of them are quiet, but more often they are among the loudest employees because they have learned that the more they complain, the more they will be left alone. A number of them will become union officials, and they will use that role to promote their own agenda. Others will file equal employment opportunity (EEO) complaints so that if management takes action against them, they can claim retaliation.

Many are good people, but either they don't have the ability to do the job, or they've simply been corrupted by the most outspoken cynics. The goal of this group is to lower the organization's standards and to break management's will, so they will be left alone. Many do not want to succeed; they merely want to survive. They constantly complain about management to other employees because they know there is strength in numbers: The more people who see that things are really bad, the more difficult it will be for management to deal with them as individuals. These individuals constantly admonish other employees to slow down, because if other employees are excelling, they will look even worse by comparison.

The remaining 80 percent of the workforce tend to be a more heterogeneous group. Some of them, of course, have the potential to rise into the top 10 percent, while others have the potential to fall into the bottom 10 percent. This group is generally composed of all types of employees, but for the most part, this group is quieter than the extreme groups, and tends to take a wait-and-see approach to the work. Each is capable of meeting and/or exceeding the performance expectations, and generally does. What characterizes this group is the fact that its members are always looking at both overt and covert messages for guidance as to how they should act. In some cases, they take their cues from management, especially in those organizations that have strong systems and reliable consequences for failing to meet or exceeding expectations. However, since most government organizations do not appear to work with that degree of sophistication, far too often, the employees take their cues from either the top or the bottom 10 percent. Whichever group ultimately wins the battle for the hearts and minds of the middle 80 percent will go a long way in determining the future of the organization.

Let's look at this more closely. The top 10 percent's primary goal is outstanding performance. They expect everyone to try and improve and will not accept the bottom 10 percent, since they see that group as working at odds with their vision. What frustrates this group more than anything else is seeing the bottom 10 percent flourish at the worksite; that is, they continue to see the worst employees skate by, doing poor work and poisoning the environment, with virtually no consequences.

If this scenario is allowed to continue for an extended period of time, the top 10 percent will continue to get frustrated and will eventually leave. Once that happens, the top 10 percent from the middle 80 percent will become the top 10 percent, and the quality of the organization's workforce will clearly diminish.

I once worked in an organization that had this exact situation. The prevailing mentality of our organization was that while we were bad, there were good reasons that explained why we were bad, and the people in Washington simply didn't understand what we were up against. Although it was clearly a tough organization to manage (a high-cost-of-living area without competitive pay, a weak workforce, difficult labor relations, etc.), the organization had stopped trying to cope with its problems. As a result, poor performers thrived, the top performers left, and the organization continued to spiral downward until the top management team was changed.

Jack Welch advocates firing the bottom 10 percent.[5] His rationale is that they are nonproducers and that they drain the workforce of energy. Firing the bottom 10 percent of a government organization's workforce would be extremely difficult to do on a consistent basis, given the rules, regulations, and labor agreements under which we work. It would also be incredibly costly and time consuming. Moreover, from a philosophical standpoint, I do not see the need to remove such a high percentage of the employees. To me, our first goal should be to pull them up and make them productive employees. This is clearly achievable as long as people recognize that (1) we will make a good-faith effort to try and help them improve; and (2) if they do not, then failure to perform and/or misbehavior could lead to their removal.

Earlier in my career, I became the leader of an organization where the bottom 10 percent was clearly winning. Shortly after my arrival, I fired an employee whom virtually everyone considered to be the worst employee on station. Knowing that a removal was highly unusual for that organization, I walked around to gauge the employees' reaction to the dismissal. To a person, the reaction was the same. "What took you guys so long to fire her?" "It's about time someone showed some strength in this organization." The fact of the matter is, most people want to be part of a winning organization and do not want management to tolerate the poor performers.

As word of this removal action spread, positive changes started to occur. For the first time, the bottom 10 percent realized that they could no longer continue to merely get by, and many of them started to improve their performance. They immediately understood that failure to meet the performance standards carried with it negative consequences. The supervisors recognized that senior management would finally support them if they took a well-documented performance-based action, so they became more willing to deal with employee performance issues. The net effect of this one action was to send a powerful message throughout the organization that management was serious about performance.

In contrast to the earlier example where the top 10 percent eventually left the organization, the action of removing that one employee had the opposite effect. Several of the bottom performers eventually were removed, while others got the message that they would not be able to survive, so they left of their own volition. More importantly, many of the marginal low performers decided to improve their performance, because they wanted to stay with the organization and had the ability to perform at a much higher level. The top performers also benefited from this approach because they were pleased that management had finally developed the backbone to deal with its long-standing performance problems. The result of this approach was that the bottom 10 percent either left or moved up, resulting in an organization that performed better with fewer performance problems to deal with.

Winning the battle for the hearts and minds of the middle 80 percent of an organization's employees is crucial to an organization's success. The best way to accomplish this is by applying the overall philosophies described in the first section of this chapter, while never forgetting that the ultimate objective is performance.

Avoiding Confrontation with the Bottom 10 Percent

Many supervisors make the classic mistake of beating up on the top 90 percent of the employees in order to avoid dealing with the bottom 10 percent. If you do this, you will play right into the hands of the bottom 10 percent, and will undermine much of the goodwill that comes by following the principles described in the last section. The reason why so many people do this is simple: They want to avoid confrontation. That is not surprising, because in my experience, very few people like confrontation. However, by avoiding confrontation at this stage, you will place yourself in a trap that will sow the seeds for much greater discontent down the road. Let's look at a typical example of how an inexperienced or poor supervisor might wind up in such a trap.

Confrontation with a Tardy Employee. Several times a week, Employee A arrives later than his starting time. Some days he is only 5 minutes late, while other days he arrives as much as 20 minutes late. His excuses vary, ranging from problems with his car to a broken alarm clock to congested traffic. Every one at the worksite is aware that he is frequently late, and they all look to see what time he will arrive each day. Employee A's supervisor is also aware of the continuing lateness, and he knows that the other employees are watching, since many of them have commented to him about this.

Finally, the supervisor decides that enough is enough and that he is going to do something about it. He calls a team meeting, wherein he states, "Some of you have been coming to work late. That is not acceptable and will not be tolerated. Effective immediately, the next person who comes to work late will be charged AWOL (absent without official leave) and disciplinary action will be taken."

From the supervisor's perspective, he has dealt with the problem, because he has placed the employee (and everyone else) on notice that he will take action against people that are late. From the employees' perspective, the supervisor is (1) a coward, because he is not dealing directly with the employee who has been late; and (2) beating up on them for a problem that they had nothing to do with. Some of them will actually interpret the supervisor's message to mean that it is okay to be late because no action has been taken against Employee A. In the battle for the hearts and minds of the middle 80 percent of the employees, the supervisor clearly lost this round.

The supervisor should have handled this situation in a private manner. As soon as he noticed that Employee A was coming to work late, he should have counseled him and put him on notice that continued instances of lateness could lead to AWOL and possibly discipline. If he continued being late, the supervisor should have taken disciplinary action in a manner consistent with the organization's table of penalties. By doing this, the supervisor would ensure that there were reliable consequences for Employee A's misbehavior. Although the employee might have complained about the counseling/AWOL/disciplinary action, the supervisor would quickly learn that as long as he had appropriate written documentation for his actions, these cases rarely go to third parties and hardly ever get overturned.

Another benefit of taking the action both promptly and privately is that the proper message will get out to the troops. Once Employee A is put on notice that management is serious about dealing with his behavior, it is likely he will complain to his fellow employees. While they may give him lip service, they will secretly cheer management for dealing with Employee A, and will conclude that management is truly serious about having people come to work on a timely basis. Accordingly, management will win this round for the hearts and minds of the middle 80 percent.

Don't Rely Only on the Top 10 Percent—Pull Others Up

We've talked about how important it is to win the hearts and minds of the middle 80 percent of our employees and how critical it is not to beat up on the vast majority of people. We also have to be careful not to give every critical, time-consuming, and highly pressurized assignment to our top 10 percent. Certainly, these individuals are our stars, our go-to people, and we do want to turn to them when necessary. The challenge is to utilize these individuals when needed, but not overextend them to the point where they become exhausted and lose some of their enthusiasm and effectiveness. The better approach is both to use their talents for special projects and to build additional capacity within the organization so we have even more go-to people to turn to.

Several years ago, I worked for a charismatic leader who was looking to reinvent the national administration that he was charged with leading. He was interested in changing almost every aspect of that administration, ranging from the way it was organized, to the manner in which work was performed, to the way it was measured. Clearly, this was an enormous undertaking. In attempting to accomplish his objectives, he turned to a relatively small inner circle of senior officials he could trust, including myself. We all had multiple assignments and worked incredibly hard to achieve our mission. I flew coast-to-coast virtually every week, while others made similar sacrifices.

Although, collectively, we were able to accomplish many things in the short term, over time, the strain took its toll on the inner circle. I got sick on a number of occasions and also began to experience back pains. The ongoing pressure wore some down, while others simply got tired and lost some of their initial energy. The lesson here was that you can rely on your top people for some things, but eventually you will have to add others to the mix—and that was exactly what happened down the road.

I worked for a different organization that also relied on only a few people. One of the individuals who was not part of the inner circle was a female employee who was anxious to advance. She had bounced around the government in several different positions, but had never made her mark. The fact that she was not a college graduate seemed to hold her back. She later came to work directly for me, and immediately started peppering me with questions.

She was obviously a highly motivated individual who desperately wanted to break into the inner circle. One day, she asked me what she could do to improve. I advised her that she needed to improve her writing skills. Shortly thereafter, she went back to school and took several courses that enhanced her ability to write. This impressed me, and I began spending more time mentoring her. Eventually, she became a trusted member of the inner circle, and was later selected to be an assistant director. By investing time in someone who was part of the middle 80 percent, I was able to add another employee to our top 10 percent.

You would be surprised how many people can improve if given the right opportunity. In fact, sometimes people are in the bottom 10 percent simply because they are in the wrong position or are given a set of tasks that don't quite fit them.

I once took over an organization and was advised that I would probably have to get rid of our chief of information resources. When I first started working with him, I noted that he was a bit nervous, and was afraid to make any mistakes. I eventually concluded that this was due partly to his personality and partly to the way he had been treated in the past.

I also came to realize that he had exceptional graphic arts skills that had never been utilized. Since I am a big proponent of visual management (see my discussion on this topic in Chapter 3), I began giving him a few assignments that would leverage his unique graphic skills. Immediately, others began to recognize his talent. He was eventually asked to develop a newsletter for the western part of our organization, and later developed a series of posters that were distributed nationally. He went from being someone who was considered to be in the bottom 10 percent to an individual who was nationally recognized for his unique skills. He demonstrated that many people could be pulled up and become exceptional employees if given the chance by management.

Key Points to Remember

- Treat people with respect and keep them in the loop, and they will respond accordingly.
- When your systems are properly aligned, they will drive the right employee behaviors.
- The more your systems are reliably applied, the more reliable will be your employees' behavior.
- Win the battle for the hearts and minds of the middle 80 percent of your employees, and your organization will succeed.

CHAPTER 3

Strategies and Tactics for Managing Government Employees

THE STRATEGIES AND TACTICS described in this chapter are relatively easy to apply. However, far too often they are not applied, or simply ignored, for a variety of reasons (time constraints, other priorities, philosophical differences, etc.). When they are utilized together as part of an integrated approach, they help foster a climate of teamwork and mutual support. More importantly, these strategies and tactics will inspire the workforce and increase its commitment toward achieving the organization's goals.

Communicate with Employees as Much as You Can (Visually, Whenever Possible)

This seems like a no-brainer. After all, who can possibly be against communication? The answer is nobody. Everyone I've ever met in management tries to communicate with the employees. The problem is that few do it successfully.

In my experience, the best way to communicate with the workforce is through a *whole brain approach*. This approach is based on the work of Ned Herrman, who developed the Whole Brain Model, which purports that there are four learning styles as follows:

1. *Theorists:* These are people who prefer lecture, fact, and details, critical thinking, textbooks, and readings.

47

2. *Organizers:* These are people who like to learn by outlining, checklists, exercises, and problem solving with steps, policies, and procedures.
3. *Innovators:* These are people who prefer brainstorming, metaphors, illustrations and pictures, mind mapping and synthesis, and holistic approaches.
4. *Humanitarians:* These are people who like cooperative learning and group discussion, role playing, and dramatization.[1]

Given the fact that people have four separate learning styles, it is essential that we attempt to communicate with them in different ways. Simply issuing a memo and expecting everyone to read it, absorb it, and remember it will not work, especially in this age of information overload. We need to get the message out in different ways: certainly in writing, but also through speeches and lectures, both in a group setting and, at times, in a more informal setting. Sometimes we need to communicate with illustrations and pictures, while other times we need to have employees actually attempt to implement the information being transmitted. There is no best way to communicate. Rather, the ideal is to use some combination of the approaches described above.

I once served in an agency's headquarters where my role was to implement a complex series of new performance measures on a national basis. I developed a lecture that explained the concept, but given its complexity, people had a hard time grasping its intricacies. Eventually, we had to add exercises to the class and repeat them multiple times in different settings (at conferences, in classrooms, at the worksite, on television, and one on one) before people began to understand what this new system was all about. We later added a detailed handbook that people could refer to, so the employees would have all of the information they would need.

In plotting a communication strategy, it is essential that repetition be part of the plan. Early in my career, I would issue a memo or give a speech, and later be amazed at how little of the information was grasped by the workforce. I constantly found myself in a position where I had to explain what I really said and meant. I learned that a one-time effort to communicate an important message in any form was simply not enough; that the key was to communicate the same message multiple times, in different ways, in order to accommodate the employees' different learning styles.

One of the most powerful ways to communicate and/or reinforce a message is through visual management. Visual management is a novel approach wherein an organization's physical plant is transformed to do the following:

•   Connect the employees to the mission by turning the space into a living, breathing tribute to its mission/customers

- Celebrate the employees
- Share information
- Hold the employees accountable
- Shape the outside world's view of the organization—with the overall goal being improved performance

In essence, visual management combines tried-and-true management tools along with the tools of an artist to help make an organization work great.[2]

When I became the leader of a government organization that adjudicated veterans' claims for benefits, it had the lowest customer satisfaction score out of 57 offices. The root cause was that the employees were not connected to the mission, so in many instances, they looked to deny benefits when they should have granted them (our grant rate was 50 percent below the national average). I constantly exhorted the employees to grant more benefits, but I found that this approach was not sufficient.

We then started redesigning our office in an effort to reinforce our message of granting benefits whenever possible. Banners were hung up with this message; we built a display depicting the history of the benefits we were supposed to administer. We added large artifacts typically used by soldiers (e.g., a scale model of an Abrams M-1 tank, a Huey Helicopter, a Willey Jeep, etc.), private reflection areas (a field hospital, a bunker, etc.), and personal memorabilia from veterans (artwork, photographs, letters, medals, etc.) in order to continue get the message across.

We also built a Hall of Fame honoring our employees of the quarter and transformed our training room into a general tribute to all of our folks. Lastly, we added television monitors that gave daily performance and rewards information to all of our employees. The net effect of this communication effort was to increase our grant rate by 50 percent (to the same level as the nation) and our customer satisfaction rate by 37 percent. In honor of this approach, the director of the United States Office of Personnel Management gave our office the prestigious PILLAR (Performance Incentives Leadership Linked to Achieving Results) Award.

The better an organization communicates with its workforce, the better the organization will work as one, united entity. Those organizations that communicate with a whole brain strategy will clearly have an advantage. Incorporating visual management as part of that strategy will ensure that the message is constantly in front of the employees.

Let's now turn to a couple of areas that often get overlooked in the communication process, yet are essential for maintaining morale and building credibility with the workforce.

Figure 3-1

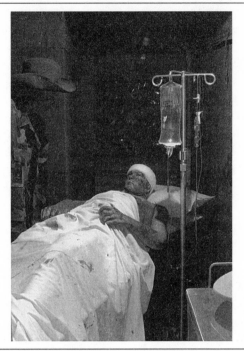

A 3-D display using visual management principles that is designed to connect the U.S. Department of Veterans' Affairs employees to the mission—serving veterans.

Teach Them the Big Picture
(The Political Climate)

The first area is the big picture. All government employees work for organizations that are influenced by a variety of political forces. In the federal government, some of the influencers are the White House, the organization's headquarters, Congress, the public, unions, special interest groups, and the media, just to name a few. At the state or local government level, the influencers can include the governor or mayor, the state assembly, the board of supervisors, as well as many of the same groups that affect the federal government. All of these groups play a role in the political process, and each of them influences the policies of their organizations.

Sometimes, unanticipated events force government to change its course. For example, a war, a terrorist attack, a natural disaster, or a scandal can quickly force a change of direction.

With so many groups and events influencing government, frequent change is virtually inevitable. An Inspector General report may point out problems with Social Security's claims processing; the media may write a series of articles criticizing a county hospital; a hurricane could develop that would require the sudden redeployment of resources to the affected area; or a budget crisis may trigger a drastic cutback in state spending. These types of events occur all the time at every level of government and inevitably trigger a response by management officials.

From the employees' perspective, change seems to be constant. They are continuously asked to change their priorities and/or focus to the point where they begin to question management's competence. We often hear, "If management would only leave us alone and let us do our work, we could get the job done far more effectively." What the employees don't realize, however, is that management feels the exact same way. Managers don't like to constantly alter the course any more than the employees do.

Although the employees and management both get frustrated by the constant changes, the overall reaction is generally different. Since most managers are normally in the political loop, at least to some extent, change is easier to accept. They understand the forces at play and recognize that their role is to implement the inevitable changes as best they can.

To the employees, each additional change is one more indication that management doesn't know what it is doing. From where they sit, management is constantly jerking them around for reasons that seem unfathomable. These differing reactions to change by the employees and management undermine trust and credibility between these two groups, and pose a danger to the organization.

The solution is to teach the employees the big picture, so they will understand the forces that affect them in the same way that management does. If management does this successfully, it will defuse an enormous amount of tension during periods of change and will ensure that change is implemented smoothly.

One of the lessons I learned early on was to always begin my employee meetings with a discussion of the big picture. I would start with a discussion of the current forces in play. For example, during FY 2005, some of the key influencers in the field of veterans' benefits were the war in Iraq, the number of soldiers expected to return home, and the national budget deficit. I explained to the employees that these three factors would probably lead to more claims for veterans' benefits being filed, but conversely, we were likely to have fewer resources with which to process these claims. By giving the employees this sense of context, I knew they would be more understanding and supportive of our local plans and initiatives.

Teach Them What's Going On in the Local Organization

Knowing what's going on locally goes hand in hand with understanding the national political picture. In most cases, local plans and initiatives flow from changes at the national, state, or county level. If employees can understand and appreciate both perspectives, they are much more likely to support management. This, in turn, will result in the organization's available energy being more sharply focused on the mission and the goals.

So how does management go about informing the employees about what's going on in the local organization? First of all, as stated earlier, it needs to communicate in a way that addresses the employees' different learning styles. Second, it needs to ensure that the employees understand the big picture. After covering these two bases, management needs to inform the employees about the organization's local strategy, goals, and expectations. If the employees have this sense of context, they will be able to understand a wide variety of management decisions and will generally be supportive. Conversely, if they don't understand where the organization is going, they are likely to devote a large amount of time speculating among themselves about what management is really doing and why. This wastes a tremendous amount of the organization's time and energy, as the employees will become less focused on work and more focused on idle speculation.

I once worked for a local organization that was very secretive. Senior management held virtually all of its decisions very close to the vest. When decisions were finally announced, little, if any, rationale was provided for the decisions. The employees were not given any opportunity to question management about the decisions they made, and there was little interaction between the employees and management. For the vast majority of employees, it felt as though all key decisions were made behind closed doors in smoke-filled rooms, by the "in crowd."

After the decisions were announced, the rumor mill took over, with people spending an inordinate amount of time on the phone or around the water cooler, trying to figure why that particular decision was made and what it portended for the future. Since almost everyone felt frozen out of the process, many felt disenfranchised from the organization. As a result, all senior management got was compliance from its employees. What it did not get, however, was commitment, and we all know that the difference between mere compliance and commitment is huge.

In another organization, I encountered the opposite approach. In this organization, senior management held periodic meetings with the employees wherein the chief executive and his key assistants explained what was going on, what his goals and strategies were, and discussed any changes in the political wind. He also gave the employees the opportunity to question the rationale behind the decisions that were being made in the organization.

This executive made it a point to walk around the worksite on a daily basis (more on this approach later) so he could get his message across and hear the concerns of the people. Finally, he published a monthly newsletter that contained additional information as to what was going on at the office (promotions, birthdays, changes to policy, etc.). This open approach to communication, which was an intentional part of the overall communication strategy, bought that executive a tremendous amount of employee commitment.

Give Them Feedback as to How They Are Doing

So far, we've generally talked about communication at the group level. Another key piece to this equation involves one-on-one communication. Although it is essential that employees know what's going on both inside and outside of their organization, it is equally important that they know what's going on with respect to them.

If an employee believes she is doing well, while her supervisor believes the opposite, trouble will be brewing. In addition, if an employee does not receive any feedback, she is likely to become anxious and/or cautious, neither of which is good for the organization.

Periodic one-on-one feedback sessions will address these issues because employees will know how they are doing relative to the organization's expectations. These sessions provide an excellent opportunity to nip problems in the bud, or to reinforce excellent performance and/or behavior. Naturally, management also needs to ensure that these sessions are reliably applied, as discussed earlier.

When done correctly, these sessions will let employees know what they are doing well and where they need improvement. In most cases, people want to know how they are doing so they have an opportunity to improve. They will appreciate honesty and will attempt to address their limitations.

If someone has a performance or conduct problem, once he is placed on notice regarding the problem (and it is documented), it becomes very difficult for him to later argue that he didn't know about the problem. Moreover, if he can see what the consequences are for continuing to have the same problem, he is likely to address it. By the same token, if he cannot improve, and management has to take a certain action, he will be more accepting of the consequences because he can see the action coming.

Handling an Employee with Performance Problems. An employee was promoted to a position that was beyond his competence. This was a good individual who was well respected for the work he did in his previous job. The new position was simply too complex for this person, and he clearly struggled. As soon as his problems became apparent, management intervened and sincerely tried to assist him. However, despite multiple counseling sessions, additional training, and the help of a mentor, this individual continued to struggle. Since it was apparent to everyone, especially the employee, that he was not going to make it, he voluntarily requested an assignment back to his former position, which was immediately granted. The employee felt that he was treated fairly and honestly, and returned to his former position in good spirits, because he could read the writing on the wall. Management handled the situation well and prevented this employee from becoming cynical and anti-management, which happens far too often when the employee cannot see an adverse event coming.

Mishandling Employee Performance Reviews. The exact opposite once happened to me. I worked for an organization that distributed a total of 31 written performance targets to its senior executives. These targets were all given equal weight, at least on the written performance plan. Many of the targets appeared to be out of reach, because we (as well as many other offices) were in the middle of an extended hiring freeze that had been going on for several years. We worked extremely hard to achieve as many targets as possible, and at the end of the year, our office met or exceeded a much higher percentage of the targets than the nation as a whole.

When I was informed that my rating for the year was "fully successful," I was shocked, because I did not see it coming. While a "fully successful" rating is a good rating, my previous ratings were almost always "outstanding," and that's what I expected. I was obviously caught by surprise, and felt that I was not treated fairly.

This rating hurt my relationship with my supervisor and left me upset and frustrated for a while. Whether it is a senior executive or a trainee, when an individual does not see a management action coming, it invariably angers that individual and weakens the person's sense of commitment to the organization.

Manage by Walking Around (MBWA)

This approach to management, first described by Tom Peters,[3] is another form of communication that is extremely effective and is a perfect complement to the other communication strategies we've described so far. Since I have spent many years managing by walking around, I want to reinforce this approach and explain why it is an excellent communication and management technique.

From my perspective, MBWA accomplishes three main goals that are completely consistent with my philosophy:

1.   It allows management to see what's really going on in the organization.
2.   It can streamline communication and improve access to information.
3.   It can improve morale by letting the employees know that management is truly interested in both their needs and the needs of the organization.

It has been my experience that if you sit in your organization's ivory tower, you can convince yourself of anything. That is, you can always find one number or statistic that will support your desire to believe that everything is going well. Over time, if all the information you receive is filtered in such a way as to support your belief that things are going well, you will fall deeper and deeper into denial. Reports of problems will be quickly dismissed, and you will become further and further isolated. History has shown that this fate can befall anyone, from first-line supervisors to presidents who become more and more isolated.

Early in my career, I did not manage by walking around, but tended to be a "numbers guy" who would look for all of the answers in our organization's metrics. When the employees did not share my view of things, I simply assumed that they did not understand what was really going on. In retrospect, I had only one side of the story, and it cost me dearly, since I often made decisions based on a false sense of reality.

After exposure to a leader who walked around the workplace on a daily basis, I very quickly began to realize that there could easily be a disconnect between our statistics and reality. It soon became evident that management by walking around was a necessary reality check.

At the time I was working for an organization that processed claims for benefits. Our statistics on average time to process claims were pretty good. That was the number that we were focusing on. What I didn't understand, until I start walking around, was that the number of unprocessed claims was climbing, which was a leading indicator of future timeliness. By walking around, I could see that a large number of claims folders were sitting on the desks of our employees waiting to be worked, and that the stress on the work floor was building. Moreover, I could see the tension and frustration on the faces of the employees, who were unhappy that our backlog was increasing. I quickly learned that statistics were one indicator of an organization's health, but not the only indicator.

Another benefit to MBWA is enhanced communication. When I first started walking around, people were very suspicious of me. Since they hadn't seen me very often, they assumed that I must have an ulterior motive for walking around. As they began to realize that I was determined to walk around on a daily basis, they started opening up. Initially, when I asked how things were going, the answer I always received was "fine." However, the answers began to change once people realized that I was serious, and was truly interested in what they had to say. Suddenly, people started telling me what was really going on. They would discuss concerns ranging from the ventilation system, to workflow issues, to the rumor mill. I would then cross-check this information with others, and, where appropriate, would immediately act on it.

During one of my rounds, I learned from several employees that they were experiencing problems with the mail. When I looked into this issue, it turned out that they were right, as a number of our mailroom employees were out on extended leave. If I had stayed in my office, I probably would not have learned about this until several weeks later, when the damage was done. However, because I had greatly increased my stream of information, I was able to quickly address this issue by detailing several people to the mailroom.

MBWA produces information in several different ways. As we've discussed, looking at the work is one source of information, and speaking to the employees is another. A third source is through the employees' body language. Sometimes, the employees simply don't feel comfortable telling someone in management that there is a problem. They may feel that it is not their job or that they will be punished if they disclose negative information. However, after walking around for a while, I began to realize that people often disclose information through their body language.

When an employee shrugs her shoulders or rolls her eyes, she is giving me a message. After a while, I began to read this unspoken language and understood that it was another way for employees to communicate with me and another way for me to learn about what was really going on.

I also found that MBWA provided me with an opportunity to communicate directly with the employees in a way that I couldn't during large group meetings. Those meetings are certainly an excellent way of passing along information. A few people will typically ask questions, but many will not because they are uncomfortable speaking in front of large groups.

It eventually became my practice after these meetings to walk around and ask the employees what they thought of the meeting. First of all, it gave me the chance to see if they really understood my message. It also gave me the opportunity to see if my lower-level managers were giving them the same message that I was. Finally, it gave me the chance to address any lingering questions from the meeting. Naturally, I was aware that if I answered the questions of a few of the employees, they would pass on my responses to others, which would further ensure that my message was getting out.

The third reason I manage by walking around is that it provides me with the opportunity to be visible—that is, to show the employees that I am there for them and that I am willing to do whatever it takes to help them succeed. When people see you on a daily basis, and they then see you reacting to their concerns, you build instant credibility. They realize that you are a person of your word, and they appreciate you for it—because that is not something they see often. If they realize that you are willing to go the extra mile for them, they, in turn, will go the extra mile for you.

For example, I once took over an organization that was very dissatisfied with the landlord. One of the biggest problems was the air conditioning, or lack thereof. In order to address this situation, I walked around with the building manager and his maintenance team. In full view of the employees, I pointed out the areas of dissatisfaction. Quickly, the ventilation improved, and the employees realized that I was willing to do whatever it took to improve their working conditions.

This simple action on my part built an enormous amount of goodwill, for everyone realized that I was there to help. They now recognized that if I walked around and identified a problem, I would do everything in my power to try and address it.

As time progressed, all sorts of problems were brought to my attention, and I did whatever I could to address them. Computer issues, copier problems, security concerns, you name it; I tried to address them all. Although people knew I couldn't solve every problem, at least they knew that I was trying. At the same time, I also wanted people to follow the chain of command, and I emphasized that in my conversations. Otherwise, the employees would begin to bypass their supervisors/managers and always go directly to me.

As time went by, many of the supervisors began to see the success of MBWA and they modeled that behavior. This built a stronger and more robust communication loop between management and the employees.

Ask Your Employees for Advice

Another strategy for enhancing communication, improving performance, and building morale is to periodically ask the employees for advice on key issues. This approach can be taken during large group meetings, in smaller settings, or while walking around. I have found this to be an effective approach because: (1) the people who do the work are often in the best position to tell you what the problems are as well as the solutions; and (2) by going directly to the workers and asking their advice, they will feel valued as long as you truly listen to what they say and carefully consider their ideas.

This approach fits well with the overall philosophies stated earlier (people want to do a good job, they want to be part of a winning organization, always treat people with respect, etc.) because you are including everyone in the effort to improve performance. When everyone feels valued, the level of effort and focus increases, leading to a more productive organization. Moreover, when people see that their advice is valued, they look more closely for ways to improve and seek to give even more advice, which creates a positive domino effect. Let's look at a few examples.

One organization I'm familiar with had as its mission to rehabilitate its clients and find them jobs. Basically, we had to determine if they had an employment impairment and, if so, place them in an appropriate program of education or training, and then help them to find a job. The people who did these jobs were highly educated and skilled professionals who knew that they could make a major difference in the lives of their clients. The problem was that while many people went through the system and received some services, the vast majority did not find jobs, which resulted in a very low rate of rehabilitation.

We sat down with the employees and asked them for their advice. The consistent message we received from virtually everyone was that they were stretched far too thin and were unable to concentrate on the bottom line—finding their clients jobs. They all had too many clients to manage (some were trying to case manage as many as 300 to 500 clients), so they were simply moving them along through the system. To a person, they emphasized that we needed to offload some of their work, so they could concentrate on their core mission (i.e., finding their clients jobs).

After listening to the employees' advice, we decided to reorganize the way we did the work. Much of their clerical work was moved to other parts of the division so the professionals could focus on the most complex parts of the job. Moreover, we hired a number of outside contractors to assume a portion of the workload so we could reduce the caseload of our professionals to a manageable number (1:125). We also improved the way we tracked our work to make sure that each of the professionals was pulling his own weight. Over time, they became much more effective at performing their core work, and the number of clients they rehabilitated increased by over 600 percent. The employees in that division now feel valued, and for the past few years, they have received a number of national awards. Moreover, during my last year there, every professional far exceeded his performance standards.

A second case involves an organization that had unusually low productivity. As is my custom, I asked the employees for their advice. Many of them immediately complained about the workspace design. They indicated that because they were sitting virtually on top of each other, with no partitions, and because there were many visitors to the worksite, they were constantly being distracted and had little opportunity to concentrate on the work. As I examined the design, I immediately realized that they were right. The employees were all seated together with no privacy, in the middle of the office. Interestingly, the file cabinets were situated against the windows so they had the best view of the outside world. The layout promoted a high degree of socializing and wandering around the office, and afforded little opportunity for the employees to concentrate on the work.

As soon as we could, we changed the layout, which created natural barriers that reduced the amount of wandering around and socializing. (Note: The natural barriers were intended to allow teammates to interact whenever necessary, but to prevent wandering from team to team, which was generally unnecessary.) The layout change also allowed the employees to concentrate on their work, which was highly technical in nature. The first month that we changed the design, our productivity increased by 8 percent, which was entirely due to our taking the advice of our employees.

Sometimes we are unable to implement the advice that our employees give us. It may be because the employee does not understand how a proposal will affect other parts of the operation; the resources may not be there to implement what is being suggested; or the advice may simply not make sense. Whatever the reason, as long as we explain to the people making the suggestion why we cannot implement it, they will normally understand, will feel that their ideas have been considered, and will continue to make suggestions.

On occasion, many of us will find ourselves in a group setting where a particularly strident individual will criticize whatever management is doing. This person invariably falls into the bottom 10 percent category and usually tries to put management on the defensive. If that happens, I first try and explain my side of the story. If the person continues to attack me, I will turn the tables on her and ask her publicly what she would suggest we do. In most cases, the response will be, "That's not my job. That's the job of management." This approach accomplishes two things:

1. It lets everyone know that you are open to the opinions of others, no matter how difficult a particular employee may be.

2. If the person gives you the typical response, it demonstrates to the group that the employee is attacking management for the sake of attacking management, and that the employee does not have any better ideas. Conversely, if the employee has a good idea, I'm all ears.

Say "Thank You" as Often as You Can

Asking people for their advice also entails thanking them when you accept their input. Saying "thank you" to someone (whether it is for giving good advice, outstanding performance, excellent behavior, etc.) is one of the best ways for reinforcing good behavior, as long as it is delivered and accepted as being sincere. When done properly, saying "thank you" is a powerful technique for motivating people and improving the bottom line. According to Jennifer Newman and Darryl Grigg:

> It sometimes seems difficult to extract a thank you from someone at work. Many employees we hear from complain of a dearth of appreciation for their efforts. They long for a pat on the back, even an appreciative smile or some indication they've done something that has helped out.
>
> Unfortunately, thank yous happen infrequently. Yet research indicates organizations that value gratitude benefit through increased performance. Customer retention increases, staff loyalty, and job satisfaction are heightened and . . . people are more helpful to their customers when they feel appreciated.[4]

It is important to note that we should thank only people that truly deserve our thanks. Otherwise, if we thank people for their work, whether they deserve it or not, it will dilute the value of the "thank you." Moreover, by thanking only the employees who truly deserve our thanks, the people who are left out will get the message that management does not believe that they deserve to be thanked.

Early in my career, I served as personnel officer in an organization that was really struggling. The performance statistics were very poor, morale was low, and there was a general sense among the management team that our organization was unmanageable. Within this context, I was trying to deal with a wide variety of difficult personnel and labor-relations issues.

After a while our central office became increasingly concerned about the performance of our organization, and sent a special team to review our operation. Naturally, at that point, there was a lot of fear among our management team, since we were concerned that we would all be labeled as being poor managers. When the team surveyed our office, they found plenty of blame to go around. However, they made a point of calling me aside and telling me that they thought I was doing an excellent job and thanking me for my good work.

This simple gesture made a world of difference to me and made me realize that if you do a good job, even under difficult circumstances, people will notice it, appreciate it, and recognize you for it. To this day, I still recall with great pleasure the simple thanks I received during a difficult time in my career.

On another occasion, I was detailed as acting director to an office that had been experiencing a lot of problems. An arrogant leader, who abused the employees in many different ways, was responsible for the bulk of the problems. In fact, he eventually retired after being accused of sexual harassment by one of the employees.

When I arrived, I tried to walk around and get to know the employees. As you could imagine, they were reluctant to say much because they were used to being treated poorly. However, it quickly became apparent to me that the employees of this office were exceptional, especially since they had a well-earned reputation for high productivity.

I still recall one particular group of employees that made a large impression on me—the folks in the mailroom. These people were serious, hard-working individuals who never received any respect. As I looked into their performance, I noted that they always seemed to deliver the mail on time, and with excellent accuracy. No one really had anything bad to say about them; they were simply ignored by their more highly educated co-workers. I therefore decided to speak with them both as a group and individually, and thank them for their efforts. Their reaction to my simple gesture shocked me. They said that I was the first director who had visited them in almost 20 years (except for the day before Christmas). They were incredibly appreciative that someone had recognized their good work, and advised me that they would do anything, and they emphasized the word *anything*, for me.

Be Sensitive to People's Sensitivities

Communicating with the employees, particularly when walking around and saying "thank you," poses some risks, as management's actions can easily be misinterpreted. Every word you say, every gesture you make, even the expressions you have on your face will be closely scrutinized by the employees, because of the inherent power that rests with management. More often than you can imagine, they will attempt to "read the tea leaves" and give far too much meaning to something where no meaning was intended. This can easily lead to confusion, mixed messages, or worse.

By nature, I am a very serious person. While I have a good sense of humor, it tends to be dry. Moreover, whenever I am concentrating on something, I seem to wear an expression that makes me appear to be angry. That expression has sometimes gotten me in trouble because people have assumed that I was angry with them, which was not the case at all. I learned that as a senior leader, I have to control my expression at all times, at least when I am with people, if I want them to get the right message.

Most workforces these days are pretty heterogeneous, meaning that our employees bring a wide variety of experiences, cultural preferences, and biases to the workplace. This makes our job even more difficult, as one approach clearly will not work for all. The answer is to keep our eyes and ears as wide open as possible, to constantly read the workforce (both by what they say and by what they don't say) and gauge what they are thinking, and to have as many sources as possible that are willing to give us the unfiltered truth. Let's look at a few examples.

It is my practice to try and walk around every day at work and talk to the employees. I generally don't talk to everyone on a daily basis, but I do try and speak to a representative sample. Sometimes the office layout can cause unexpected challenges.

In one particular office where I worked, it was difficult to approach the employees who sat near the windows, since they were often surrounded by carts or files cabinets. As time went by, I became a bit sloppy and tended to talk only to the people in front—because it was convenient for me. What I didn't realize was that many of our African-American employees sat near the windows because that was the most desirable space and they had the longest tenure with our office. Since it appeared to them that I was ignoring them, they began to question whether my actions were intentional. While they were not, I was not as sensitive to their impressions as I should have been. Fortunately, our union president, who had always served as a reality check for me, pointed this issue out to me early enough that I was able to change my practice. Once I ensured that I was talking to a true representative sample of the employees, the issue went away.

It is amazing what management can be accused of. One time, a Jewish member of our workforce accused me of being, or at least acting like, an anti-Semite. This accusation struck me as being a bit unusual, since it was no secret that I am Jewish. When I asked the employee what formed the basis for her accusation, she replied, "You are bending over backwards to hurt the Jews, so the non-Jews will not think you are prejudiced in favor of the Jews." While her reasoning struck me as a bit convoluted, I did recognize that perception could be reality for some. We sat down and went over the basis for her accusation, and I eventually convinced her that I had been even-handed. However, I came away from this meeting with the recognition that I had to be constantly on my guard in an effort to both treat and appear to treat our employees in a fair and equitable manner.

We not only have to be sensitive to every race and ethnic group, we also have to be sensitive to the different personality types of our employees.

Most people prefer to talk with positive, upbeat individuals. It's simply not as enjoyable to talk to someone who is angry, depressed, or cynical. However, we have to make sure that we attempt to talk to everyone, regardless of his or her personality type. First of all, it's the right thing to do. Second, it will insulate us from any charges of disparate treatment. Third, by talking to these individuals, we may be able to change their behavior or we may find that they are as not as negative as they appear to be.

Early in my career, I shied away from talking to a female employee who never seemed to want to talk to me or anyone else. I thought she was an unhappy person who didn't get along with anyone. One day, I got up the nerve to talk to her. It turned out that she was a delightful person who was extremely shy. She was very happy to learn that someone, particularly at my level, had taken an interest in her. From that moment on, she slowly but surely opened up to me and eventually became a positive force in our organization.

Your Human Resources Management Advisors

If applied fairly, the strategies and tactics discussed here for managing government employees will greatly improve our chances of having a high-performing, well-motivated workforce. However, we all come across situations that require the advice of others, someone who is knowledgeable in the field of human resources and is not emotionally involved in the situation. That individual is the human resources (HR) specialist. HR specialists wield an enormous amount of power in government organizations, because the personnel rules and regulations are so complex and convoluted that line managers can't possibly be expected to become experts in the field. As a result, they have to frequently turn to HR experts for advice and assistance as to how they should deal with their employees.

The Two Types of HR Specialists

I was an HR specialist for years, and have also served in line management wherein I interacted with HR specialists on a daily basis. Those experiences have taught me that HR specialists tend to have two different schools of thought. The first school says, "If the personnel rules don't say you can do it, don't do it." The second school of thought says, "If the personnel rules don't say you can't do it, do it." These two schools of thought reflect different mindsets among HR specialists. The first group tends to take a strict constructionist interpretation of the personnel manual; the second group takes a much more liberal interpretation. The difference in these two philosophies is profound. I strongly believe that the extent to which either philosophy infiltrates an organization will have a major influence on its success.

The first philosophy is generally held by HR specialists who see their primary role as protecting the personnel rules and regulations. They want to ensure that they never make a mistake, that every rule and regulation is complied with to the letter, and that they look exceptionally good on a personnel audit of their records. They also want to be certain that only airtight, perfect cases go to a third party.

In my view, these individuals are technocrats, since their primary loyalty is to the HR manual, not to the organization's mission. They rarely take the time to learn the organization's mission, because they spend most of the time trying to comply with the personnel rules. As a result, when line managers come to them for advice, the advice they provide is designed to ensure that the line manager does not break any rules. They do not try and assist the line manager in accomplishing her mission, because they do not really understand the mission. For these types of HR specialists, the mission is secondary to the personnel rules and regulations.

As an example, an office where I worked was desperate to hire some trainees. Since we were located in a high-cost-of-living area, and the salary we were offering was not competitive with the private sector, we knew that recruitment would be tough. We did a lot of advertising and received a reasonable number of applications. However, the personnel office that was servicing our office took a conservative approach toward qualifying the applicants, and more than half of them were disqualified, even though many of them appeared to be good candidates.

It was particularly galling from our standpoint, because the qualification standards merely required general experience in the same or related field as the job we were recruiting for. Instead of taking a flexible approach to qualifications determinations, recognizing that it was in the best interests of the government to have a large pool of candidates, the HR specialist took an overly rigid approach and greatly pared down our pool. The net result was that we were unable to bring on as many highly qualified individuals as we would have desired.

The second philosophy is generally held by HR specialists who see their role as being there to support the organization's mission. They understand that the rules and regulations are important, but they interpret them more flexibly, recognizing that they were not written to cover every situation. They are willing to take chances and are prepared to make an occasional mistake, knowing that they are trying to help the organization achieve its mission.

These individuals take the time to learn the organization's mission and see themselves as key contributors to that mission. For them, human resources management is not separate and distinct from line management; it is closely integrated with them in an effort to accomplish the organization's mission.

To my mind, these are the HR specialists who truly add value to organizations. When a supervisor comes to them for help, they do not immediately say no. They start with a question, "What are you trying to accomplish?" Once the goal is clear, they figure out ways it can be accomplished, so they can achieve management's objectives while flexibly and appropriately interpreting the governing rules and regulations.

There was once a very tense situation in my organization. Three employees were involved in a love triangle that was polarizing the office. At any one time, two of these individuals seemed to be romantically involved, leaving the third person out in the cold. The third individual in the equation frequently changed, creating a situation where one of the three always seemed to be angry. Almost on a weekly basis, one of them would file a complaint against one or both of the remaining two individuals. As you can imagine, the situation became very personal, and many people were dragged into this mess. Moreover, an enormous amount of time was wasted looking into and trying to resolve these never-ending complaints.

No one could figure out how to address this issue until I proposed that we counsel all three individuals and advise them that continued problems relating to their love triangle would result in all three of them being disciplined, regardless of who complained. The traditionalists were shocked by this approach because there were no personnel manual references that allowed management to take such an action against all three individuals; there was no precedent for the action; and they were concerned as to what would happen if the action went to a third party.

Despite these concerns, management decided to take my advice and proceed with the counselings. Once the employees received the written counselings, they realized that management was serious and was prepared to do what it had to do to stop their nonsense. Immediately, they stopped bringing their problems to the workplace, and the issue went away.

Toward the beginning of my career, I was interviewed for the position of personnel officer. During the interview, the director and assistant director constantly complained to me about an employee in the finance department. This individual held a black belt in karate and was intimidating both the employees and management. He frequently made subtle threats of bodily harm to people; however, because the threats were deemed by the HR office to be difficult to prove, no action was taken, which only reinforced his belief that he was invulnerable. No one knew what to do about this individual, but it was clear to everyone that he was having an adverse impact on the organization. I promised my interviewers that I would immediately deal with this individual if selected, and shortly thereafter, I got the job.

During my first week on the job, he made one of his veiled threats to management, which was immediately relayed to me by his division chief. I suggested that we propose his removal. The division chief was shocked. "We can't do that!" he said. "Why not?" I replied, He said, "Personnel has told me time and again that if we take action based on these types of threats, we will lose before a third party." I then asked him how many times he had gone to a third party, and the answer was never. In essence, they had avoided taking action out of fear of later being overturned, so they had given up before they had even started.

I asked the division chief if he thought that removing this individual was the right thing to do. He responded, "Absolutely." I therefore asked him to try things my way and see what happened. He agreed. Once the employee received the proposed removal, his entire demeanor changed. He went from being a confident bully to being genuinely afraid of losing his job. He blamed his behavior on a long-time mental condition, and we eventually negotiated an exit strategy wherein he took a disability retirement.

All of the senior managers were amazed that a long-standing difficult personnel problem went away virtually overnight. They realized the value of having an HR specialist who was not afraid to recommend a risky approach. After that, I was always at the table when key HR decisions were made.

Getting Good HR Advice Is Harder than Ever

By now it should be clear that a top-notch HR specialist can make an enormous difference in an organization. Unfortunately, managers often find themselves saddled with a local HR specialist who is either inexperienced or a rigid thinker, or who does not understand their mission or their needs.

This problem has been compounded by the push to centralize HR activities in an effort to reduce the size of government. On paper, this approach makes perfect sense. After all, does every organization really need its own HR staff? The answer is probably not. However, as so often happens in government, the push to reduce staffing resulted in so much centralization that few HR jobs were left at the local level.

This has resulted in two distinct problems. First of all, where HR jobs were consolidated, HR ceased being viewed as a valued career field at the local level. Smaller HR offices resulted in fewer career opportunities, causing the most talented and experienced HR specialists to leave their local organizations for greener pastures (usually in the same area of the country, with an HR office that had not been centralized). At the same time, the remaining pool of available talent began to shrink, because these folks also took the message that HR was not a valued career field. As a result, they simply looked for other career fields to enter. This left the remaining HR specialists in the difficult position of having very few individuals at the local level to turn to for guidance and mentoring.

The move toward centralized HR activities also created a different set of problems. Since these large offices serve so many different organizations, it is hard for them to provide the individualized level of service that local HR offices used to provide. They devote most of their energies toward filling positions for their largest customers and, to some extent, become almost HR recruitment factories. Moreover, because these offices are usually not co-located with the organizations that they service, they are rarely in tune with what is happening at the local level.

The net result is that many managers are unhappy with the level of HR advice they are receiving today. This is particularly troubling given the fact that it is more difficult to manage government employees today than ever before, for three reasons:

1. The demand for performance and accountability is incredibly high, creating more and more pressure on everyone.
2. People are more litigious than ever.
3. Government employees have more options than in the past because retirement programs are more portable, making them less likely to stay if they don't want to.

With all of these challenges, how does a government manager survive if the organization has a poor HR advisor? The answer is simple: either *change* your advisor or change your *advisor*. If the person at the worksite is weak, try to find a mentor who can help develop the advisor to become more aggressive and action-oriented. If that doesn't work, find someone else, either at the current worksite or at another location, who has the expertise to help you.

You've probably met such a person at conferences or on project teams. While she may not be able to assist you on a daily basis, you can definitely turn to her when key decisions need to be made. There are still plenty of people around who are skilled in HR. The problem is, there are not nearly as many out there as there used to be.

Finding someone with the right skill sets and attitude to help you through the difficult situations is absolutely crucial, because without the right person, you are likely to be paralyzed by inaction.

Key Points to Remember

- Communicate as much as possible, in a whole brain fashion, using visual management techniques.
- Let employees know what's going on in the organization and how they are doing; say "thank you" as often as possible.
- Manage by walking around; learn what your employees are thinking.
- You need an HR advisor who is flexible, creative, and mission-oriented.

Dealing with Difficult People

IN THIS CHAPTER I will begin to focus on one of the hardest tasks a government manager can face—dealing with difficult employees. The task is hard for several reasons:

- No one likes to be the bad guy, and no one likes confrontation.
- It takes a lot of work to take action against an employee.
- Because of the protections afforded government employees, any action we take against a difficult employee can be overturned at a number of different levels.
- Supervisors who take action may be labeled or even ridiculed by some as being overly tough or not people friendly.
- Many supervisors will face personal attacks through grievances, EEO complaints, or even lawsuits.
- Supervisors are subject to political attacks, whereby the difficult employee brings his alleged plight to a local congressman or other official, forcing the supervisor to justify actions to powerful individuals outside the chain of command.

With the difficulties facing supervisors who want to take action, many choose the path of least resistance, which turns out to be no action at all. The difficulty with this approach is that the problem lingers, and begins to metastasize. Others take the message that unacceptable behavior is acceptable, and they begin to act accordingly. Before they know it, the supervisors who try to avoid one problem now have to deal with several issues.

Overall Philosophy

A Problem Employee Tends to Stay a Problem Unless Handled

Wherever I've worked, everyone has known who the problem employees are. People talk to each other all the time, and they quickly recognize and point out the slackers. In fact, these are the individuals that employees talk about the most, because these are the people who are the loudest and most demonstrative.

Employees look to their supervisors to deal with these individuals. Unfortunately, for the reasons described earlier, far too many supervisors do nothing. They take no action because taking action is difficult, and because they mistakenly hope that the problem will go away. However, the problem rarely goes away because problem employees tend to stay problem employees, unless management deals with them. The same principle applies when rearing children, and in the classroom. Unless unacceptable behavior is addressed timely and firmly, it will continue. If it is dealt with promptly and appropriately, the offender will generally get the message and change his behavior.

I once worked at a government office that employed a particularly difficult employee. She was loud and belligerent and could be quite intimidating. She could also be very charming when it suited her purposes. Early on, people knew she was a problem, but no one did anything about her. She was eventually moved to different parts of the organization because no one was willing to deal with her. Finally, a strong and determined supervisor proposed her removal. However, when the deciding official met with her, she turned on her charming side and claimed that she had been under a great deal of stress, and he decided to give her another chance.

She stayed on her best behavior until about a year later, when her loud and belligerent side took over again, and she again misbehaved. When a different supervisor proposed her removal, she claimed that she was having personal problems, and the deciding official again let her off the hook.

Meanwhile, behind the scenes, she felt that she was invulnerable and boasted to others that she had again pulled the wool over management's eyes. She continued intimidating others and drove several employees out of the organization. It took management years to finally get rid of her. Along the way, she inflicted an untold amount of damage upon the organization, because the organization did not properly deal with her.

A few years ago, having become the leader of a government office that had just hired many trainees, I was walking around and noticed an older employee verbally thrashing one of the trainees. I later found out that this was her modus operandi, because she both was angry with her plight in life and resented having to teach others, who invariably moved ahead of her in the organization. It was obvious to me that her behavior was harming the trainees, and I was concerned that if it continued unabated, many of them might leave the organization.

I asked her division chief to counsel her and to advise her that her behavior was unacceptable. He was very reluctant to do this because he was concerned about her reaction to such a counseling. However, I insisted that he go through with the counseling. After he told her that her behavior would not be tolerated and of the consequences of future misbehavior, he braced for her reaction. To his surprise, she replied, "No one ever told me that my voice was loud or that I had been saying anything inappropriate. Had I known that, I certainly wouldn't have said anything wrong. I have four years to go before I can retire, and I can't afford to lose my job." From that day on, she was a much better employee, because management had finally dealt with her.

Beware of the Employee Who Continually Uses the Same Excuses

Sometimes we deal with employees who have multiple issues, while other times we deal with people who always have the same problem. In most cases, we have to deal with both types of employees in the same way—fairly and firmly. The key is to *deal with the issue(s)* in front of us before it gets out of hand.

Employees with one recurring issue are generally better employees than those with multiple issues. Employees who have multiple issues usually have similar problems in their personal life, and they bring these same issues to the job. One might be angry because of a divorce or due to financial pressures. Another might have multiple issues because of personality defects. The reason doesn't really matter. Management must make it clear that all employees must check their problems at the door before coming to work.

Employees who have one continuing problem (which is often personal in nature) generally have it because they perceive the problem as being outside their control. They tend to see themselves as victims and invariably bring the problem to the attention of management with the hope that management will solve the problem. If management takes the bait, the problem becomes management's and not the employee's. The solution is to push the problem back to the employee by letting the employee know that it is his or her responsibility to solve personal problems and to conform to the agency's rules, regulations, code of conduct, and expectations.

I once had an employee who had a difficult time coming to work on time. His continuing excuse was that his car was old and kept breaking down. He said that he couldn't afford to buy another car and that public transportation wouldn't work for him because it would be too time consuming.

His continuing lateness was clearly having an adverse effect on our office. Others had to stop what they were doing and take over his work. Moreover, people were getting frustrated with his continued lateness.

I sat down with him and advised him that continued lateness was unacceptable and would not be tolerated. I further advised him that additional lateness could lead to disciplinary and/or adverse action, including his removal. He protested that it wasn't his fault that his car kept breaking down and that he couldn't afford to buy another car. I responded that it wasn't my fault either, and that it his was his responsibility to come to work on time.

The next time he was late, we disciplined him. He realized that we were serious about his lateness, and searched in earnest for a solution. Shortly thereafter, he joined a vanpool that dropped him off just two blocks from the office.

A continuing personal problem for this employee and our organization was finally resolved because the issue was addressed firmly and directly. The employee started coming to work on time and within a year was promoted to a higher-level position.

In another instance, we received complaints from several employees that four employees were leaving work at 2:15 p.m. each day, which was 15 minutes earlier than our earliest departure time. They were all part of a carpool in which one of the employees had to pick up his son from a childcare center before its 5:00 p.m. closing time (they all lived an extreme distance from the office).

We advised the employees that the earliest time they could leave work was 2:30 p.m., unless they each wanted to take 15 minutes of vacation time every day. They all agreed that they did not want to exhaust much of their leave in this fashion, but insisted that we were being unreasonable by requiring them to stay until 2:30 p.m., especially since the care of a child was involved. We responded that the starting and ending times were flexible (employees could start as early as 6:00 a.m. or as late as 8:45 a.m., as long as they were on a preset schedule and worked 8 hours each day), but that the rules applied to everyone. We emphasized that it was up to them to find a solution to the childcare issue. We also added that future early departures would result in appropriate disciplinary/adverse action.[1]

Once the employees recognized that we were serious about treating everyone equally, they found a solution to the problem. The employee with the young son enrolled his child in a childcare center that had longer hours, and the issue was resolved once and for all.

You Can Successfully Deal with a Difficult Government Employee

There are many reasons why managers do not take action against difficult people. They may believe that it is too hard to deal with difficult employees; they may feel that it takes too much work; they may think that they will get too much political heat; or they simply do not want to take the chance of losing an appeal. Whatever the reason, this negative mindset against taking action seems to prevail in government. As we all know, if you don't believe you can take action, you simply won't be able to take action. It's that simple.

In order to have an effective HR program, government organizations must possess the will to deal with difficult people. Having the will is an organizationwide dedication to taking the right action, which sometimes means having to fire a poor employee. It's a recognition that firing a difficult employee, when it is the appropriate thing to do, simply has to be done, even if it is hard. It is a commitment to taking action, even when you may occasionally lose on appeal. Once government organizations develop the will, employees get the message, and it becomes a self-fulfilling prophecy.

Developing the will to take action does not come overnight. It evolves through training and experience and is usually accompanied by a number of mistakes. However, if managers are prepared to learn from their mistakes and to support each other, even if they occasionally lose a case, they will develop the requisite mindset that will enable the organization to have an effective HR program.

We once had a large male employee who was intimidating two female employees. He was angry with them because they had testified against him on a prior disciplinary matter. In order to make his displeasure known and to prevent them from ever testifying against him, he began staring at the two women in a threatening manner. Although several lower-level members of management were aware of this situation, they did not believe they could take action against the male employee. Their rationale was that it would be hard to prove that he was staring at the women with an intent to intimidate them.

Fortunately, upper management did not see things the same way. They believed that he was trying to intimidate the women and were not going to tolerate such behavior. They decided to deal with the situation by proposing the employee's removal, even though they knew that the outcome of such an action was risky.

For his part, the employee was shocked by the proposed removal. He begged to keep his job and promised to reform. In essence, management had turned the tables on the bully and learned that he wasn't so tough. Eventually, management settled this case by offering him a temporary job at another facility. By having the will to deal with this individual, it was possible to resolve a tense and difficult situation.

Here's another example: An employee who had transferred from another agency was constantly giving us problems. Her production was low, her accuracy was poor, and she did not seem to pay attention during training. Part of the problem may have been due to some personal problems she was having, as well as her weight and her age. While we granted her a reasonable amount of leave in order to assist her, we still expected her to meet her performance standards.

Every time her supervisor tried to deal with her, she alleged age and racial discrimination. She also kept arguing that her training was inadequate, even though every other member of her training class was performing in a satisfactory manner. In order to address her concerns, we gave her extra training, but we also made it clear that training was a two-way street.

Since her performance problems continued, we placed her on a performance improvement plan, which she failed, and then proposed her removal. She eventually retired, and her EEO complaints were dismissed.

Tactics

Utilize the Probationary Period

Many of the problems described in this book would never appear if management utilized the probationary period as intended. Virtually every government organization has a probationary period for newly hired employees. This period, which is generally a year, is designed to give management the opportunity to observe a new employee and determine if the person is a good fit for the organization. If new employees demonstrate during probation that they possess the necessary skills, abilities, attitude, and behavior that the organization requires, then they are converted to a permanent status.

However, if performance and/or behavior during probation indicate that an employee is likely to be unsuccessful, then management should terminate him. Naturally, prior to taking termination action, management should first make a good-faith effort to try and assist the employee in an effort to address identified weaknesses. If such assistance does not work, the employee should be promptly terminated. This is the best opportunity to nip a problem in the bud, because once a poor employee is allowed to complete probation, all of the requisite civil service protections apply and it becomes much more difficult to terminate the person.

Many years ago, we hired a class of trainees, most of whom were exceptional. However, one of the people in that class was a female who had difficulty keeping up with the other students. She was often late for class, rarely took notes, and was frequently disruptive. The class instructor was very concerned about her behavior and brought it to the attention of her division chief. However, instead of dealing with the employee, the division chief advised the instructor to try and deal with the disruptive trainee as best she could.

When the training period was finished, all of the trainees were assigned to teams and expected to begin performing. Naturally, the female was unsuccessful, but she claimed that it was management's fault because her training was inadequate. In order to avoid a confrontation with the employee and the union, her division chief decided to put her back in training. By this time, the employee was approaching the end of her probationary period. Since her supervisors had virtually no documentation that they had ever counseled the employee, they reluctantly decided that she had successfully completed probation and converted her to permanent status.

As you might expect, this employee became a thorn in management's side, as her career was marked by constant moves from team to team, as well as by a series of disciplinary actions. Had management dealt firmly with this employee from the beginning and, if necessary, subsequently terminated her during probation, none of those subsequent problems would have occurred.

Several years later, that same division hired a new class of trainees. Again, most of the trainees were excellent, but one particular trainee had problems almost from day one. She had difficulty grasping the most basic concepts and often gave her instructor a hard time.

However, this time a new division chief was in place, and he handled the case differently. He ensured that the trainee was put on notice regarding her deficiencies, both orally and in writing. He also ensured that the employee received extra one-on-one training, because he wanted her to have every opportunity to succeed. As time went by, it became obvious to everyone that she was not going to make it. As a result, the division chief reluctantly terminated her during probation. Interestingly, the other trainees were very supportive of the decision to terminate her because they knew she would not be an asset to the organization.

The employee filed a discrimination complaint (as a probationary employee, she had no other recourse) alleging that her termination was based on race and sex. However, her complaint was dismissed because managers had documented the fact that (1) they had treated everyone in the same manner; and (2) they had made a good-faith effort to assist her. A potential long-term problem was averted because management had utilized the probationary period exactly as it was intended.

Keep It Simple, Stupid

In dealing with difficult people, many supervisors make things much more complicated than need be. A simple rule to remember is that the more complicated a case becomes, the more difficult it will be for management to prevail. Far too often, a straightforward case of unapproved absence or insubordination goes off on a series of tangents, to the point where it becomes difficult to remember what the original offense was. The key for management is to focus on the offense, and to treat all other issues as secondary, not primary issues.

This is not as easy as it may seem, because mitigating circumstances are usually involved. In addition, unions will often add other issues to the equation (allegations of contract violations, disparate treatment, etc.) that will make things more difficult for management to sort through.

To make matters even worse, supervisors, often working in conjunction with HR specialists, frequently write charges that are far more complex than they need to be and that are difficult to prove to a third party. On many occasions, they also ask for unnecessary information, delaying their cases and muddying the waters even further.

Naturally, supervisors have to gather their facts before taking action. However, they need to keep the charges and the focus of the case as simple as possible. Remember, we are talking about an administrative action, not a legal action that has to be proven beyond a reasonable doubt.

Simple versus Complex Charges. An employee submits a travel voucher that claims reimbursement for $42.00 in expenses she did not incur. Once this comes to the attention of management, it decides that the employee should be suspended. In the body of the disciplinary action, management charges the employee with "intentionally submitting a fraudulent travel voucher in violation of Section X of the federal law." Although the charge may be factually accurate, it is overly complex and difficult to prove. As written, management must prove that the voucher was false, the employee intended to defraud the government, and the employee's actions violated the law. This clearly places an unnecessarily heavy burden on management.

A better approach would have been to simply charge her with submitting a false travel voucher. This charge would be much easier to prove and would still justify a suspension.

Getting Sidetracked from the Real Issue. An employee is absent from work for several months due to a leg condition. He uses up all of his sick leave and requests leave without pay (LWOP) for another month. Accompanying his sick leave request is the following doctor's statement: "The employee is unable to return to work for another month." Since the doctor's statement is rather sketchy, the supervisor decides to challenge the note by claiming that it does not contain enough information to justify another month of LWOP.

While this approach may at first seem reasonable, let's play it out to its logical conclusion. The supervisor has predicated his disapproval of LWOP on the need for additional information from the doctor that the employee was truly incapacitated. The implication of such an approach is that if the employee comes back with a more detailed note stating that he is incapacitated, the supervisor will approve the leave. Since government health insurance plans generally provide employees with a large number of doctors to choose from, the odds are that the employee will be able to get a more detailed note from his current doctor or another one. Thus, the supervisor has boxed himself in, and has complicated what should have been a simple case of leave denial.

What the supervisor should have done is simply denied the request for LWOP based on workload, and not on the quality of the doctor's note. After all, the employee has no legal entitlement to LWOP, and approval is at the discretion of the supervisor. By taking this approach, the only issue is whether the workload justified the denial of leave. Since the supervisor is the expert in this area, if the case ever went to a third party, the supervisor would be in a much better position to explain denial of LWOP. Moreover, third parties have consistently upheld the principle that management may deny an incapacitated employee's request for LWOP if the workload requires the employee's presence.

If Poor Employees Never Cross the Line, Change the Line

Human beings are amazingly flexible creatures. We seem able to adapt to almost any situation. The same concept holds true in our working lives. We find a way to adapt and get used to whatever faces us. Unfortunately, this means that over time, the abnormal can become normal to us, and what once was unacceptable can become acceptable.

In the late 1970s, the United States was facing an unprecedented oil embargo by Iran. Fuel was in short supply, and prices skyrocketed. In an effort to conserve energy, President Jimmy Carter ordered that half of all lights in federal buildings be turned off. While this made the lighting in most federal buildings pretty dim, people accepted it as an appropriate sacrifice for the crisis we were in.

When the crisis passed, most federal buildings turned all of the lights back on. However, the federal building in West Los Angeles, California, did not, and no one seemed to notice. Over time, the people got used to the dimly lit space, and nobody complained. The unacceptable had become acceptable.

When I became director of an office in that building, I was shocked at how dark the building was. Moreover, I was just as shocked that no one seemed to notice that fact other than me. I quickly met with the building manager and insisted that the lights be turned on. Shortly thereafter, the lights were turned on throughout our space—the first time in over 15 years! People were amazed at the difference, and for the first time began to realize how bad the lighting conditions had been.

The point of this story is that we in management need to be cognizant of what we consider to be normal. If we are not careful, we will slowly, without recognizing it, begin to allow the unacceptable to become acceptable.

When I was an HR specialist, I was amazed at how often a supervisor would come to me and complain that an employee had approached the line of misbehavior, but had not crossed it. Such supervisors would obviously be frustrated, because while they wanted to do something about the conduct of poor employees, they felt that their hands were tied because the employees had not crossed the line. Invariably, when I asked a supervisor to describe the problem employee's conduct in detail, I would point out that in fact, the employee *had* crossed the line, and had probably been crossing the line for months, if not years. After looking at things from my perspective, the supervisor would immediately agree with my assessment.

What normally happens, just like with children, is that employees will test the supervisor to see what they can get away with. Meanwhile, the supervisor, in an effort to promote harmony, will slowly allow the unacceptable conduct line to move further and further from where it originally was. Eventually, the supervisor and the other employees will get used to the new line and will not even recognize as unacceptable, conduct that is clearly inappropriate. Once this happens, management must redraw the line back to where it originally was, and must advise the appropriate offender(s) accordingly.

I worked for an organization that employed a particularly difficult employee.

He was very angry, emotional, and defiant of management, and management went out of its way to avoid confrontation with him. Recognizing management's reluctance to deal with him, this employee became more and more brazen. He began to turn other employees against management and was becoming a major negative influence on the entire organization.

One day, while serving as personnel officer, I made a series of PowerPoint presentations to large groups of employees. This aforementioned employee attended one of these sessions and immediately closed his eyes and paid no attention to my presentation. He acted in such a cavalier manner that it was obvious to everyone in attendance that he was defying a senior management official. I decided to confront him in front of the group by saying, "John [not his real name], please pay attention to my presentation." He angrily refused, and eventually stormed out of the room.

I reported this incident to his supervisor, who finally took disciplinary action against this individual. Moreover, he also gave John a written counseling wherein he placed him on notice that certain behaviors that had been tolerated in the past would no longer be tolerated. Once the supervisor had changed the line, John did not magically become an outstanding employee. However, because he now understood where the line was and that it was not to be crossed, he behaved in a manner that was much more consistent with the organization's code of conduct.

Make Sure You Control the Situation

Another reason why supervisors are reluctant to confront difficult employees is because once they take action, the situation can quickly spin out of control. Before they know it, a difficult employee exercises rights under one or more of the government's statutory, regulatory, or contractual employee protections. From that point on, the supervisor is on the defensive. More and more time is devoted to responding to the employee's complaints, placing the supervisor in the unenviable position of wondering why she went down this path in the first place.

Burdened by a Difficult Employee. An employee is charged as absent without official leave (AWOL), and the supervisor counsels the employee that AWOL is unacceptable. The employee takes official time to go to the union to complain and eventually files a grievance against the supervisor, requiring both a grievance meeting and a written response from the supervisor. The following week, the employee is again charged AWOL for unauthorized absence. This time the supervisor issues a written counseling. In response, the employee files an EEO complaint, contending that the action was based on his race, age, and sex. This triggers the involvement of an EEO counselor, a formal EEO investigation, and eventually an EEO hearing, all of which require an enormous investment of the supervisor's time.

Several weeks later, the employee is again charged AWOL, and this time, the supervisor gives him an admonishment. In response, the employee files another EEO complaint, alleging that this AWOL charge was in retaliation for his last EEO complaint. In addition, the employee informs his supervisor that he is now a union steward, and will require official time to tend to union business.

The following month, the employee is AWOL once again, and this time the supervisor issues him a reprimand. The employee then files another EEO complaint and again alleges retaliation. The employee concurrently files an unfair labor practice (ULP) charge and alleges that the reprimand was also retaliation for his union activities.

During this period, the employee also starts filing complaints that are unrelated to the AWOL charges. He files a grievance because he is denied overtime, he files an EEO complaint alleging that his desk was moved in retaliation for his filing an EEO complaint, and so on.

From the supervisor's perspective, she has done everything by the book. She has attempted to correct the employee's behavior by following the principle of progressive discipline. What she has gotten in return are two grievances, four EEO complaints, and a ULP, all of which will require a considerable amount of her time defending her actions. Moreover, the employee is now a union official, so he is no longer working for her on a full-time basis.

As the supervisor looks ahead, she sadly concludes that she is knee deep in a big mess, with no end in sight. She feels helpless and frustrated and feels like the situation is totally out of control. She decides to try and settle his complaints by withdrawing all of the counselings and disciplinary actions, so she can finally get back to focusing on her regular job.

This example is not an exaggeration. It happens at every level of government at some point in time. Although it does not happen in every case, or even in most cases where a supervisor attempts to take corrective action, it occurs often enough to frustrate supervisors and to make them think twice before taking future action.

The best way to handle difficult employees is for management to firmly take control of the situation. This will happen only if the employee reacts to management rather than management reacting to the employee.

In the preceding example, the employee concluded that his job was not in jeopardy. Since the actions that management took against the employee were minor and incremental, the employee decided that there was no need to change his behavior. He decided that the best defense was a good offense, so he kept hammering management with more and more complaints until the supervisor was ready to give up. He controlled the situation, not the supervisor.

Let's look at a real-life situation where the exact opposite occurred.

Several years ago, I was asked to visit a government office to assist with an extremely difficult personnel situation. One employee had filed multiple complaints against several management officials, and had virtually tied up that entire office in paperwork. Half the employees were on management's side, while the other half sided with the employee. The point is that everyone was so involved with this employee's situation that little time was being spent on accomplishing the organization's mission. Management was incredibly frustrated because the employee felt invulnerable and was clearly in control of the situation.

After interviewing a representative sample of employees and management officials, I concluded that the situation was intolerable and needed to be addressed immediately. Although there was plenty of blame to go around, it was essential that management regain control of a steadily worsening situation. Accordingly, after conferring with our headquarters, we decided that it would promote the efficiency of the government if we reassigned the employee to another office several hundred miles away. We knew that this was a risky proposition, and that a third party could overturn us. However, we also believed that it was the right thing to do.

The employee was shocked when he learned about the reassignment. At the same time, he suddenly realized that management was now in control of the situation, was serious, and that he couldn't afford to lose his job. Instead of devoting his energy toward attacking management, he now worked furiously to protect himself. Within two weeks, he found another job in a different state, and the problem was solved.

Bring Your Problems to a Head

Perhaps the biggest mistake that supervisors make when dealing with difficult employees is that they allow the problem to linger. A simple rule of thumb is this: The longer a problem is not addressed, the more difficult it becomes to deal with. More issues arise, more complaints ensue, more supervisory time is spent, and more employees get sucked into the middle of the situation.

With virtually every problem employee, the best approach is to bring the problem to a head as quickly as possible. Sometimes, a simple counseling session with the employee is enough to identify the root cause of the problem and to come up with a mutually satisfactory solution. However, in many cases the problem is much deeper and requires stronger action. In these situations, the employee must understand that management is serious about changing the behavior. The employee must also understand that should unacceptable behavior not change, management is prepared to terminate the person. It's been my experience that a problem employee will generally change only when convinced that his job is on the line.

Once an employee is in a vulnerable position where his job truly is at risk, he is most likely to lay his cards on the table. He may confess what the true problem really is (alcohol, drugs, marital problems, etc.), or he may make it clear that he will continue to be a problem no matter what management does. If management then plays its cards right, only two outcomes should occur, both of which are acceptable: (1) The employee changes his behavior and becomes a productive employee (the preferred option); or (2) management terminates the employee. The only outcome that is unacceptable is the status quo, and that's why the problem needs to be brought to a head as soon as possible.

The best way to bring a problem to a head is through strong and decisive action on the part of management. Unfortunately, the biggest mistake that supervisors invariably make in these situations is that they misapply the concept of progressive discipline. Progressive discipline means that you should take the lowest disciplinary or adverse action that you need to take that will change an employee's behavior.

Many supervisors (and particularly union officials) seem to believe that for each transgression committed by an employee, you have to slowly up the ante of discipline (first an oral counseling, then a written counseling, then an admonishment, then a reprimand, etc.). Although this approach makes sense for a good employee whose behavior has inexplicably changed, it does not make sense for a poor employee. She has usually been a poor employee for quite some time and has not tried to change, so why would a minor action cause her to change at this point?

In my view, for this type of individual, you need to take a much stronger action from the start and let her know you are serious. Only a strong action will change her behavior. Moreover, by taking a strong action(s), you will bring the problem to a head much more quickly and avoid all of the time, energy, and pain that is involved in a protracted action.

In an organization that employed a number of vocational rehabilitation counselors, one of the counselors was clearly troubled. He seemed to be constantly angry, upset, or unhappy. A series of incidents occurred (furniture damage, pictures defaced, etc.) that everyone attributed to him, but no one could prove it at the time. His co-workers went out of their way to avoid him, and his first- and second-level supervisors were actually afraid that he might physically harm them.

Finally, his division chief had had enough, and she proposed his removal for several incidents that were sketchy at best. She wanted to bring the problem to a head. As the deciding official on this employee's proposed removal, I sat down with the employee and his representative and discussed the case. Clearly, he was worried about losing his job. By the same token, he confessed that the job was not a good fit for him and that he had been experiencing emotional problems for quite some time. The proposed removal was the catalyst for this discussion, and we wound up settling the case by supporting the employee's application for disability retirement, which was approved.

In another workplace scenario, we had a very talented management official who was constantly causing problems. She was frequently absent, often pitted one employee against another, and, worst of all, started undermining her immediate supervisor, whom she did not respect. Her actions created a great deal of anxiety and tension within our organization, and it was clear that something had to be done.

The problem was that while we knew her behavior was unacceptable, we also knew that it would be difficult to formally describe and document specific charges against her. However, since we also knew that the worst thing we could do was to maintain the status quo, her supervisor decided to bring this issue to a head by proposing her demotion.

She was shocked by this action, and indicated that she would do anything to keep her job. She eventually accepted a change to a lower grade with another organization.

Fear

There is one other factor that can quickly undermine management's ability to deal with difficult people, and that is fear. Fear seems to exist among supervisors and managers at almost every level, and that fear can easily lead to inaction. This fear can manifest itself in many forms: fear of losing a case; fear of being criticized by upper management for either taking or not taking action; or fear of an employee filing a complaint.

Although all of these fears certainly exist for many people, I think the bottom line is that supervisors and managers fear the unknown. Since very few of these individuals are experts in the government's personnel rules and regulations, they believe that once they begin taking action against an employee, they will be marching down a path that is vague and unclear, and can place them in a very public and perilous position. Moreover, because many, if not most, people feel that it is incredibly hard to fire a government employee, the mentality of management is often to not waste time dealing with difficult employees. Instead, managers choose the path of least resistance and decide to simply work around these employees. Thus, fear becomes a self-fulfilling prophecy in the sense that management often gives up before it even starts.

If supervisors and managers understood that the system provides plenty of protections for management, as well as employees, they would begin to see things in a different light. If they understood how a grievance, disciplinary action, or EEO complaint plays out, they would see that management has numerous opportunities along the way to either settle a case or withdraw an action, if it is not justified. The key is for the individual taking action to bring both supervisors and the HR advisor into the loop, in an effort to get political and technical support. Once that happens and the action goes forward, it is not merely the supervisor's action; it is the organization's action.

Let's look at a few examples as to how some actions might play out.

Getting Your Ducks in a Row. A supervisor, after consulting with all of the appropriate individuals, proposes to suspend an employee for five days because of insubordination. The employee then responds to a higher-level official who makes the final decision on the suspension. If the official sustains the suspension, the employee can then grieve the suspension through one or more levels of the organization. If the grievance is denied, the employee can request arbitration, which must be approved and may be paid for (at least in part) by the union.

As you analyze this scenario, the grievance is reviewed by management at multiple steps and will go to a third party only if it is not resolved earlier and the union decides to pursue it. If it goes to arbitration, the entire process can easily take six months or longer. If there is a problem with the case, management has many opportunities to settle it. However, if the supervisor has done his homework and lined up the requisite support beforehand, it is highly likely that his actions will be supported throughout the process. Even if the case is resolved at some point, some form of action is likely to be sustained, and the supervisor will still have made his point. In essence, if the supervisor has lined up his ducks, he will have little to fear.

Hanging In for the Long Haul. A supervisor places an employee on a performance improvement plan that causes the employee to file an EEO complaint. The complaint process generally involves informal counseling, a formal investigation, a hearing, and a final agency decision. In addition, the parties are also encouraged to attempt alternate dispute resolution, which requires the assistance of a mediator. If the entire process plays out, resolution of the complaint could easily take one to two years, if not longer. Meanwhile, if any weaknesses in the case appear, management will have plenty of opportunities to resolve the matter. Moreover, should the employee's performance improve to the successful level, the complaint will become moot way before it gets to a hearing.

The point is that management has nothing to fear except fear itself. If a supervisor believes that taking action against an employee is the right thing to do, she should take the action. As long as she has done her homework, the organization will generally support her and the system will protect her. Moreover, she will earn respect for her willingness to deal with a difficult employee.

The Key Players in Having an Effective Program of Discipline

The best way to have a strong, organizationwide program of discipline is to have a consistent philosophy at every level of the organization. This is easier said than done, because each level of the organization has a different perspective on things. However, all levels must work together, toward the same goal, if the program is going to work at its optimum level.

If the levels do not work together, one or more will work at odds with the others, and will frustrate the overall intent of the program. When this happens, consistent discipline becomes difficult to administer and enforce, and the program breaks down. As a result, management becomes discouraged and stops taking action, while the vast majority of the employees become frustrated because the bottom 10 percent are skating by, without consequences.

In many government organizations, there are five key players that must be on the same page:

1. The first-line supervisor, who deals directly with most employee issues
2. The head of that employee's organization, sometimes referred to as the division chief or service chief
3. The leader of the organization, who generally makes the final determination as to whether an employee should be terminated
4. HR advisor(s)
5. The organization's attorney(s), who normally represent the organization at third-party hearings

All of these players have a key role in a government organization's program of discipline and must be on the same page.

I took over an organization where many of the first-level supervisors were unwilling to take action. They had been burned on several occasions by the prior leadership team and were unwilling to go through that headache again. As a result, difficult employees became even more difficult because they knew that their supervisors were unwilling to take action. On the surface, things seemed to be okay because there were no disciplinary actions taken, nor were virtually any grievances filed. However, as I walked around, I quickly learned that (1) there were no grievances *precisely because there was no discipline;* and (2) there was a deep undercurrent of frustration among many of the employees because they believed management to be weak and in bed with the union.

In order to address the situation, I personally conducted a series of training sessions for all of our supervisors on employee discipline. These sessions included an extensive amount of case studies and role playing. I also walked around, met individually with the supervisors, and encouraged them to take action when appropriate. Lastly, when a few courageous supervisors finally took action, I publicly praised them so the other supervisors would get a consistent message. Although it took several years to build a can-do mentality with respect to discipline in the organization, once it took hold, we were able to change the behavior of many individuals and make our office much more professional.

Another reason why the organization described earlier had many problems in dealing with difficult employees was its relationship with its attorneys. The attorneys were good people, but they always seemed to emphasize the weaknesses in management's cases to the point where management never took any action. Over time, their advice added to the office's culture of inaction.

I sat down with our attorneys and explained my philosophy to them. Although we initially had several heated discussions over my approach, I repeatedly emphasized that my role was to make decisions for the good of the agency and that their role was to represent us. I wanted them to know that I respected their legal opinions, but that my decisions took into account many factors, not just the odds of prevailing before a third party. I also emphasized my belief that if I took a strong action for the right reasons, I would generally be in a good spot to negotiate from a position of strength.

As time went by, they began to see things from my perspective. On some occasions, I decided not to settle a case, and we almost always prevailed. On other occasions, they would negotiate on my behalf, and the settlements almost always resulted in the employee not returning to our organization.

Lessons Learned

Document, Document, Document

Once you've identified problem employees, it is essential that you begin documenting their performance and/or conduct, as well as your own actions. Documentation is crucial in the event that a dispute with an employee winds up before a third party. Many cases never go to a third party, but you never know in advance which cases will require litigation and which will not. Therefore, you need to always prepare for that possibility.

One advantage of a well-documented case is that it can sometimes preclude a case from going to a third party.

Documenting to Ward off Third-Party Action. Management gives an employee a reprimand for AWOL. The employee is unhappy with the reprimand and decides to seek assistance from the union. On the one hand, if the union official reviews the case file and sees that management's action is well documented, the official will usually advise the employee that he has a weak case and should consider not pursuing a grievance. On the other hand, if the employee insists on pursuing the grievance, the union will almost certainly represent the employee, but without the same enthusiasm that it would on a case that was poorly documented.

Another reason for having good documentation is that if a case goes to a third party, you want that individual to have a favorable first impression of your case based on the contents of the case file. It's been my experience that most third parties usually prod management, the employee, and the employee's representative to try and settle a case before it gets to a hearing. Accordingly, if the third party believes your case to be strong, she is more likely to try and force the employee to settle the case on terms that are more favorable to management.

My office was involved in prehearing settlement negotiations involving the removal of a particularly troublesome employee. During the negotiations, the administrative law judge let everyone know that after reviewing the case file, he believed that management had a strong case and that the employee should try and negotiate the best deal possible, because she was likely to lose if the case went to a hearing, Using his guidance as leverage, we settled the case by allowing the employee to resign. This would not have been possible except for the fact that the case was well documented.

The best way to document a case is to ensure that it addresses all of the issues contained in the charges. This means that the case file should include evidence that explains "who did what," "how they did it," "when they did it," and "where they did it, " as described in the charges. It should also indicate why what the employee did was wrong, and, if not obvious, show how the employee's action(s) related to and adversely impacted upon the job.

In essence, you want to clearly paint the picture of what happened so that all those reviewing your case understand your position to the point they can at least conclude that the action taken was reasonable. The more clearly you paint the picture, the more likely that the action taken will stand.

You Don't Need a Perfect Case to Take Action

Documentation is very important, but do not fall into the trap of waiting to have a perfect case. In reality, there are no perfect cases. Every case has its weaknesses and can be picked apart, at least to some degree. If you wait until you dot every *i* and cross every *t*, it is likely that you will wind up taking no action. In short, you will be in a state of paralysis caused by overanalysis.

When you are convinced that action needs to be taken to correct someone's behavior or improve her performance, the best approach is to (1) gather the evidence as best you can; (2) consult with your advisors (both technical and political) to determine if you have a reasonable case; and (3) if you believe you do, take action.

In many cases, even if your case is weak, setting an action in motion will still have the desired effect. First of all, the employee may simply accept the action taken. Second, the employee and his or her representatives may not see the same weaknesses in the case that you do. Third, even if they do, they may decide that it is not worth the time, energy, and money to pursue the case before a third party and may look to settle. Finally, you may still prevail before a third party or you may wind up settling the case.

The point is that too many supervisors give up before even taking action. If you believe you are right, you are better off taking an action and seeing it through.

An employee was frequently loud and contentious. He often made subtle threats, but instead of dealing with him, management tried to placate him. All this did was make the employee bolder and make the other employees realize that management was not going to protect them. Finally, he made an overt threat that was overheard by several employees. Word got back to his division chief, who decided to propose the employee's removal.

Unfortunately, when the division chief asked the employees who heard the threats to provide him with a written statement, they all wrote wishy-washy statements. Despite the weaknesses of their statements, the division chief decided to proceed with the proposed removal, and included his own written statement listing what the employees had told him regarding the threat. This time, instead of caving in, he decided to take a stand and at least elevate the employee's conduct problems to the next level.

When the employee and his representative sat down with me, the deciding official, to discuss the proposed removal, it was clear to me that (1) he knew his actions were wrong; (2) he was afraid of losing his job; and (3) he feared having a removal from the government on his permanent record. I eventually settled the case by allowing the employee to resign and by giving him a settlement of several thousand dollars. In this case, the settlement was more than reasonable from my perspective, because it would have cost us far more money to litigate the matter, and I knew that we had a decent chance of being overturned if the case went to a third party. However, because the division chief did not give up before he started, he wound up ridding himself of a problem employee.

Avoid Third Parties When You Can, but Don't Be Afraid of Them

As you read this chapter, you'll note that I have settled a number of cases. I've done that because it is usually cheaper to settle a case than to go to a third party. Moreover, once you go to a third party, you lose control of the outcome, because you never know what a third party will decide.

One of my rules of thumb is this: I'm generally willing to settle with a problem employee if it will result in the employee's departure. I'm far less willing to settle with a problem employee if the person will remain with the organization, because that may encourage other employees to file frivolous complaints. Obviously, if the employee has a good case and management is wrong, I will try and promptly resolve the issue at hand. However, if I feel that we are right, I will be prepared to go to a third party.

On the one hand, if you settle all cases out of fear of losing before a third party, you run the risk of compromising your values. Moreover, you send a message to others that you are weak, and that you will fold as soon as the pressure is turned up. On the other hand, if you settle cases when it is in the best interests of the government to settle, and go to a third party when it does not make sense to settle, then you are doing the right things for the right reasons, and you will be respected for it.

Two employees filed EEO complaints against our office. The facts in each case were very different, but it was clear that both individuals were working together to help buttress each other's case. We were convinced that we would probably lose the first case and be liable for a large amount of money, primarily because the first individual had a number of friends among the employees who were willing to testify on her behalf, and the paper trail was not favorable to management. Moreover, it was equally clear that the supervisor was very worried about the case and was distracted from his day-to-day activities.

We decided to settle the case for a fraction of the money she was asking for. In fact, the cost of the settlement was probably less than the cost of going forward with the hearing, even if we prevailed. As part of the settlement, she agreed to resign, so she never returned to our office.

With respect to the other employee, we decided to fight her case, because our case was much stronger and it was the right thing to do. The case was ultimately dismissed before it ever got to a hearing, and we eventually fired the employee for AWOL.

It's Better to Lose an Occasional Case than to Never Take Action

If you are prepared to go to third parties when necessary, you must also be prepared to lose an occasional case. That is simply a fact of life. If and when you lose such a case, you should treat it as the cost of doing business. It is not the end of the world, nor does it insulate the prevailing employee from future action.

The big mistake that management makes is to be so fearful of losing a case that it takes no action at all. That is the mentality that you want to avoid at all costs. If you go to a third party and lose, it will surely hurt for a while, but you will get over it. By the same token, the employees will respect you for taking the action, because they do not want to work for a management team that will not even attempt to deal with problem employees.

Many years ago, I worked for an organization that removed five employees for the possession and/or sale of drugs. Although several of the employees appealed their removals, all were sustained except for one, which was overturned for technical reasons.

When the local union learned that the employee would be reinstated, it hung up several pictures of the employee triumphantly returning to work. From the union's perspective, it had saved a downtrodden employee's job, and it wanted to take credit for its actions.

Unbeknownst to the union, many employees resented the pictures and the fact that an individual involved with drugs was returning to work. Several resigned from the union, while others came up to management and told us that they appreciated the fact that we had tried to deal with a serious drug problem at work. In essence, while we had lost the case, we had actually won, since we had gained additional respect from the workforce and had sent a message that we would not tolerate inappropriate conduct.

Later on, the same employee again misbehaved and we removed him a second time. This time he was not so lucky and did not win his job back.

Let Them Fight You from Outside the Organization

When you are engaged in a protracted battle with a problem employee, and you cannot change that person's behavior, your best bet is to let that person fight you from the outside. Otherwise, he is going to spend most of his time collecting information to support his case. He will photocopy everything he can get his hands on that is helpful to him and will keep copious notes of all the wrongdoings you are allegedly committing. In short, although the government is paying him, he will do everything he can to undermine your organization.

The longer this goes on, the worse things will get from management's perspective. Other employees will be drawn into the battle, and more and more attention will be diverted away from the mission. If there is no other solution, you will be in much better shape if the employee is no longer at work.

From the employee's perspective, he doesn't really want to be there, either, because he knows he is not successful and is not wanted. However, because he does not want to lose his job for economic reasons, he will do everything he can to prevent that from happening. However, as soon as the employee leaves the job, he normally moves on and looks elsewhere for another position.

One of our supervisors was managing an activity that included 10 people. Two people within this group were very difficult employees and did everything they could to undermine the organization and promote their ongoing complaints. The supervisor constantly complained to me that (1) he did not have enough people; (2) he was constantly distracted having to deal with these two individuals; and (3) given his current resources, he would be unable to meet the performance goals.

He eventually fired those two individuals, but was unable to replace them. Despite now having only eight people, he was able to meet every performance goal. Without these two individuals constantly undermining him and the team, they were able to accomplish their mission. He learned that sometimes you can have addition by subtraction. Meanwhile, it took years for the complaints of the two employees to be adjudicated. During that time, the employees moved on to other activities. When their cases were finally adjudicated (one was dismissed and one was settled), neither of them had any desire to return to our office.

Key Points to Remember

- Deal with problem employees as quickly and as firmly as possible, by bringing these problems to a head.
- Let the employee react to management rather than having management react to the employee.
- Make sure that all of the key players are on the same page.
- Better to occasionally lose a case than to never take action.

Performance Management

Principles

A performance appraisal system is designed with three overriding principles in mind:

1. To align and communicate organizational goals
2. To improve organizational, group, and individual performance by holding everyone accountable
3. To serve the customer

The better the system achieves all three goals in an integrated manner, the more effective the organization will be. Let's look at each principle in greater detail.

Many organizations make the mistake of rarely explaining what their performance goals are. They may include them in a report or in a chart, but that information rarely cascades down to the individual employee.

The most effective way of doing this is to first ensure that there is a clear line of sight from the organization's goals down to the individual's performance standards. This is essential because if the performance goals are properly aligned with employee and team performance standards at all levels of the organization, everyone will be working toward achieving the organization's goals.

Once the standards are aligned, they must be written in a manner that is clear, understandable, fair, measurable, and achievable. Last, the employees need to understand how the standards relate to the organization's goals, so they recognize how their actions fit into the bigger picture. This should be accomplished using the whole brain method of teaching described earlier in this book.

Several years ago, I worked for a national organization whose productivity had declined. In order to address this situation, national productivity goals were established, and goals were given to every office. Each director had a productivity goal written into his performance standards, as did each division chief, each team, and each employee. Everyone understood the goals, why they were important, and how they fit into the national picture. The net result of this unified approach was that national productivity increased almost immediately, and continued at a high rate.

Improving performance at the organizational, group, and individual levels requires a commitment to using the appraisal system as intended, a willingness to provide employees with the training and tools that they need to do the job, hard work, consistency, a desire to address any problems that may develop, and the ability to hold everyone accountable. By applying the system fairly and firmly at every level, you will make incremental improvements along the way that can easily add up to significant improvements in their totality. The key is to view this approach as a two-way street—that is, while we are expecting employees to achieve the goals we've set for them, we must do everything we can to make sure that they succeed.

In the case just cited regarding productivity improvement, the organization did more than simply align its performance goals. First of all, it also established national performance standards for every key position, which meant that it would have the same minimum expectations for each employee at every one of its facilities. This approach helped to reduce the variability in performance across the country. Second, it established a national computer-based training system that was given to both new employees and employees that were experiencing performance problems. Third, it developed an Intranet-based performance management system that tracked the performance of each employee, so that (1) everyone could easily see how he was doing relative to their standards; and (2) upper management could ensure that throughout the country, anyone whose performance was below expectations would be dealt with appropriately.

When applying the first two principles, you need to ensure that they also have an impact on the customer. After all, as government employees, we are here to serve the citizens of our country, state, city, or county. However, if the appraisal system does not address the needs of the customer, the organization can easily become too internally focused and lose sight of the customer. When that happens, you will eventually see a disconnect between the organization's perception of its service and the perception of that service from the people the organization is serving. Once that happens, trouble usually follows.

The same organization that made major strides in productivity did not have performance standards emphasizing customer satisfaction. As a result, slowly but surely, problems started developing. For example, over time, when people called that organization for assistance, they found employees to be less courteous and less willing to help. Moreover, the rate at which that organization's decisions were being appealed doubled, because the focus was on increasing productivity, not on making decisions that satisfied its customers. Lastly, the media wrote a number of uncomplimentary articles regarding that organization because they did not believe that it was as customer-focused as it should have been. Had that organization made customer satisfaction a part of its performance appraisal system, many of those problems would have been alleviated, at least to some extent.

Goals

There are three major goals when implementing a performance appraisal system: (1) The system will drive the right behavior; (2) people will be treated fairly and by the numbers; and (3) employees will know where they stand at all times. If you can achieve these three goals, the system will help foster strong performance, the right culture, and the sense that everyone is on a level playing field. Let's look at each goal in a bit more detail.

A successful performance appraisal system means that employees are trying to perform in a manner that helps the organization achieve its goals and objectives. If everyone is working in that direction, the organization will function both smoothly and effectively. However, if the system is poorly designed or implemented, just the opposite can happen—the employees may be working at odds with the organization's goals. The clearer the link between the standards and the goals, the better and more focused will be the overall performance.

I once worked for a government organization that said it placed a premium on making quality decisions. However, because that organization had heavy backlogs, management did not feel that it could afford to perform monthly quality reviews of its employees' work. As a result, for all intents and purposes, there was no quality element in the employees' performance standards.

The employees quickly recognized that management wanted them to push the work out in order to reduce the backlog. They gave the organization exactly what the performance appraisal system said that management wanted—high productivity at the expense of good quality. In this instance, the performance appraisal system drove the wrong behavior.

Management eventually recognized the error of its ways and understood that high output with low quality translates into low productivity, because of all the rework that is involved. Accordingly, it reinstated the quality reviews and struck the right balance between productivity and quality.

If a performance appraisal system is not perceived as being fair, it will eventually implode. In my experience, the one issue that upsets government unions more than anything else is disparate treatment of bargaining unit members. If employees know that their careers are subject to the whims of their current supervisor, they are likely to become angry and/or cynical or simply leave the organization, any one of which is bad for the government.

Employees expect and deserve fair treatment. The best way to do this is by consistently applying the numbers to everyone, regardless of whether or not you like a particular employee.

I once took over an organization that was perceived to have many difficulties with its local union. When I discussed this matter with the union representatives, they complained that managers tended to go after employees they did not like, and protected poor performers who were their favorites. When I looked into this, I reluctantly concluded that they were right.

In order to address the situation, I instructed each division chief to rank the performance of employees by position, from top to bottom, and to share this information with all supervisors who had a need to know. I wanted to ensure that we were dealing with the bottom performers fairly, and that we also identified the top performers. Once this happened, the supervisors realized that their actions could be easily scrutinized, so they began taking a closer look at the way they treated each employee. This resulted in the employees being treated in a much fairer and more even-handed manner.

The third goal of a good appraisal system is that employees know where they stand at all times. In this way, they will know when problems arise and will diligently try to address them. The more information that employees receive about the context of their individual performance, the better they will perform.

In this organization that started ranking its employees, we later added two additional pieces that further enhanced the application of the appraisal system. First of all, we gave the employees monthly feedback that let them know exactly what their monthly and year-to-date performance was relative to the standards. We also let them know how they were doing relative to their peers so they had a sense of context with respect to their performance. By demystifying the appraisal system, we let them see things a bit more from management's perspective, which served to further motivate most of the employees.

Involvement

The best way to develop and implement a performance appraisal system is to include all of the key players: line management, HR staff, the affected employees, and the union. All of these players have a stake in the standards, so it is much better to involve them early on in the process and get their perspective. Otherwise, complaints may arise throughout the development and implementation of the standards that will slow down the process and, quite possibly, preclude management from taking timely action.

At the very outset, line management should consult with human resources regarding all technical aspects of the standards. At a minimum, management wants to ensure that the standards will be in compliance with all legal requirements as well as the agency's rules, regulations, policies, and procedures regarding performance management. Once this is clear, management should get copies of standards written by other organizations for similar positions. After all, there is no need to reinvent the wheel.

As soon as that is done, management has two choices: (1) it can write the standards and then float them by the union, which will most likely canvass the employees for their thoughts; or (2) it can include the employees and the union in the actual development of the standards. I prefer the second approach. Although it is up to management to actually set performance standards, including the employees and the union at that stage gives them a greater stake in the standards, and a sense of inclusion. Potential problems are identified early on, and they are easier to iron out before positions harden. Lastly, it becomes much more difficult for an employee and/or the union to challenge the standards at a later date if they have been involved in the process from the beginning.

Union Relations. If management simply develops the standards and then sends them to the union for comment, the union's usual reaction will be resistance. From its perspective, the new standards seem to come out of left field, so it tends to view them with suspicion, thinking that management is out to get the employees. Inevitably, the union will try to delay the process and do everything it can to put up barriers along the way.

Of course, sometimes the relationship between the parties can be poor, and in that case, a less-inclusive approach may be better. However, management should ask itself, which came first, the chicken or the egg? In other words, have management's actions caused the relationship to sour, or is it simply dealing with a difficult and unreliable union?

Performance Appraisal

What Is It?

A performance appraisal is a written method for assessing how well an employee is performing, usually on an annual basis. It is the primary means by which a government organization holds its employees accountable for achieving desired outcomes.

How Does It Work?

Each year, employees are given a written set of measurable performance expectations (standards) that are directly linked to the achievement of the organization's goals and objectives. During the year, management provides them with feedback as to how they are doing relative to the standards. If an employee fails to meet any of the standards, management is expected to intervene early in an effort to help the employee improve his performance. If the employee continues to perform below par, management should take further action.

At the end of the appraisal period, each employee receives a formal written appraisal that assesses his performance against each one of the standards and assigns him an overall rating.

There are two primary types of appraisal systems in government. The first one is called a pass/fail system. Under this approach, at the end of the year, employees receive one of two possible ratings: pass or fail. The goal of this type of system is to simply weed out poor performers. Some supervisors prefer this kind of system because it is simpler to use and does not require the supervisor to make meaningful distinctions between employees, which can be both painful and difficult and can often trigger hard feelings, grievances, and EEO complaints. The other side of the coin is that the system has limited relevance beyond performance appraisal.

I worked under this pass/fail system for several years. It was relatively easy to use and trouble free. However, because meaningful distinctions were not made between the employees, there was no real linkage between the appraisal system and the other management systems. Moreover, the top employees resented the system because it did not give them the credit they felt they deserved, and it did not distinguish between the better employees and the marginal employees who were barely making their standards.

The second type of system is known as a multitiered appraisal system. Under this approach, employees can receive a number of different ratings, depending on how they perform relative to their standards. The advantage of this system is that you can make meaningful distinctions between employees and can use those distinctions when making other management decisions. The disadvantage of this approach is that it requires more work and more documentation, and forces supervisors to make some decisions that they would prefer to avoid.

Having worked under a multitiered performance appraisal system for most of my career, I have learned that supervisors are generally uncomfortable with such a system when the standards are unclear or when they have a difficult time measuring the performance of their employees. They feel that way because they know when it comes time to issue their end-of-year appraisals, the overall ratings will be difficult to justify. As a result, they often have to rely on their gut, which frequently triggers dissatisfaction among the employees and a perception that the system is not fair.

However, when the standards are clear and the employees' performance is easy to measure, such problems are less evident. Under these circumstances, you can make meaningful distinctions between employees based on solid data, and this gives the system credibility. Moreover, it becomes possible to clearly and fairly apply the results of the system to other management decisions (rewards, promotion decisions, etc.).

Most government appraisal systems use a multitier approach. The remainder of this chapter will, for the most part, address performance appraisal under a multitier system.

What Is It Used For?

An appraisal system is used to improve the performance of the organization and its employees and to provide assistance to people whose performance is unacceptable. It is also used to help reward organization, team, and individual performance and to make determinations with respect to within-grade or step increases. Lastly, it can be used for making retention determinations, to assess training needs, and to make selection decisions.

Linking Performance Appraisals. Many performance appraisal plans in government are directly linked to the rewards and recognition system. In those cases, people who receive high performance ratings can expect to be rewarded.

In the federal government, employees who receive outstanding ratings get extra credit in the event that there is a reduction in force. In this way, high performers are more likely to be retained in the event that cutbacks occur.

Many high-performing organizations track the errors that its employees make during their performance reviews in order to identify gaps in their training. In this way, they can customize the training and address those errors accordingly.

Many government promotion plans take into account an individual's appraisal, particularly during the rating and ranking phase. Using this approach, when candidates are assessed against each other, people with high appraisals will have a better chance of being referred to the selecting official for further consideration.

What Is in a Performance Plan?

Performance plans are usually composed of elements and standards. The elements reflect the components of a job that are sufficient to require appraisal. Elements may include, but are not limited to, productivity, accuracy, timeliness, customer satisfaction, and manner of performance. Elements may have one or more performance standards.

There can be two different types of elements. The first one is commonly referred to as a critical element. This involves a job responsibility of such importance that failure to achieve the performance standards of the element would result in a decision that an employee's overall performance is unsatisfactory.

The second type of element is often called a noncritical element. This pertains to a job responsibility that is important enough to appraise, but not important enough that failure would trigger an overall unsatisfactory rating.

Government organizations that use a pass/fail system have only critical elements in their performance standards. That is because the only determination they wish to make is whether an employee should be retained. Organizations that use a multitiered approach to appraisal also use noncritical elements. In this way, they have more levels at which to appraise their employees.

Using Noncritical Elements. One way to use a noncritical element is to require that employees who fail such an element (but no critical elements) will be appraised at the minimally satisfactory level. At this level, such employees do not get removed from their position. However, they would not receive a within-grade or step increase, either.

The performance standards describe the minimum performance requirement(s) that must be achieved in order to be appraised at a certain level of performance.

A multitiered appraisal system features several overall levels at which an employee can be appraised. Some possible levels would be outstanding, highly satisfactory, fully satisfactory, minimally satisfactory, or unsatisfactory. The number of levels and the criteria for appraisal at each level should be described in the organization's plan and/or its negotiated agreement.

Setting Rating Criteria. A plan usually specifies that to receive an outstanding rating, an employee must far exceed every critical element. It may indicate that a highly satisfactory rating requires the employee to far exceed all critical elements and to fully meet all noncritical elements.

It may indicate that you need to far exceed all performance standards in an element in order to far exceed the element, or it may be silent in this area and allow the rater to make that judgment. Similarly, it may indicate that you need to fail one or all of an element's standards in order to fail that particular standard, or it may stay silent on that point.

As you can see, there are many ways to develop an appraisal system and all of its components. The key is that it be in writing, be shared with everyone, and be applied fairly and reliably.

Most performance plans require annual appraisals and at least one mid-year progress review. In addition, a minimum period of time is usually established for an employee to occupy a position and be under the performance plan before he can receive a performance rating.

How Do You Write Performance Standards?

Performance standards should be challenging, yet realistic and sufficient to permit accurate assessment of the employee's performance. They should be written in terms that are clear and understandable.

Standards should not explain what an employee is supposed to do; that is the role of a position description. Rather, they should describe *how* an employee is to perform those duties. Ideally, numbers should be incorporated into the standards, because they make it easy to measure an individual's performance.

Measurable Performance Goals. A good, clear, and defensible standard might contain language requiring an employee to make five decisions a day, with 90 percent accuracy. It might even require that employees make 85 percent of their decisions within 21 days. Another standard might require that people make three field visits per day and that they issue reports within 30 days of the visit, containing no substantive errors 90 percent of the time. All of these standards are easily measurable and can clearly be understood by the affected employees.

Unfortunately, some positions do not lend themselves to measurement as easily as others. For those positions, a bit more creativity may be required.

Abstract Performance Goals. Every level of government seems to have analyst-type positions. These positions rarely require the incumbents to produce the same amount of work on a daily basis, because the nature and type of work varies so frequently. However, with a little bit of effort, these positions can also be measured.

One way to do this would be to use a logbook or spreadsheet to track each assignment and due date given to that individual. Every time the person completes an assignment, the completion date would be recorded so management and the employee would know whether she met the deadline. In this way, the employee could have a measurable standard that requires her to complete 85 percent of assignments on time.

We could take the same approach with respect to her quality. Every report that is submitted to the supervisor could be graded either on a scale of 1 to 10 or on a pass/fail basis. In this way, we could assign a minimum performance standard for quality of either an average of 8.5 per report or that 85 percent of the reports have to be acceptable.

For a job that is primarily advisory in nature (e.g., an attorney, an HRM specialist, etc.) you could build a customer survey into the standards. For instance, a minimum standard might require that 85 percent of the employee's customers must rate the employee's advice as being helpful or very helpful.

Dealing with Problem Employees

Identify Them Early and Let Them Know There Is a Problem

Once you develop and distribute performance standards, the next step is to track each employee's performance relative to those standards. In most cases, you already know who the problem employees are, and the performance appraisal system should merely confirm that. As soon as you have enough data to identify who the problem employees are, you should begin a dialogue with them. This has four purposes:

1. It puts problem employees on notice that there is a performance problem.
2. Supervisor and employee mutually identify the root cause(s) behind the problem.
3. Strategies for resolving the problem are identified.
4. Problems can be nipped in the bud in order to prevent further management action down the road.

Remember, the initial goal is never to fire employees; after all, you've already made an enormous investment in them. The goal at first is always to try and get their performance up to an acceptable level.

Having an open and honest dialogue at the very beginning will often pay big dividends. At the early stage, positions have not yet hardened and people are generally more open to suggestions. As a rule of thumb, the sooner you address a performance problem, the sooner you will know what you are dealing with and the easier it will be to fix the problem. Moreover, if you can fix the problem up front, you can avoid all the time, energy, and costs of litigation that may come later.

In one notable case, we identified an employee who was struggling to meet her performance standards. Her supervisor met with her and her union representative and learned that she was having a difficult time working with her assigned mentor. From the employee's perspective, the mentor was gruff and unresponsive and was unwilling to help her in the areas where she was weak. The supervisor asked her to give him a list of acceptable mentors, which she provided. The supervisor then assigned her a mentor from that list. The two hit it off right away, they were able to iron out her performance difficulties, and she became a productive employee.

Trying to resolve a performance problem up front is always a good thing because: (1) in many cases, you will solve the problem and wind up with a good employee; and (2) in the event that you are unable to improve the performance, you will be able to document the fact that you tried to help the employee.

Always Make a Good-Faith Effort to Help Your Employees

There is a big difference between going through the motions and truly attempting to help an employee in trouble. Some supervisors simply go through the motions of assisting employees because it is required by some rule, regulation, or labor agreement. In reality, they do not really care because they believe that it is the employees' problem and responsibility to fix their own performance.

Although this approach will probably work on some occasions, the more the supervisor truly attempts to help employees, the better for everybody. First of all, some employee performance problems can be resolved only with the intervention of management, such as the case just described where the employee simply needed a different mentor. Second, other employees and the union watch management to see if it will attempt to assist employees in trouble. When people see that supervisors will go out of their way to help an employee in trouble, they will reciprocate in kind.

There are two other reasons why you want to make a good-faith effort to help a struggling employee. The first reason is that it is the right thing to do. If you were in the shoes of the struggling employee, you would want your boss to try to help you improve. The second reason is that it is good business. If you wind up having to take a performance action against the employee, it could potentially take hundreds of hours of your and others' time, and could cost the government thousands of dollars to defend your actions. It is always better to try to get the employee to perform successfully, especially at the beginning of the process, when minimal effort is required by management.

One of our employees kept getting involved in automobile accidents. He was a very nervous individual who simply couldn't drive very well. He was also very knowledgeable about the technical aspects of his job, but it was clear that he could not continue to drive.

We sat down with him and explored other avenues. We realized that he was a long-term employee who had skills that were needed by our organization. Accordingly, we reassigned him to a job where we could leverage his technical skills, but did not require him to travel by car. By making a good-faith effort to address his situation, we were able to retain a valuable employee and demonstrate to the other employees that we were a compassionate employer.

Don't Wait Too Long to Take Action

You've made a good-faith effort to assist the employee and have given him a reasonable amount of time to improve. If you do not see any improvement, then it is time to take further action. At this point, your informal efforts have not paid off, so it is time to move on to the next step.

A common mistake that supervisors make at this juncture is to do nothing, because they hope that the problem will simply go away. Unfortunately, it almost never does. If early intervention does not succeed, that is generally an indication that the performance problem is far more serious and needs to be addressed immediately. If you made a good-faith effort to sit down with the employee and identify what the problem was, the employee made a good-faith effort to try and improve, and the performance remains unchanged, then the performance problem is serious and needs to be addressed immediately. This means placing the employee on a performance improvement plan.

A performance improvement plan is a written document that advises employees regarding four specific aspects:

1. How their performance is unacceptable
2. What specific assistance will be provided to assist them in improving their performance
3. What they need to do to bring their performance up to the acceptable level
4. How long they have to bring their performance up to that level

This is the formal phase of the process, and the place where the rubber meets the road. In other words, once employees are placed on an improvement plan, they either meet their performance standards or action is taken to remove them from their job (by reassignment, demotion, or separation). This is the time when management finally brings the problem to a head, because earlier informal efforts have failed. The sooner we bring the problem to a head, the sooner it will go away.

I can cite the case of an elderly employee who was failing in both her quantity and her quality standards. Because of her advanced age, her supervisor was uncomfortable dealing with the situation, and she let the problem linger. Finally her division chief insisted that appropriate action be taken. Despite management's informal attempts to help the employee, she was unable to come close to meeting her standards, so she was placed on a performance improvement plan. During the performance improvement period, the employee failed miserably, in part because she was unwilling to take virtually any direction from her supervisors. Accordingly, management proposed her removal and I eventually terminated her.

At first, the local union grieved the removal and accused us of terminating her because of age discrimination. However, her family eventually intervened, realized that it was time for the employee to retire, and convinced her to withdraw the grievance. By using the appraisal system in the proper matter, we were able to bring this matter to a satisfactory resolution.

Another example: Looking to boost our organization's productivity, we raised our individual production standards by 17 percent. Although it was a bit of a stretch for many people, we felt that almost all of the employees were capable of reaching that standard. At the beginning, almost half fell short of the new standard. The supervisor sat down with each employee who was failing and tried to provide assistance. Over time, many of these folks achieved the new standard and no further action was taken. However, a few could not make the grade, so they were placed on formal performance improvement plans.

Once they recognized that management was serious about the standards, was willing to continue to help them, but was prepared to take further action if necessary, almost all of the remaining people came around. Overall productivity increased, and the few employees who couldn't make the grade were demoted to lower-graded positions.

Document Your Actions

I've made this point before, but need to reiterate it because the documentation requirements for performance-based actions are a bit different. For actions involving misconduct, you primarily need to document what, where, when, and how an employee did something wrong. You also need to show why the conduct was wrong; to establish a connection between the employee's job and the misbehavior; and to demonstrate that the action taken by management was reasonable.

For performance-based actions, you have to show that the employee was aware of the performance standards and was placed on notice that the standards were not being met, that the employee was given the opportunity to improve, that management made a good-faith effort to provide assistance, and that, despite this, the standards still were not met during the performance improvement opportunity period. Furthermore, you also have to demonstrate that whatever action you wind up taking (reassignment, demotion, or separation) was reasonable under the circumstances. In my experience, the two areas that generally come under attack when a performance-based action is taken are the standards themselves and whether management truly made a good-faith effort to assist the employee.

In most cases, if management simply keeps good records, there should be no dispute that the employee was aware of the standards (the employee should have signed her appraisal form at the beginning of the year indicating that she received her standards). In addition, there is rarely disagreement as to whether the employee made her performance standards. Either she made the standards or she didn't. If the standards are based on numbers, then the performance should not be in dispute, especially if she is receiving periodic reports regarding her performance.

Unions invariably attack the standards, claiming they either are too difficult or are unclear. The best way to counter this claim is to be prepared to demonstrate (1) the connection between the organization's goals and the standards; (2) that the union and the employees were involved in the development of the standards; and (3) that most of the employees were able to achieve the standards.

The area where management is generally the most vulnerable is in its obligation to assist the employee. Most government labor agreements contain detailed procedures outlining what management is to do when an employee has performance problems. It is vital that all supervisors familiarize themselves with these requirements so that they can both comply with them and document their compliance. Otherwise, they can easily expose themselves to charges that the employee was not truly given the chance to improve as agreed to in the labor contract.

We demoted an employee for poor quantity and low quality. From our perspective, this was a no-brainer, since (1) he was historically our poorest employee in his particular occupation; and (2) there was little dispute that his performance was unacceptable. However, the union argued that the labor agreement required management to identify the root cause of an employee's performance problems and to take appropriate action to address that root cause. Since his supervisor was not aware of that provision and did not document her efforts to identify the root cause of the employee's problems in the case file, an arbitrator overturned the employee's demotion, finding that we had not complied with the contract.

In another instance, we took a performance-based action against an employee who occupied a position that required a high degree of concentration. This was a more complex case than the one just described because he had difficulty sleeping at night due to a medically documented condition. His defense was that he was always tired at work through no fault of his own, so he should not be penalized for health reasons that were beyond his control.

In this situation, management fairly and methodically dealt with the employee's concerns, so that by the time he was demoted, management had a strong and well-documented case. His supervisor first asked for medical information that would document the employee's sleeping problem, as well as a list of reasonable accommodation(s). Although the employee ultimately did not request any accommodations, his supervisor did allow him to get up from his desk and walk around briefly whenever the employee became drowsy. He also allowed the employee to change his work schedule so he could come to work later in the morning.

As his performance problems developed, the supervisor followed the contract requirements with respect to performance-based actions, and documented his actions accordingly. Once management proposed to take action against the employee, the union knew that management had a strong case and requested that the employee be demoted to a position that did not require so much concentration. The employee did much better in his new position, which created a "win-win" situation for everyone.

Keep Your Focus

If you have to formally place an employee on a performance improvement plan, do not allow the employee's complaints to cause you to lose focus. Many times, employees will try to turn the process around and place the onus on management. If that happens, you will wind up in a reactive mode and will be constantly responding to the employee's issues. Once that happens, you tend to veer away from the performance improvement process, and that's when things get out of control.

Always stay focused on the process, because if you do that, you will be much more likely to treat everyone in the same way. The more you allow allegedly unique circumstances to intervene in the process, the more you will be open to charges of disparate treatment.

That is why I am a strong advocate of early intervention. It allows you to identify issues early on in the process and then respond to them accordingly. By the time you have to proceed formally, you should have addressed the employee's main complaints, which will then allow the process to proceed unimpeded.

Clarifying Expectations. A supervisor notes that an employee has a problem meeting timeliness standards. The supervisor counsels the employee that his timeliness is unacceptable and needs to be improved. He also asks the employee if there is anything wrong, and the employee responds that he has been having a lot of personal problems lately. Wanting to be fair, the supervisor refers the employee to an employee assistance program and offers to approve leave if it will help the employee take care of the problems. At the same time, in a follow-up letter of counseling, he again makes it clear to the employee that he expects performance standards to be met.

In this situation, the supervisor has treated the employee in the same manner as any other employee who was failing his standards, and has made a good-faith effort to help the employee. By dealing with the situation firmly but fairly, he is in a good position to take further action if the employee's performance doesn't improve. In essence, he has (1) attempted to help the employee; (2) documented his actions in the event he has to take further action; and (3) stayed on course with the performance improvement process.

Training Is a Tool to Improve Performance. A large number of employees are failing their quality standards. A review of the reasons why so many people are failing suggests that many of them are making multiple errors on the same procedure. In this situation, the appropriate thing to do would be to give additional training to everyone on that procedure, monitor how people were doing, and then take further action against the people who are still experiencing problems (presumably, a lot fewer people).

Although this approach delays the process a bit, it is the right thing to do. First of all, you want to take action only against people who truly have performance problems. Second, if you proceed against a large percentage of the people, all of whom are experiencing the same problems, for the same reasons, the process will eventually get sidetracked, and at some point you will wind up back at square one. Better to fix the problem early on and then move forward in a manner that is sure to stay on track.

Best Practices

Examine the Performance Trends

In reviewing the performance of your employees, it is important to look at which direction they are trending. If the performance of most of your employees is relatively consistent, that tells you that you have stability in your process. If it is getting better, that is obviously a good thing, but you need to know why. Perhaps many of them are becoming more experienced, or maybe some recent training helped to clarify a few issues. If things are trending poorly, you also need to know why. Maybe a process has changed, or possibly morale has dropped for some reason. Whatever the cause for the sudden change, you need to know the reason so you can address it if necessary.

The same principle holds true for individual performance. You need to look at each employee's performance with the same pair of eyes, since the direction they are trending should influence the action you take.

Picking Your Battles. An employee with performance problems who is trending better every month should probably be treated a bit differently from someone who is getting worse each month. That's not to say that they shouldn't both be treated fairly. However, I think it is fair to delay issuing a performance improvement plan to someone who is trending well and will soon be meeting his standards. At the same time, it is also fair to issue the plan to someone who is not meeting his standards and getting worse each month.

It is important to pick and choose your battles. On the one hand, in this case, the second battle is worth fighting, and the first battle probably need not be fought, since the employee seems to be doing a good job of raising his performance. On the other hand, if the employee trends positively but is still unable to meet his standards, then a performance improvement plan would probably be warranted.

Look for Common Causes of Performance Problems

When analyzing performance, you need to determine if there are common causes of the performance problems. If most employees are making the same mistake, that tells you the problem may not be an employee problem but a system problem (training, process, etc.). First try to solve that system problem before treating it as a series of employee performance problems.

Faulty Training. Our organization hired several classes of trainees during a six-month period. The training that the first class received was not nearly as good as the classes that followed (e.g., a national computer-based training program was not available to the first class). As time went by, the first class started experiencing performance problems that the second and third classes did not. Instead of simply taking action against the members of the first class, we analyzed the reasons for their performance problems and determined that their initial training was the root cause of their problems. As a result, we gave them all the opportunity to go through the computer-based training and supplemented the training with mentors, and that resolved most of the performance problems.

You may also discover that one person has actually caused what appear to be multiple employee performance problems. That person may have done a poor job of training, given out misinformation, or otherwise hurt the performance of many people. If that is the case, first address it with the employee before going down the performance improvement route with a large number of employees. You do not want to devote all of the time and energy that is required to fix a problem that does not really exist.

We seemed to have a smooth quality review system, which was designed to assess each employee's accuracy. Our organization had competitive quality, and we successfully dealt with the occasional employee whose performance was below par.

Eventually we changed the individual who conducted the quality reviews, and all of a sudden, the number of errors that were called began to skyrocket. The employees were up in arms, since far more errors were being called on them than in the past, even though the quality of their work had not changed.

Fortunately, instead of overreacting to the situation and issuing a bunch of performance improvement plans, we first rechecked the errors that were called by the new quality reviewer. We found that he was being overly strict, so we reversed a number of the errors that he called. Ultimately, we replaced him with a reviewer who was universally recognized as being fair.

Use Spreadsheets to Track Employee Performance

You should keep performance spreadsheets by position, with each employee ranked from top to bottom. This will accomplish a number of things:

- Employees can be compared to their own performance standards and to each other.
- You will clearly know who are your top employees, your middle group, and your low performers.
- You will be able to ensure that people are being treated fairly, by the numbers, and with no favoritism.
- Supervisors will understand that they are accountable for their personnel decisions, because their actions can be easily compared with the spreadsheet.
- You will be in a much better position to justify your personnel decisions.
- Spreadsheets can be used for trend analysis, training determinations, and rewards and recognition decisions.

The best type of spreadsheet is one that is electronically linked with the employees' work so that their performance is automatically recorded by the appraisal system. If that is not possible, manual input is the next best thing, but you need to have a process in place to validate the accuracy of the employees' input.

Using Tracking Software. Government organizations that answer large numbers of phone calls normally record the performance of each employee in the system's computer. Some of the information they capture includes number of calls answered per day, number of calls answered per hour, average length of each call, and so on. This information can be easily uploaded into a performance spreadsheet, and then supplemented with a manual input by management that records each employee's quality. The spreadsheet could then be manipulated to rank employees by their output, their quality, their timeliness, and so on.

Post Performance Data

Spreadsheets can also help to both motivate the employees and improve their performance, especially if they are posted. In my experience, the more the employees know how they are doing relative to the standards and their peers, the better they will perform. Posting performance spreadsheets is a great way to accomplish this objective.

I also believe in posting attendance data along with the performance information because attendance is tied to performance. Even if you are a highly productive employee when you are present, if you do not come to work, the job simply doesn't get done.

When you post performance/attendance spreadsheets, several things will happen:

- The employees will suddenly have access to much of the same information that management has.
- Employees will be better informed as to where they stand within their peer group.
- If their performance is good, employees will feel proud to see their recognition up on the wall.
- Poor performers will realize that they cannot hide anymore and will be motivated to improve.
- Peer pressure will develop and force the bottom 10 percent to either improve or leave the team.

The initial reaction of most people to this idea is that you can't do this in a government organization. Some of the objections are that (1) it violates the employees' privacy; (2) the employees will not like it; and (3) the unions will oppose it. Let's examine all three objections more closely.

I'm not aware of any law, rule, or regulation that prohibits management from posting this type of information. However, regardless of whether one exists or not, my preference would be to post the information anonymously, that is, Employee A, Employee B, Employee C, and so on. In this way, no one gets formally embarrassed, and to some extent, each employee gets to retain privacy. That being said, everyone would know which letter represents him or her, because they would know their own individual statistics. Moreover, since employees invariably talk to each other, over time, everyone will eventually know who each letter represents.

I've learned that the only employees who don't want information posted are the poor performers. If I were in their shoes, I would not want that information posted, either. However, most other employees do want to see that information because they want to see the organization succeed, they want to know where they stand, and they want the top performers rewarded and the bottom performers held accountable.

From the union's perspective, this is also a good thing. Posting the information ensures that people will be treated fairly, since management's actions will be more easily transparent. It makes the union's job easier, because instead of going out and trying to dig for information, the information is suddenly out in the open for all to see.

I was working for a government organization that serviced delinquent home loans. In essence, the mission of that organization was to help certain citizens avoid foreclosure. There were three ways to accomplish this: (1) the citizen would make a repayment agreement with the lender and would eventually become current on the payments; (2) the government would assume the loan from the lender and become the loan holder; or (3) the citizen would convey the deed to the property to the lender in lieu of foreclosure. Whenever an employee servicing the loan could achieve one of these three actions, it was known as a successful intervention. The higher the number of successful interventions relative to the number of foreclosures, the higher our foreclosure avoidance through servicing (FATS) ratio became.

Although our goal was to have at least a 45 percent FATS ratio, our actual ratio was closer to 20 percent. Accordingly, I asked the division chief to begin posting on a weekly basis the number of successful interventions for each loan servicer. During the first week alone, the disparity in the employees' performance was remarkable. Our best employees had nine successful interventions, while our poorest employees had none. The employees were flabbergasted. How could several of the employees have no successful interventions?

Immediately, peer pressure began to build, and the lowest performers started cleaning up their act. The number of successful interventions began to steadily increase, and by the end of the quarter, our FATS ratio increased to 48 percent!

Team Performance Spreadsheets. Look at Figure 5-1 for an example of a team performance spreadsheet that might be posted. For this particular job, the minimum standards are as follows: productivity—at least 5 decisions per day; quality—15 percent error rate or lower; and timeliness—85 percent or better.

For productivity, Employee D is right on the borderline, while Employee E is well below. The supervisor will need to work closely with these two, especially Employee D. However, note that while Employee F has the highest average productivity, his overall output is by far the lowest because he rarely comes to work. This should be handled as a leave issue, and is something that the other employees are certainly aware of.

Figure 5-1

	Team Member Monthly Performance					
	Productivity		Quality	Timeliness	Attendance	
Employee	Total Output	Average Output	Error Rate	% w/i 21 Days	Hrs on Duty	Direct Labor Hrs
A	115	5.75	5%	91%	160	160
B	99	5.5	2%	88%	160	144
C	97	5.39	7%	95%	144	144
D	75	5	11%	77%	152	120
E	59	3.93	15%	83%	120	120
F	24	6	6%	55%	32	32
Average	78	5.21	8%	82%	128	120

Note 1: Average output represents total output divided by (direct labor hours divided by 8).

Everyone is achieving the accuracy standard. However, Employee E is right on the borderline. Given the fact that he is also failing the productivity standard, he will require a good deal of supervisory attention.

Concerning timeliness, more than half the employees are failing this standard, although several are close (excluding Employee F). In this situation, the supervisor might want look at the process to see if there is something that is causing so many employees to fail. The supervisor should also discuss this matter with the employees, to see if there is anything else that could be done to ensure that both the organization and the employees succeed.

Issue Monthly Report Cards

Another technique that works extremely well is the use of monthly report cards. Under this approach, employees are given short, monthly reports that tell them exactly how they are doing relative to their performance standards and, in some cases, against their peers.

The report can be as long or as short as you would like, but the key is that it contains information that is clear and directly relates to the employee's standards. At a minimum, you should include information related to the employee's performance under both the elements and standards. You may also wish to include other pertinent information showing the average performance for all employees for each element/standard, and information related to attendance. All of this information will provide the employee with a sense of context and will force the employee to see things from management's perspective.

Monthly Report Cards. Figure 5-2 shows one kind of monthly report card that could be used. It shows employees exactly how they are doing relative to the per-

Figure 5-2

Report Card for Employee A								
	Productivity (Number of Decisions Made)				Accuracy		Timeliness	
	Total Output		Average Output					
	Month	FYTD	Month	FYTD	Month	FYTD	Month	FYTD
Standard	N/A	N/A	5	5	15%	15%	85%	85%
Employee	84	488	5.2	5.2	9%	10%	89%	87%
Team	80	477	5.2	5.3	11%	12%	85%	85%

Attendance						
	Month		FYTD		Leave	Leave	Leave Balance
	Hrs on Duty	Direct Labor	Avg Hrs on Duty	Avg Direct Labor	Month	FYTD	
Employee	144	129	137	125	16	138	838
Team	139	123	131	120	21	174	603

"Team" represents the average for all team members.
"Hrs on Duty" represents the number of hours that the employee was actually on the job.
"Direct Labor" represents the number of hours on duty that the employee was performing the primary duties of her job. It excludes training, meetings, special projects, etc.
"Leave Balance" could be either the employee's remaining sick leave and/or annual leave.

formance standards and their peers, on both a monthly and a fiscal year-to-date (FYTD) basis. It also provides detailed information regarding their attendance, the time they are spending on direct labor activities, their leave balances, and how that compares to the team averages.

The employee whose performance is documented in the report card in Figure 5-2 appears to be a slightly above-average employee. His output is about average, while his accuracy and timeliness are slightly better than average. He also comes to work on a regular basis, which is a definite plus.

The challenge with this employee is to help raise his performance to the exceptional level. While meeting the minimum standards is a good thing, we all want our employees to do better than that. One way to accomplish this would be to list the higher-level goals on the report card. In this way, the employee will be on notice as to what she needs to do to excel and will have something to shoot for.

Another advantage of a monthly report card is that it allows far more communication with the employee (and documentation) than the usual twice a year meetings. If the employee is doing well, it's always good to put a note on the employee's report card thanking her for her good work.

By doing this, management can recognize the employee far more frequently than normal. By the same token, if the employee is not doing well, you should also note that on the report card. This will allow you to build a strong case that you have kept the employee informed of her performance problems. As a result, if you have to later take action against her, it will prevent her from arguing that she did not see it coming.

Key Points to Remember

- Align and communicate your organization's goals.
- Identify, address, and try to resolve performance problems as quickly as possible.
- Always make a good-faith effort to help struggling employees.
- Let people know that you are serious about dealing with problem performers.
- Post performance statistics and issue report cards.

CHAPTER 6

Rewards and Recognition

Overview

Government rewards and recognition programs have two primary purposes:

1. To recognize both individuals and groups of employees who make contributions in support of the mission, organizational goals and objectives, and strategic plan
2. To help motivate employees to make contributions that support and enhance organizational goals and objectives

Programs that accomplish these twin goals are built on a set of core principles. In my experience, the following are the key principles behind a solid performance appraisal system:

- The closer the rewards and recognition system is aligned with the organization's mission, goals, objectives, and performance management system, the more effective it will be.

- The more reliable the rewards and recognition system, the more it will drive the right behavior.

- Recognition is most effective when it is given as soon as possible following the accomplishment.

- The type of recognition given should be consistent with the contribution that was made.

- Employees and their representatives should be involved in the development and implementation of the system.

- When a group or team effort produces the desired results, all contributing members of the team should usually be recognized. The level of recognition per team member can vary, depending on each person's overall contribution.
- Proper presentation and strong publicity are important to the program.

The closer a rewards and recognition program follows these principles, the better will be its results.

Rewards and recognition programs generally fall into two distinct but related categories. The first category involves money, which could be a bonus or a pay increase. These are the most complicated rewards programs to administer simply because money is involved. When applied properly, programs containing financial incentives can motivate employees to accomplish the organization's goals and objectives. However, if people believe that rewards money is not being distributed in a fair and equitable manner, the program can actually serve as a disincentive, because people will believe that the money is distributed based on whom you know, and that achieving the goals does not really matter.

The second program involves nonmonetary forms of recognition, ranging from time off to a formal certificate to a simple "thank you." Although not as complex or emotional as programs that involve money, this type of recognition can go a long way toward driving the right behavior if it is administered properly. The key is that nonmonetary recognition must (1) follow the same principles already described; and (2) work hand-in-hand with the monetary awards to influence the right behavior. Let's look at each category, starting with nonmonetary forms of recognition.

Nonmonetary Recognition

There are many ways to recognize employees. One of the best ways, of course, is to simply say "thank you." In my experience, you can never thank employees enough. This simple token of appreciation, whether it is verbal or in writing, goes a long way toward letting employees know that they are appreciated. In fact, many studies indicate that a simple thank you from their supervisor is the number-one desired form of recognition.[1]

Unfortunately, most supervisors thank their employees far too little. Maybe they don't think of it, maybe no one ever says "thank you" to them, or perhaps they are simply too busy. It's hard to say. However, thanking someone takes less time and energy than virtually any other form of recognition, yet has an enormous payback, so it is hard to understand why this form of recognition is so rarely used.

In one case, I was working with a young manager who was under a great deal of stress. She was obviously a hard worker who was eager to learn and cared a great deal about the organization. Although she made some mistakes along the way, she also did many things right. To reinforce this, on several occasions, I made a point of thanking her for her good work and telling her just how proud I was of all her accomplishments, while at the same time pointing out ways that she could improve. Later on, she came up to me and told me how much she appreciated both my support and the fact that I truly appreciated her efforts.

A few years later, when we were no longer working together, I heard that her office was going through some difficult times. I contacted her to see how she was doing. She told me that after one particularly difficult meeting, she personally thanked her subordinate supervisors and told them just how proud *she* was of their accomplishments. Several of them later told me of the young manager's comments and how much it meant to them. In the same way that my simple act resonated with her, she was able to motivate her subordinates by showing her appreciation.

A good way to reinforce the right behavior is to compliment an employee in front of others, particularly high-level officials. When an employee feels that her supervisor is aware of her accomplishments, and is willing to speak about them in front of an important individual, that employee truly feels recognized and valued. Moreover, when that employee is complimented for an accomplishment that supports the organization's mission, goals, and objectives, it establishes a consistency of purpose and promotes further acts along the same line.

For example, my office would receive frequent visitors from around the country to see some of our innovative approaches to management (the use of visual displays, new computer applications, etc.). Whenever I took the visitors around the office for a tour, I made a point of stopping at the desks of the people who had developed creative programs that were consistent with the culture I was trying to establish.

Other people began asking what they needed to do to gain similar recognition. We advised them that all they needed to do was develop a unique contribution to our organization, and they would surely be recognized. Thus, a simple form of recognition began to drive a positive form of creative competition within our organization.

An easy but powerful way to reinforce the right behavior is to use bulletin boards to display success stories. The success stories could be thank-you letters from satisfied customers, or they could be letters of appreciation from management to the employee. One of my favorite approaches is to post photographs of the customers and/or the employees along with the success story. Any time you add a face to the story, it seems to connect with people even more.

We once posted the picture of a young woman who had just graduated from school under a government-sponsored program of vocational rehabilitation. The picture showed her smiling broadly while wearing her graduation cap and gown. The following note accompanied the photograph:

> I'm a little late at writing my cards this year because I have more on my plate, which I am very thankful for. Thank you so much for believing in me even before I knew how to believe in myself. . . . You [her counselor] truly are a positive inspiration to me and every veteran you have served and have yet to serve! God made someone very special when he made you!

This story remained on the board for quite some time and, as you could imagine, was a source of pride for her counselor. Moreover, whenever a visitor came down to that division, I always pointed out her picture and retold her story, which gave the counselor even more recognition.

A more formal way to recognize employees for their accomplishments is to build an employee wall of fame. Based on Major League Baseball's model in Cooperstown, New York, an employee wall of fame is a simple yet elegant way of recognizing your best employees. It could be a permanent display or rotating displays highlighting the employee(s) of the month or quarter, the team of the month or quarter, the supervisor of the month or quarter, etc. One way to do this is by posting the employee's photograph, along with a brief biography and statement of accomplishments, in a prominent location that employees typically pass by. Such displays can now be done very cheaply, since they can be created with a computer.

During my tenure with one particular government organization, I established an employee wall of fame. The wall displayed the employees/supervisor/team of the quarter, which qualified them as nominees for our employee/supervisor/team of the year program. The winners were announced at our annual employee breakfast. It was strategically placed outside our main training room so that whenever employees attended training, they could read about the accomplishments of their fellow employees. Employees really liked this display because they felt it showed that we truly cared about our employees and that we were determined to recognize those people who had made significant contributions to our organization.

Shortly after I left that organization, the staff took that wall of fame to another level. They replaced the employee photographs with individual PowerPoint slide shows of each recipient. The staff recognized that you need to always raise the bar with respect to employee recognition, and this new display received instant acclaim. Once other offices saw this innovative display, several of them indicated that they wanted to replicate the concept.

A complementary approach to an employee wall of fame is a room dedicated to celebrating the employees. Such a room could contain photographs of the teams, the management staff, employees serving their customers, former award recipients, previous employees, the families of the employees, or similar personal touches. It would also be a good place to display trophies, plaques, and proclamations. A properly designed employee room could reinforce the right behavior by emphasizing some of the organization's core values, such as excellent performance, teamwork, the importance of the employees, a sense of family, and so on.

Most government organizations provide minor articles of value to employees on certain occasions. For example, employees who stay with the government for at least 10 years typically receive a 10-year pin, and then receive additional pins of greater value every 5 or 10 more years that they serve. The problem with these pins is that they are often handed to the employee with little fanfare, which gives the impression that the government does not really value the employee's service.

A better approach is to leverage these occasions by presenting the pin to the employee as part of a recognition ceremony. In this way, the employee and his peers will see that the government truly values each employee's service, and that it is a big deal when someone reaches a particular milestone.

For the first 20 years of my career, I received service pins in the same manner that many other government employees received their pins. Twice my supervisor simply gave them to me in private, while the other time, it was merely left on my desk. Needless to say, the way these situations were handled did not instill much pride in me regarding my government career.

I later came to work for a leader who took a different approach. Every time an employee became eligible for a service pin, he insisted that the employee be given the pin at the director's staff meeting. Before giving the employee the pin, he first gave a recap of the employee's career to date. This recap gave us a sense of perspective regarding the employee's career, and frequently put the employee in a different light than we were used to seeing.

Once the senior leaders at the meeting heard about the employee's career, they invariably applauded as the employee received the service pin. It was obvious to all that the employee appreciated the pomp and circumstance that accompanied the service pin. Moreover, a summary of the meeting was later sent to all employees, which meant that everyone knew that the employee had achieved a career milestone.

Employee recognition does not always have to come from management. Sometimes, the most effective form of recognition can come from the employees. One way to do this is by establishing organizational thank-you cards that are given to each employee. These cards, which are tied to the organization's mission and vision, goals and objectives, or core values, are designed to enable one employee (either a supervisor or a nonsupervisor) to thank another employee for helping the person achieve a specific objective or for exemplifying a desired core value. They are very effective because they give everyone a sense that she is important. That is, everyone's thank-you cards count as much as anyone else's.

We shamelessly stole the thank-you card concept from another organization. We customized it to our organization by placing the road map we had developed on the cover of the card (see Figure 6-1). We then added our core values to the inside of the card and gave each employee 10 cards for his personal use. We advised them that anytime a fellow employee exhibited one of those values, they should place a check mark next to the core value, add a personal note, and give it to the employee.

This approach took off like wildfire, as people started thanking each other in ways that we had never seen before. Suddenly, signed cards started appearing on the desks of our employees, as well as on bulletin boards throughout the office. A simple, nonmonetary gesture seemed to touch a nerve with our workforce.

Another program that involves employees recognizing their peers is an employee lotto program. Under this program, employees are given a number of lotto tickets that they can present to fellow employees for a job well done (see Figure 6-2). Once an employee identifies another deserving employee, he writes the employee's name on the ticket, signs it, and gives it to the individual he wants to recognize, who then places the lotto ticket in one of a series of designated lotto boxes. At the end of the quarter, six tickets are randomly selected from the lotto boxes, and the winners are given prizes such as movie tickets or restaurant vouchers.

This is an effective, low-cost method for recognizing employees for the right behavior while ensuring that everyone is involved in the process.

Whenever I used to receive a letter from a customer acknowledging the good work of one of my employees, I would forward the letter to the employee along with a note from me thanking her for her good work. Once we implemented the thank-you cards and the lotto program, I began writing my thank-you note on the card, checking off the core value that the employee exemplified, and including a lotto ticket with the card. By making this subtle adjustment, I was able to recognize the employee with something a bit more tangible, and the employees really seemed to appreciate this new approach.

Figure 6-1. The front and inside cover of a government organization's "thank you" card that is tied to its mission, vision, and core values.

Thank you for exemplifying our core values

- Veterans have earned our respect and are our reason for being, our common purpose. All our efforts are directed toward meeting their needs.

- We are committed to communicating to our veterans and employees in a timely, thorough, accurate, understandable, and respectable manner.

- We listen to the concern and views of veterans and our employees to bring about improvements in benefits and services, and the climate in which they are provided.

- We value understandable business processes that consistently produce positive results. We foster an environment that promotes personal and corporate initiative, risk taking, and teamwork.

- We are open to challenge and flexible in our attitudes.

- Respect, integrity, trust, and fairness are hallmarks of all our interactions.

- We value a culture where everyone is involved, accountable, respected, and appreciated.

- We will perform at the highest level of competence, always, and take pride in accomplishment. We are a "can do" organization.

To

Thanks for

Figure 6-2

A government organization's "lotto" ticket that employees can give to each other in order to recognize a job well done.

Monetary Recognition

Rewarding government employees always seems to be a struggle. First of all, governments usually set aside a very small percentage of their budget for this purpose. One reason for this is that, unlike the private sector, governments are not in business to make profits. As a result, even if a government entity performs at a high level, the government usually does not make any more money. Since no additional funds become available to reward the employees for high performance, especially at the local level, it tends to foster the perception that no matter what they do, it is never enough, and they will never truly be rewarded for their good work.

From a political standpoint, it is also difficult to pay large rewards to government employees. Many members of the public believe that government employees are overpaid, while others feel that government employees have a level of job security that does not exist in the private sector. To then issue large bonuses to these same individuals would be an extremely difficult sell, especially during an era when we have unprecedented deficits in many branches of government.

Another challenge to giving large bonuses is the scrutiny it would command. Large bonuses for government employees invariably trigger negative headlines in the media, which is something that every government leader tries to avoid. Moreover, once a large rewards program hits the spotlight, the inevitable investigation ensues. The Inspector General or some other entity becomes involved, and at that point, trouble begins to brew.

By contrast, many private-sector organizations allow employees to earn 10 percent, 20 percent, 30 percent, or more of their salaries in bonuses, which adds an enormous incentive for employees to succeed. That is because the more money an employee brings into the company, the more money the company will make. In essence, the better they do, the better they will get rewarded. It's as simple as that. Of course, the private sector is not burdened by all of the rules and regulations that are part of government. Moreover, because the bottom line for business always involves profit, it makes sense to pay people more when profits are good and, conversely, to pay them less when profits are down.

By contrast, if the Social Security Administration improves the quality of its decisions or its level of customer satisfaction, it will not make any more money. Nor, for that matter, will a library or a school system that does a better job from one year to the next. In fact, if a government organization is able to do more with less by becoming more productive or eliminating certain costs, the likelihood is that you will be told, "Thank you, but it is your job to save money," and nothing else will happen in the form of rewards or recognition.

Once, having taken over an organization that had excess space, we came up with a creative solution to give up even more space than was first anticipated. This resulted in a net savings to the government of about $600,000 per year in rent. Over 10 years, the government would save $6,000,000, not counting any rent increases that would surely come during that period.

Perhaps naively, I asked if a portion of that savings could be given back to our office so we could hire extra people or buy goods and supplies. Such a payback, I reasoned, would serve as an incentive to other offices to also give back space. As you might expect, the request was denied, and I was told that rent money came from a centralized account that could not be used for payroll or to buy goods and services at the local level.

Here's another example: I once managed 1 of about 40 government offices that were responsible for selling foreclosed properties. This was an expensive and time-consuming process that involved hundreds of millions of dollars. At the time, all properties were advertised in the newspaper, after which prospective purchasers were required to submit bids to the office selling the property. A typical advertisement in the newspaper cost us more than $10,000 and required several employees to evaluate each bid that we received.

We decided to reengineer the process by advertising all of the properties via the Internet, and by using an Internet-based computer program to evaluate all of the bids we received. This approach saved us about $70,000 per month in advertising costs and allowed us to redirect the services of the employees who were manually reviewing the bids to other areas of our operation. Many other offices adopted this approach, which ultimately saved our organization millions of dollars on a national level.

However, because the savings were in a centralized account that was not transferable to other accounts, we never saw a penny. From my perspective, the reaction I received was, "Thank you, what have you done for me lately?"

Sometimes, when an organization saves money, its budget will actually be cut. This occurs because once Congress, the state, or the city legislature sees that a government entity can get by with less, it will inevitably make sure that it does in the future. That is why most government officials try to spend their surplus money prior to the end of the fiscal year. They'll buy new computers, replace their furniture, paint their office, and so on, to make sure that they don't have to turn back excess money. They want to avoid being criticized by their headquarters for not using all of the resources they've been given for the year, and they want to show the people who appropriate and allocate their budget that they could not get by with less.

For example, we changed our telephone system, which saved our office tens of thousands of dollars in phone charges. Although the new system had a few less features than the old one, we figured that it was worth it, given all the money we were saving. However, the bean counters in our central office noticed the savings as well, and cut our telephone budget the next year. In essence, by saving the government money, we wound up hurting ourselves, because we ended up with a system that was as not as good as the previous one.

The cases in point cited here show how frustrating it can be for managers to do something positive, and then receive virtually no reward or recognition, or perhaps even wind up being penalized. In my experience, poorly designed and/or operated government rewards and recognition systems have frequently proven to be *disincentive* systems, as they have frustrated both the employees and managers with whom I have worked. Once that happens, cynicism begins to set in, because when people see that the wrong behavior is being rewarded, they conclude that management is not serious about living up to its core values.

Other implementation problems may be caused by unrealistic goals or by a lack of resources. Rewards programs will work well only when people believe that the goals are achievable and they have enough resources with which to attain them. Otherwise, people will get discouraged and will simply give up and go through the motions.

In my experience, rewards programs can be very fragile. They are intended to encourage people to perform better but frequently wind up discouraging people, which will hurt the organization in the short term and, perhaps, the long term.

I worked for an organization that, on a national level, frequently set goals that were unachievable. Sometimes the goals were set too high because of political pressure, while other times, they were set too high because of poor management decisions. Whatever the reasons may have been for setting the goals so high, when they were stratified down to the local level, people often became extremely frustrated and discouraged. To compound matters, resources were normally distributed based on projected workload rather than on what an office needed to achieve its goals. As a result, some offices had more than enough resources to achieve their rewards targets, while others had virtually no chance of making them. This created an organization of the "haves" and "have-nots" and wound up turning off many of the organization's key players.

One year, however, that same organization received more resources than usual and set its goals in a manner that was commensurate with the resources it received. Even though resources were still not linked to the performance targets, everyone felt that the goals were challenging but reasonable, and that they had enough resources so that they had a chance to attain the goals. Sure enough, that organization had a banner year, as everyone was motivated, worked hard to achieve the goals, and in many cases did just that. In this instance, the rewards system accomplished exactly what it set out to do.

Well-designed and properly implemented rewards and recognition systems can reinforce the right behavior and ensure that everyone is working toward the same goals—even if a lot of money is not involved. After all, people want to see their organization do well and will try and achieve the organization's goals, even if the rewards pool is relatively small. As long as they feel that the organization is doing right by them, the employees will try to do right by the organization.

Alignment

One of the keys to any good rewards and recognition system is to align the system with the organization's mission, vision, goals, objectives, and budget, along with its other management systems. The more aligned the systems are, the more everyone will be working in the same direction. Keep in mind, however, that alignment can be a very tricky and difficult task.

Rewards and recognition is a very emotional topic for many employees. Most think that they are excellent employees and deserve to be rewarded. If they perceive the system to be unfair, or believe that management is saying one thing and then doing something else, they can easily become turned off and lose the commitment that the organization so desperately needs.

A properly aligned rewards system should flow from the other management systems and be the final piece of the puzzle. Once you hire and train your employees, provide them with the proper tools and resources, make them aware of the organization's goals and objectives, and issue them performance standards that have a clear line of sight (the input), you need to ensure that employees and/or teams that exceed your expectations (the output) will be rewarded. The clearer, more consistent, and more reliable the relationship between the input and the output, the more successful will be your rewards program. In addition, the more this relationship holds true up and down the organizational chain, the better the employees will perceive the system to be working and the more it will drive the right behavior.

Conversely, if people believe that rewards determinations are based on whom you know or how well you are liked, or are simply hypocritical, they will not trust management, nor will they trust the rewards program. If that happens, the employees will continue to comply with the organization's requirements, and will still strive to succeed, but with less energy and less commitment.

As a case in point, one of our divisions received its yearly goals and rewards targets from headquarters. We immediately built those goals into the division chief's standards, then stratified them down to the employee level, and included them in the employees' standards. We felt confident that at every level there was a clear line of sight for the performance goals.

We carefully monitored everyone's performance with the goal of having each employee hit his or her rewards targets, which would mathematically result in the division meeting its rewards targets as well. Although there were a few bumps in the road, that's exactly what happened. Every employee performed in an exceptional manner, and the division received additional rewards money. All of our systems had been properly aligned and managed, and this translated into the right behavior and the desired performance.

Headquarters established national rewards targets for offices that were responsible for managing regional housing programs. The targets were both clear and fair, and every office worked hard to reach them. However, late in the fiscal year, the people overseeing this particular rewards program made an adjustment in the way they were counting certain errors. As a result, only five out of the nine offices achieved the rewards goals, even though two additional offices had been under the impression that they would also be rewarded for their efforts. Although the five offices that received the money were pleased, many people felt that it was terribly unfair to change the rules so late in the game.

I later visited one of the two offices that were expecting to be rewarded for achieving the performance targets. In a nutshell, they were devastated by the way they had been treated. The employees all felt betrayed, and the office's performance suffered for quite a few months.

I decided to try a novel approach to rewards and recognition. Recognizing that employees want to be involved in key decisions that affect them, I tried to incorporate a peer review program into our rewards program. The premise behind this approach was that the people doing the work know how their peers are doing, so incorporating their perspective into the rewards program would add another positive dimension to the program. This program was fully negotiated with our local union, so I had its support as we moved forward.

Under the new program, employees could receive rewards money based on three elements: (1) accomplishing individual goals; (2) achieving group goals; and (3) receiving high scores from their peers. (Employees could still be rewarded for one-time special acts.) The maximum amount of money that could be earned from each category was capped, with the lowest amount being set aside for peer review. I intentionally did this because I knew that type of review could be very emotional for some people, as it involved having their peers evaluate them.

When we first implemented the peer review program (prior to tying it to rewards), it worked well. People appreciated the feedback and tried to address the constructive criticism that they received. However, once we tied peer review to rewards, the program simply fell apart. Suddenly, people became angry at each other, and felt that their peer reviews were unfair. Many believed that their peers were intentionally giving them low scores in order to make themselves look better. Even though relatively little money was at stake, it didn't seem to matter. As long as people felt that the system was unfair, it was never going to work. Needless to say, we quickly scrapped the peer review aspect of our rewards program.

As you can see from these cases, rewards and recognition systems can be very damaging to an organization if they are not carefully designed, closely aligned with the organization's goals and objectives, and fairly implemented. In the last three cases in point, the employees who were affected by the rewards program believed that the program was either unfair or unreliable. As a result, in each case, the rewards program hurt the organization, rather than helped it.

Unfortunately, in my experience, these cases in point are reflective of the rewards programs that I've seen throughout my career. Most rewards programs have failed on one or more counts and have probably caused more harm than good. The lesson learned in all of this is that when you distribute rewards money, you have to follow the principles described at the beginning of this chapter. If you do, then you can have a rewards program that facilitates improved performance, rather than causes you more problems.

Having seen rewards programs fail time after time, both in offices that I managed and around the country, I set out to design a program that would be consistent with the principles of a solid rewards program. In designing such a program, I recognized that I would always have the burden of a limited rewards budget at my disposal. That being said, I also felt that the vast majority of government employees wanted to do a good job and be part of a winner. In short, even if I couldn't offer them rewards commensurate with the private sector, I still believed that a fair and open rewards and recognition program could motivate them to excel. Let me share that program with you now.

A Simple Rewards Program That Works

As with most government organizations, we received an annual awards budget. Typically, the budget ranged between 0.5 percent and 1.0 percent of our budget for employee salaries. We set aside a third of that budget to reward employees who committed special acts that were worthy of recognition. It was important to set aside money for special acts because we wanted to reward our employees as soon as possible after they had made a special contribution or an unusual accomplishment.

Of the remaining budget, one-third was set aside for group accomplishments and the remaining third was set aside for individual achievements. I did this because I had learned that if you weight your rewards too heavily toward individual performance, people will focus almost exclusively on their own performance and will not be as interested in the performance of the group or in assisting others as the organization would like. Conversely, if the rewards are weighted too heavily toward group performance, people will focus so much on the group that you probably will not see them trying to exceed the performance standards of their individual positions as much as you would like.

Once we established the budget mix, the next step was to establish rewards targets. It's been my experience that many government managers do not like to establish the rewards targets in advance. They believe that doing this will limit their flexibility at the end of the rating period to assign an overall performance rating and to issue rewards. I believe that this approach is a mistake. While it clearly provides management with flexibility, it limits the reliability and credibility of the rewards system. After all, if employees don't know what they need to do to excel, they will be working to some extent in a vacuum, which means they may not be focusing all of their efforts on helping the organization achieve outstanding performance. Moreover, if the employees don't know the criteria for excellent performance, it is likely that when the end-of-the-year awards become public, there will be a certain amount of resentment, as some people will conclude that the awards were based on favoritism rather than fairness.

This is why so many supervisors do not look forward to giving performance appraisals and awards. From their perspective, all it seems to do is foster anger and frustration among the troops. However, if the employees knew in advance what the criteria were for outstanding performance, and then received periodic updates as to how they were doing against these criteria, there would be no surprises at the end of the year, since the employees could accurately predict what their appraisal will be and whether they will be eligible for awards.

With this approach in mind, we decided to set three individual and three group rewards targets per quarter. Every time you achieved a rewards target, you earned one rewards certificate, with six being the maximum number you could earn per quarter. The number of rewards targets could be adjusted if necessary, depending on job requirements and group goals. However, because we wanted to be consistent across our organization, anytime we increased the number of rewards targets for a job and/or team, we decreased their relative worth so that everyone could earn only a maximum of six certificates per quarter. In other words, if a specific job had four rewards targets and the group was also given four targets, each time the employee achieved a rewards target, the employee would earn three-fourths of a certificate.

We wanted the supervisors to have a strong stake in the system as well, so a supervisor earned three certificates for every group rewards target achieved. We did this because: (1) in government, there is relatively little difference between an employee's pay and a first-line supervisor's; (2) a supervisor is always under a lot of pressure, and we wanted to reward them when their team achieved its targets; and (3) we wanted to show our employees that the supervisors were important and to encourage them to become supervisors down the road.

We had a different challenge when it came to our support divisions (mailroom, payroll, information resources, human resources, etc.). They did not have any formal goals or targets from our headquarters. However, we felt that it was important to make sure that they were assisting our business line divisions in achieving their goals. We also thought it was important to make them feel that they were a part of our organization and were included in our rewards program. Accordingly, we developed three individual and three group goals for these employees that were as linked to the business line goals and objectives as possible. In addition, they were advised that should any of the business line divisions achieve their national rewards targets, they would receive a portion of those rewards. This provided them with a sense of consistency as well as a stake in the performance of the business line activities.

In setting the rewards targets, we started with the mindset that these targets must clearly flow from our organization's goals and objectives down to each team and each employee. We then tried to decide what would represent outstanding performance at the organization, team, and individual levels, and use this information to set the six rewards targets. The rewards targets were always higher than the minimum performance standards and represented stretch goals whenever possible. The individual targets were the same for every employee occupying a similar position, while the group targets were the same for every member of a discrete team.

Once the targets were set, we published them and posted them so everyone would know exactly what he needed to do to succeed. We used television monitors to give daily updates on group performance, posted monthly spreadsheets so everyone could see how she was doing relative to the targets and their peers, and also provided all employees with monthly report cards.

Before you could receive any certificates, you were required to also meet the following criteria: (1) you had to be present at the job for at least half the quarter; and (2) you could not be on a performance improvement plan or receive any disciplinary and/or adverse actions during the quarter. As long as you met these criteria, you would automatically receive a rewards certificate for every individual/group rewards target that you achieved.

At the end of a quarter, you received a statement indicating the number of group and individual targets that you achieved (see Figure 6-3). You also were advised if you were going to receive additional money for a special act or contribution. (Note: You did not have to wait until the end of the quarter to receive payment for a one-time act). We provided quarterly statements to promptly recognize employees for their accomplishments and so that if an employee changed jobs or teams during the year, he or she would continue to carry over the certificates earned until the end of the fiscal year, when we would convert the certificates into cash.

We waited for the end of the fiscal year because there was not enough money in our awards budget to make quarterly rewards payments meaningful. At the end of the fiscal year, we added up all of the certificates that were earned, and then divided that total into the pool of available rewards money (roughly two-thirds of the rewards money that had been given to us at the beginning of the year). If we did not spend all of the remaining third of the money that was set aside for special acts and/or contributions, we added that money to the overall pool available for

Figure 6-3

Report Card

				Shares Earned
Quarters 1–3: Total Shares Earned				13
Quarter 4				
Individual Goals	*Target*	*Results*	*Shares*	
Goal 1	16	17	1	
Goal 2	95%	90%	0	
Goal 3	97%	97%	1	
Group Goals				
Group Goal 1	2,700	2,550	0	
Group Goal 2	95%	96%	1	
Group Goal 3	97%	93%	0	
Quarter 4: Total Shares Earned			3	3
Quarters 1–4 or Performance Appraisal Period				16

	Conversion to Money
"Share Value: $100,000/4,000 shares earned"	$25
Total Earned ($25 x 16 shares)	$400
Special Acts	$0
Total Incentive Awards Earned	$400

Comments: No performance or attendance problems during the performance year. "Thank you for all of your hard work, especially your willingness to mentor Jim."

This is an example of an employee report card that lets the employee know exactly how he and his team did relative to the rewards targets. There are no secrets and no surprises. At the bottom are comments that enable the supervisor to provide the employee with even more feedback.

rewards certificates. In a given year, a rewards certificate was typically worth be-tween $13 and $22.

The better we did, the less a certificate was worth, because the more certificates that were earned, the less their overall value. However, as I will explain later, the employees were usually able to more than make up for the difference by earning national rewards.

Scenario 1. A rewards budget is roughly $100,000 for a workforce of about 300 employees. Approximately $67,000 is set aside for the rewards certificates. A total of 5,153 certificates are earned for the year, which means each certificate is worth about $13 ($67,000/5,153 = $13).

Scenario 2. A rewards budget is roughly $150,000 for a workforce of about 450 employees. Approximately $100,000 is set aside for the rewards certificates. A total of 4,545 certificates are earned for the year, which means each certificate is worth about $22 ($100,000/4,545 = $22).

At the end of the end of the fiscal year, employees could receive anywhere from zero certificates up to a maximum of 24 certificates, depending on their perfor-mance and the group's. They do well if the group does well, but they do even better if they also achieve their individual targets. The top performers will do much better than the bottom performers (who will receive nothing if they have attendance, per-formance, and/or conduct problems), so we will only be rewarding contributions to the organization, and not reinforcing mediocrity or worse.

At the end of the year, one other element comes into play—the achievement of national goals. In our organization, if a business line division[2] achieved certain na-tional goals, that division would earn a large amount of money that was over and above our office's regular budget for local rewards. At many of the relatively small number of offices that earned this extra money, they would simply give everyone an equal share of this additional pot of money, regardless of the employee's contri-bution. From their perspective, they could not come up with another clean, defensi-ble, and reliable method for dividing up the money. The downside was that outstanding employees were receiving the same amount as poor employees, even though their contributions were vastly different.

Since we had a system of certificates, we were able to measure each person's contribution based on the number of certificates earned. Everyone knew the for-mula for distributing national rewards money, so there was virtually no room for dispute. The formula went like this: For every business line division that earned national rewards, a portion of their rewards funds were set aside for the support divisions. Since the support divisions were about 10 percent of our office's payroll, the maximum amount of the national rewards pool that they could earn would be 10 percent. If only one or two business line divisions earned rewards, the support divisions would receive a pro-rated share of those rewards.

Scenario 3. Business Line Division A contains 50 percent of the business line division salaries. The support divisions make up 10 percent of the office's salaries. Business Line Division A earns a total of $80,000 in national rewards. The support divisions' share of those rewards would be 50 percent of 10 percent, or a total of 5 percent of the rewards ($80,000 $\times$ .5 = $40,000 $\times$ .1 = $4,000). The remaining $76,000 would be distributed among Business Line Division A's employees.

Scenario 4. All business line divisions earn national rewards totaling $160,000. The support divisions are 10 percent of the office's salaries. The support divisions' share of those rewards would be 100 percent of 10 percent, or 10 percent of the rewards ($160,000 $\times$ 1.0 = $160,000 $\times$ .1 = $16,000). The better the office performs, the more the support divisions earn.

The remaining money would go to the business line division(s) and would be distributed to employees based on their percentage of the total shares earned by the employees in the division. The more shares that you earned for the year, the higher your percentage of the national rewards that you receive. It's that simple. In essence, we would distribute these rewards based on (1) a preset formula that everyone was aware of at the beginning of the year and was kept apprised of throughout the year; and (2) criteria that were fair and equitable and were linked to the organization's goals and objectives.

Scenario 5. A business line division earned $80,000 in rewards, of which $4,000 was given to the support divisions, leaving a total of $76,000 to be distributed to the business line division's employees. Within that division, the employees have earned a total of 1,250 rewards certificates, which means that for this purpose, each certificate is worth $61 ($76,000/1,250 = $61). Employee A is a supervisor whose team achieved all three goals per quarter for the year. Accordingly, he received a total of 36 certificates (12 certificates $\times$ 3 because he is a supervisor, = 36 certificates). He receives a total of $2,196 ($61 $\times$ 36 = $2,196).

Employee B works on the same team as Employee A. She received 12 certificates, since her team hit all of its goals, and another 6 certificates for achieving some of the individual rewards targets. All told, she earns 18 certificates, or $1,098 ($61 $\times$ 18 = $1,098).

Employee C works on the same team as Employee A and Employee B, but he experiences performance problems throughout the first half of the year, resulting in his being placed on a performance improvement plan in the first and second quarters of the year. He finally achieves acceptable performance in the third and fourth quarters, but never attains any of the individual rewards targets. Even though his team accomplished all of its goals throughout the year, he is ineligible to receive certificates for the first two quarters, because his performance was below the minimum acceptable level during that time. He receives six certificates as a team member for the third and fourth quarters, since he was a contributing member of that team during those quarters. As a result, he receives $366 for his efforts ($61 × 6 = $366).

In these examples, one individual received $2,196, a second earned $1,098, and a third got $366. Each person was paid for his or her contributions based on preset criteria. The top performers received the highest rewards, team members were compensated for group achievement, and low performers were given several important messages: (1) they need to increase their individual contributions if they want to be rewarded; and (2) where the team does well *and* they make a reasonable contribution to the team, they will be rewarded for the team's accomplishments. Through these clear and consistent messages, the rewards system will drive the right employee behavior and help the organization to improve its performance.

Results of This System

The year after we implemented this system, we compared our employee satisfaction score for rewards and recognition with the same measure for the prior year. Remarkably, employee satisfaction with this one measure went up by more than 20 percentage points! Without a doubt, the employees recognized that this system was much better than previous ones since (1) the criteria were announced in advance; (2) it was clear and easy to understand; and (3) it was perceived as being applied fairly and consistently.

Over time, word began to spread about our rewards program, and quite a few offices requested copies of our system.

In August 2001, the U.S. Office of Personnel Management presented our office with its prestigious PILLAR (Performance Incentives Leadership Linked to Achieving Results) Award. Our office was one of only two offices in the entire federal government to receive this award that year. The PILLAR Award recognized the integrated manner in which we used our rewards program to help drive our organization's performance.

Why Did This System Work So Well?

The system accomplished its objectives because it embodied the principles of an excellent rewards and recognition system that were described at the beginning of this chapter. Let's compare those principles to this system to see how well they were designed and implemented.

Principle: The closer the rewards and recognition system is aligned with the organization's mission, goals, objectives, and performance management system, the more effective it will be.

The System: All of the key measures that translated into rewards certificates were closely aligned with the organization's goals, objectives, and performance standards. We continually tried to ensure that we were choosing the metrics that were the drivers of our performance. On a quarterly basis, we would review the six key measures (the measures themselves, as well as the targets) in order to make mid-course adjustments where necessary.

Principle: The more reliable the rewards and recognition system, the more it will drive the right behavior.

The System: It was extremely reliable because the targets were published in advance, results were available on a daily and/or monthly basis for all to see, and decisions were based strictly on the numbers. The reliability of this particular rewards system was one of its strongest features.

Principle: Recognition is most effective when it is given as soon as possible following the accomplishment.

The System: We accomplished this goal in several ways. Special acts or contributions were paid out immediately following the accomplishment, so there was no waiting under these circumstances. When quarterly performance targets were achieved, employees received both their rewards certificates and a quarterly rewards statement, soon after the end of the quarter.

Principle: The type of recognition given should be consistent with the contribution that was made.

The System: The system was specifically designed so that the level of the reward would be consistent with the level of the contribution. The example described earlier wherein one employee received $2,196, a second received $1,098, and a third $366 is a good illustration of the system's ability to make distinctions between contributions. The use of rewards certificates, coupled with the issuance of one-time rewards for special acts or contributions and the many non-monetary awards that management has at its disposal, provides plenty of flexibility to be true to this particular principle.

Principle: Employees and their representatives should be involved in the development and implementation of the system.

The System: Our local union was intimately involved in the development of this system. In fact, when we formally introduced this system to our employees, the union actively and publicly supported it, because it understood that the new system would be beneficial to the bargaining unit as well as the entire organization.

Principle: When a group or team effort produces the desired results, all contributing members of the team should usually be recognized. The level of recognition per team member can vary, depending on each person's overall contribution.

The System: As described earlier, the system rewards teams that achieve their rewards targets. Team members are rewarded at a level that is commensurate with their contributions to the team. In those rare instances where a team member is absent for much of the year, performs below minimal expectations, and/or is a significant conduct problem, that individual may not receive any rewards whatsoever.

Principle: Proper presentation and strong publicity are important to the program.

The System: Awards are normally presented in a variety of different ways, including at team meetings, staff meetings, annual award breakfasts/luncheons, and so on. Awards are publicized through newsletters, minutes of staff meetings, on bulletin boards, and the employee wall of fame, for example.

Key Points to Remember

- Use monetary and nonmonetary rewards to recognize both individuals and groups.
- If you are not careful, your rewards program can be a disincentive to good performance.
- Make sure that people know what the expectations are, and keep them apprised of the results.
- Apply the system in a reliable manner so there are no surprises.

CHAPTER 7

Attendance Management

ATTENDANCE MANAGEMENT means ensuring that employees are at work to perform the government's mission. Obviously, the more time that employees are at work doing their job, the easier it will be to get the job done. However, this topic is more complicated than it may first seem, as it involves three interrelated areas: tours of duty (including alternate and compressed work schedules), alternate workplaces, and leave administration.

The bottom line for all three areas is that managers must ensure that the government is functioning smoothly and effectively while serving as an employer of choice by being sensitive to the needs of its employees. Trying to do both is a delicate balancing act that requires skill, strength, and an even hand. Let's look at each individual area in more detail.

Tours of Duty

Tours of duty pertain to the work schedules of government employees. When scheduling such tours, first consideration should be given to the effective and efficient management of the organization's functions, and second consideration should be given to fair treatment of the employees. Work schedules need to be established in a manner that best meets the organization's actual work requirements. For example, some government organizations are traditionally open for 10 or less hours per day (a library, a school, a court, etc.), while others are open 24/7 (a hospital, the police, the military, etc.).

In most government organizations that are not on a 24/7 schedule, the normal workweek for full-time employees is 40 hours. The usual tour of duty within the 40-hour workweek is five 8-hour days, not counting lunch or breaks, Monday through Friday. For most employees, the working hours in each day of the normal workweek are the same.

Generally, an employee's work schedule will remain fixed from week to week. However, on occasion, workload demands may require that a schedule be changed. Under these circumstances, employees should be given the opportunity to discuss how the changes to the work schedule will affect them. If the change is still administratively necessary, the employee should be given advance notice, where possible. Consider this example:

Our employees were allowed to come to work as early as 6:00 a.m., in order to avoid the southern California traffic. However, our phone hours of operation were from 7:30 a.m. until 4:00 p.m. It didn't make sense to allow the people who answered the phones to come in so early, since they would be leaving by 2:30 p.m., which was 1½ hours before we closed for business. Accordingly, we notified the employees of the change, worked closely with our local union in order to address any extraordinary personal situations, and then implemented the change because it enabled us to provide better service to the public.

Special consideration should be extended to employees who have religious beliefs that prevent them from working on a particular day. If appropriate, consideration should be given to allowing the employee to exchange her duty assignment with another employee, or to finding another solution whereby everyone's needs may be met.

Religious Considerations. Government organizations that have religious employees who observe the Sabbath may face discrimination complaints if they try and require these employees to work on Friday night and/or Saturday. On the one hand, if they can accommodate these employees within the framework of their tours of duty policy, without setting a precedent that can come back to haunt them, they can avoid the time, energy, and expense of litigation. On the other hand, if no other accommodations are possible, they should (1) ensure that all employees are aware of the policy; (2) be certain that everyone is being treated fairly and equitably under this policy; (3) document that they made a reasonable effort to try and accommodate the employee(s); and (4) stick to their guns.

From a management perspective, the easiest tours of duty to manage are those in which everyone comes to work at the same time and leaves at the same time. Under this approach, everyone's starting time might be 8:00 a.m., with all tours of duty ending at 4:30 p.m. (assuming 30 minutes for lunch). This approach is very simple to manage because everyone comes and goes at the same time; everyone is available for meetings, training, and so on.

Unfortunately, as time goes by, one set tour of duty in government seems to be a thing of the past. First of all, government is competing with the private sector for skilled labor, and hours of duty are important to potential employees. Accordingly, it needs to find ways to make it an attractive employer, and offering a variety of tours of duty can be appealing to current and prospective employees. Moreover, the pressures on two-income families, the increase in single parents, worsening traffic, customer demands for increased business hours, and other factors make it imperative that government increase the flexibility of its tours of duty. As a result, many government organizations offer alternative work schedules to the traditional work schedule, which may be either a flexible work schedule and/or a compressed work schedule. Let's look at each in more depth.

Flexible Work Schedule

There are many types of flexible work schedules. For the sake of simplicity, let's go over just a few.

One approach is to have a flexible time band that contains a designated part of the schedule whereby employees may choose one daily arrival and departure time for the week, within limits consistent with their job responsibilities. This means that employees have the option of choosing one starting time for the week, between the hours of, let's say, 6:00 and 9:00 a.m.

Another approach is a gliding flexi-tour, whereby employees may select a starting time each day, and may change that starting time daily as long as it is within the flexible band established by the supervisor. Under this concept, an employee can choose to start work at 6:00 a.m. on Mondays and Wednesdays, at 7:00 a.m. on Tuesdays and Thursday, and at 9:00 a.m. on Friday.

A third approach is a modified flexi-tour whereby the employee picks a starting time within the flexible band. This starting time determines the employee's work schedule until changed. Under this type of schedule, the employee is given a predetermined amount of flexibility on either side of the arrival time the employee selects (usually 15 to 30 minutes). The time the employee arrives then becomes the starting time for that day, and the tour ends $8^{1}/_{2}$ hours later.

There are many more options than the three I just described, but as you can see, the more that exist, the more difficult they become to manage. Let's look at a number of examples where these schedules could be used and the challenges that they would pose.

Scheduling Group Meetings. Supervisor A works for his state's Department of Labor and manages a team that is responsible for making decisions on workers' compensation claims. Within that organization, they have both a flexible time band and a gliding flexi-tour. The supervisor manages a team of 15 people, some of whom arrive as early as 6:00 a.m., while others arrive between 7:00 and 9:00 a.m.

From one perspective, the schedules are not a problem, because most of the employees are responsible for processing paperwork, so the arrival time does not have a big impact on workload management or productivity. However, the wide variety of schedules means that training sessions can be conducted only after 9:00 a.m. and before 2:00 p.m., when all of the employees are present. Moreover, team meetings can be held only during the same period of time, or there will be gaps in communication. Lastly, the times when team members can confer on specific cases or other issues are also limited because of variances in attendance caused by the work schedules.

Scheduling Field Workers. Supervisor B manages a unit that is responsible for conducting background investigations. Most of the employees that she supervises spend the majority of their time in the field. They also work under a flexible time band and gliding flexi-tour. However, because the employees' work in the field is individual by nature, the flexible schedules have virtually no impact on the unit or the supervisor's ability to manage his team. Moreover, the flexible schedules allow the employees to plan their days around the locations of their investigations as well as around traffic schedules. In this situation, the schedules work well for everybody with little or no down side.

Compressed Work Schedules

A compressed work schedule simply means that a full-time employee who normally works 10 eight-hour days in a two-week pay period will be scheduled to work the same number of hours in the pay period, but for fewer days. Compressed schedules may take the form of four 10-hour days per week, or one day working eight hours and 8 days working nine hours in the pay period, resulting in the employee working only 9 days instead of 10 (this is sometimes called 4:5:9, meaning a person would work four days one week and five days the next). Compressed work schedules can take other forms as well, particularly for firefighters or nurses, who may work as little as three days per week. However, let's look at how the first two types of schedules could play out.

1. Our organization allowed a number of our employees to work four 10-hour days. These employees were responsible for making complex decisions based on detailed written information. The employees liked the schedule because they had an extra day off each week and got to avoid the San Diego Freeway. Their supervisors were not as thrilled because the workplace was often far too empty for their taste. More importantly, over time, they began to notice that the output of the employees began to decline. While they still achieved their performance standards, the employees started to produce roughly the same amount of work in 10 hours that they used to produce within 8 hours.

I discussed this phenomenon with my counterparts in other offices and learned that they had had the same experience. Our conclusion was that this particular job required a high degree of concentration, and for most people, concentrating so hard for 10 hours per day was just too difficult.

2. We converted many of the employees who were on the four 10-hour days schedule to a 4:5:9 schedule. We found that this was more feasible because it was less tiring on the employees and did not adversely affect our productivity/performance. Although the employees would have preferred an extra day off, we were able to mathematically demonstrate why one program was better than the other one. As a result, people were able to accept our rationale and were pleased that we had at least retained the 4:5:9 schedules.

Considerations Regarding Flexible and Compressed Schedules

Flexible and compressed work schedules are complex issues that can be difficult to manage. They often sound better in theory than they work out in the real world. In deciding whether to establish and implement such schedules, you need to consider:

- The overall impact on your work
- The workload peaks that require the presence of all/most employees in the unit
- The effect of such schedules on productivity, efficiency, and overall performance
- The difficulty in managing, tracking, and coordinating the work of employees who are on a variety of schedules

- Additional costs generated by such schedules (rent, equipment, etc.)
- The employee coverage required during public hours of operation
- The impact on recruitment, retention, and morale
- The traffic patterns that affect the employees' ability to arrive at work on time
- The manner in which training will need to be delivered in order to accommodate multiple work schedules
- The ability to conduct both team and larger group meetings
- How well the employees can work during periods when their supervisors are not present
- The effect that such schedules will have on your relationship with your employees and the local union(s)

Although these considerations are similar throughout the country, each situation is different and needs to be considered on its own merits.

Area Costs. Alternate and/or compressed schedules may make more sense in high-cost urban areas where employees have longer commutes and face far worse traffic than in lower-cost areas. In high-cost areas, government salaries are generally less competitive with the private sector, so offering alternate work schedules makes sense from a recruitment and retention perspective, and also should help to reduce tardiness. In lower-cost areas, where employees can live closer to the office because government salaries are more desirable, alternate/compressed schedules may still make sense, but they should be considered within the context of the local situation.

Many times, both type of work schedules arise out of negotiations with local and/or national unions, since such schedules are highly prized by employees. Management needs to be very careful when agreeing to such schedules because their impact may not be known until they've been in place for quite some time.

I strongly recommend that organizations that agree to these types of schedules build in the following caveats before implementing them:

1. They should first be implemented on a trial basis (e.g., three months, six months, one year, etc.).
2. The criteria for retention of these schedules should be established in advance (e.g., productivity, timeliness of service, customer satisfaction, etc.).
3. Employees should be made aware of the criteria and be kept apprised as to how the organization is doing relative to these criteria,
4. In the event that performance deteriorates, management will retain the right to terminate the schedule(s) that contributes to the decline in performance.

In this way, employees will have just as much stake in, and information regarding the retention of, the schedules, so in the event that the schedule(s) have to be eliminated, the employees will be able to see it coming and will have no real cause for complaint.

There was a case in one organization I was working for in which it was agreed to try an alternate work schedule. We identified in advance the criteria for retention of this schedule, which was that our employee output be equal to or better than it was prior to the trial. We decided that the trial would last for 90 days and that we would keep everyone posted regarding the results of the trial. At the end of the 90 days, we were able to document that productivity had declined, so we eliminated the alternate work schedule with virtually no employee resistance.

Our headquarters in Washington, D.C., has a difficult time recruiting and retaining people because of the cost of living in that area and the difficulty in commuting to work. Given the fact that many of the jobs there are analyst-type positions that do not require rigid schedules, they are able to offer alternate and compressed work schedules to many of their employees. Having the capability of offering flexible schedules makes it easier for them to recruit and retain good people. Moreover, these work schedules help morale and do not seem to have an adverse impact on the work.

Alternate Workplace

Alternate workplaces give employees the opportunity to work at locations other than the typical office setting. This can include working at home, working in an out-based office, or even working in mobile offices (e.g., helping the homeless, providing simple medical care, etc.). As with flexible schedules, alternate workplaces are designed to help the government work better while meeting the needs of its employees.

In many cases, flexible workplaces can improve services to our citizens by (1) moving the government closer to them; (2) improving productivity and efficiency by creating an environment in which employees can produce more work; (3) helping to recruit and retain employees by allowing them to work nearer to or actually in their homes; (4) and enhancing the quality of life of participating employees by allowing them to work in a less-stressful environment. It also may be used as a reasonable accommodation for handicapped employees.

As with flexible schedules, alternate workplaces are usually the subject of bargaining with local unions. Accordingly, prior to implementing such an approach, management needs to (1) work closely with the union(s); (2) be sure of its objectives going into such a program; and (3) be crystal clear regarding the criteria for success. In this way, if management concludes that an alternate workplace is not working, it will be in a good position to terminate such an arrangement.

That being said, once an alternate workplace is established, you want it to succeed. The best way to accomplish this is through careful planning and analysis. Prior to establishing an alternate workplace, you should consider the same factors that are recommended for flexible work schedules (what needs to be accomplished and when; the effect on productivity, efficiency, and overall performance; the difficulty in managing, tracking, and coordinating the work of employees who are away from the traditional office; additional costs generated by such a workplace, etc.). However, given the fact that alternate workplaces involve working at locations beyond the traditional worksite, there are several other factors that you should also consider, including:

- Whether the participating employee's work duties can be effectively performed away from the work site
- If technology is needed and available to support the employee
- The manner in which the employee's performance will be measured
- The procedures for dealing with unacceptable performance
- The way that training and communication will be handled
- The impact on the privacy of the government's records[1]
- The possibility of someone getting injured at the alternate site

Assuming you want to establish one or more alternate workplaces, let's examine the plusses and minuses of two of the most common types: work at home and out-based locations.

Work at Home

Working at home is very desirable for some employees, since it completely eliminates the time, expense, cost, and hassle of commuting. It is not for everybody because (1) many jobs are simply not transferable to the home (public contact positions, jobs that require employees to interact closely with others, positions that involve frequent meetings, etc.); (2) it can greatly reduce management's flexibility, since fewer people are at the main worksite at any one time; and (3) many people miss the social interaction of working together with others. However, under the right circumstances, this can be an excellent option for both the organization and the employee, either on a permanent or a temporary basis.

One of the key positions in our organization required employees to make complex decisions regarding applicants' entitlement to benefits. The position was solitary in nature, as the employee would simply sit at her desk, review written evidence, and make decisions all day long. The job involved relatively little interaction with other employees, except for periodic training sessions that were held several times a month. Performance was easy to measure, as employees were primarily appraised based on the number of cases they completed and their accuracy rate.

Given these conditions, we allowed people who occupied these positions to work at home up to four days per week. We required them to come to work the same day each week so they could (1) bring their finished work in and pick up new work; (2) attend training and team meetings; and (3) address any other issues that might develop (computer problems, performance issues, etc.). The employees liked these arrangements because they didn't have to fight the traffic and they had more free time at their disposal. We also liked it because employees who worked at home were required to complete about 33 percent more cases per day than the employees who worked in the office (employees working at home did not have some of the same discrete tasks as the employees at the worksite, so we were able to raise their performance standards). In addition, we had happier and more energized employees.

While other employees had jobs that did not lend themselves to working at home, they understood which jobs fell into that category and which did not, and why. Moreover, they also knew that if they were selected for a position that was eligible for the work at home program, they too could take advantage of that opportunity.

For example, a long-term, exceptional employee transferred to our office. However, she had a serious disease and was finding it increasingly difficult to come to work. Since her job duties did not have to be completed at the worksite, we agreed to let her work at home for up to four days per week, just like the other employees referenced in the case just cited. However, as time went by, her condition worsened, and she was unable to come to work even for that one day.

Since she was a highly productive employee, we did not want to lose her services. Moreover, she wanted to stay with the government if possible. As a result, we had an employee who lived near her pick up and deliver her work once a week. In order to keep her in the loop, she dialed into training sessions and team meetings.

By taking this creative approach, we were able to retain her and leverage her talents. None of the other employees who had to come to work once a week complained, because they recognized that we were simply making a reasonable accommodation for a handicapped employee. In this situation, everybody won.

Out-Based Locations

Out-based locations are basically satellites of the main worksite. They may involve a few people or may be larger in size. They are more complex to establish and administer than the work at home program, since these sites often (1) perform more discrete tasks than the people who work at home; (2) require additional infrastructure (mail, supervision, storage, etc.); and (3) are generally more expensive to operate since additional space translates into more rent.

However, under certain circumstances, the additional costs can be more than offset with increased performance, better customer service, savings, and more satisfied employees.

After the 1994 Northridge earthquake, for example, many of the federal government's employees who worked north of the federal building in West Los Angeles, California, were unable to get to work in less than three hours. The earthquake had destroyed a section of the freeway that most of these employees normally took to work. In response, the United States General Services Administration opened up a Telecommuting Center in Valencia, California, for the employees who simply couldn't get to the federal building within a reasonable period of time.

One particular group of employees worked for the United States Department of Veterans Affairs (VA) Benefits Office. This group, which was less than 10 people, instantly became a team. They were so thrilled with their new arrangements that they vowed to outperform the other employees at the main worksite, with the goal of being able to remain at the Telecommuting Center for the foreseeable future. That's exactly what they did, as their performance was extraordinary. As word of their success spread, many people came to visit this office to see a successful Telecommuting Center in action. Eventually, Vice President Gore presented it with a "Hammer Award" for reinventing government.

In another case, our Oakland office was having an extremely difficult time recruiting and retaining people because of the cost of living in the Bay Area. People couldn't afford to live there on a government employee's salary, given the cost of housing. Moreover, the office was paying an exorbitant amount of money for rent. Senior management knew that it couldn't simply up and relocate the office given the fact that so many of the most experienced employees were entrenched in the area and would not relocate if the entire office moved to another part of the state. Accordingly, it decided to open up an out-based office in Sacramento, whose cost of living was much lower than Oakland's.

Immediately, the organization found a large pool of talent in the area who wanted to work for the government. Quickly, it began to build that office up, and over time, it began to excel. Productivity rose and timeliness improved. While the Oakland office was now paying dual rents, it began transferring more and more resources to Sacramento. Eventually, it was able to give up space in the main office, which defrayed the costs of the new space in Sacramento. Within a few years, the Sacramento office became virtually a full-service office and is likely to continue to grow.

Then there's the case at the Veterans Health Administration (VHA). For many years, the U.S. Department of Veterans Affairs had a reputation for delivering substandard health care. Veterans often went to private hospitals rather than receive free health care from the VA.

Part of the problem was that VHA was delivering health care services primarily through a large, bulky series of hospitals. VHA boldly transformed its organization by moving many of its employees out of these hospitals and into hundreds of community-based outpatient clinics (CBOCs). As a result, veterans had much greater access to health care, as they no longer had to drive great distances to visit a VA hospital. Moreover, the employees working in the CBOCs were generally more satisfied, as many of them wound up with shorter commutes. Today VHA is considered the worldwide leader in health care.[2]

Leave Administration

Although alternate/compressed work schedules and alternate workplaces are good strategies for improving your employees' attendance, perhaps the single most important factor is still sound leave administration. This section will focus on strategies for improving the way you administer your leave program.

There are many types of leave in government, but for the sake of simplicity, I will focus on the three most common types of leave: (1) annual leave, also known as vacation time or personal days; (2) sick leave, which covers illness, doctors' appointments, maternity, and so on; and (3) leave without pay (LWOP), which is authorized absence from work while in a nonpay status. Regardless of the type of leave that is involved, if you apply the following principles of leave administration, you will establish a strong foundation for your program.

Principles of Leave Administration

- The rules governing leave policy and administration should be communicated both orally and in writing to everyone. In addition, all employees should receive periodic training on this subject (e.g., employees should know the appropriate uses of each type of leave, whom they should contact to request leave, their phone numbers, when they should call, when a doctor's note is required, etc.).

- Leave policies should be administered in a fair and equitable manner across the board (i.e., the same rules should apply to everybody).
- To the maximum extent possible, leave should be requested in advance. This will help optimize the overall attendance patterns.
- The largest periods of projected leave should be scheduled on an annual basis in order to avoid the forfeiture of such leave.
- Employees should be encouraged to save their leave so they are prepared for an emergency (catastrophic illness, care for a family member, etc.).
- Employees requesting leave should be treated humanely.

Let's look at a few real-world examples of these principles.

Importance of Written Rules. An employee does not come to work, nor does he call in and request leave. When he returns to work the following day, his supervisor is quite upset because he did not hear from the employee and decides to charge him absent without official leave (AWOL) and take a disciplinary action. The employee responds that no one ever told him that he was required to call in and request leave for an absence of just one day. Moreover, he did not know his supervisor's phone number.

While on its face, the employee's rationale may seem somewhat silly, should (1) the employee decide to grieve the AWOL/disciplinary action, and (2) the supervisor be unable to document that the employee was aware of the leave policy and/or his phone number, the supervisor will be in an unnecessarily weak position to defend his action before a third party. The more effectively that the supervisor communicates the leave policy and all other appropriate information with the employees, the better the system will operate.

Treating Employees Consistently. An employee requests emergency leave for personal reasons. The supervisor denies the request based on workload considerations. The employee complains, indicating that the day before, the same supervisor approved emergency leave for a different employee in the same unit, which constitutes disparate treatment.

The supervisor is on firm ground to deny the leave if (1) the workload situation and/or priorities are different that day as compared to the day before; (2) there are fewer employees on duty that day than the day before; or (3) there is another legitimate business reason why the employee needs to be at work.

The key is that supervisors treat all employees in a consistent manner and are able to articulate their rationale when they deny leave. One note of caution: Do not interpret this principle too strictly. Very few leave disputes wind up before a third party, so don't operate out of fear. Just make sure that you are asking yourself whether you are treating everyone fairly, and you should be in good shape.

Dealing with Frequent Absences. An employee always seems to have personal problems that require emergency leave. Every time he does not come to work as planned, it makes things that much more difficult to manage. The more the supervisor approves the unscheduled leave, the more he encourages the employee to continue to find excuses not to come to work.

This employee is different from the typical employee who has an occasional emergency; that's to be expected. This type of employee needs to understand that frequent bouts of emergency leave hurt the organization.

The easiest way to handle this is for the supervisor to place the employee on notice that continued instances of emergency absences will not be tolerated and could lead to charges of AWOL and disciplinary and/or adverse action. He should then take appropriate action if the absences persist.

Mishandling Leave Schedules. Several employees come to you at the end of the calendar year and request the last two weeks off. Some of them simply want to enjoy the holidays, while others have suddenly realized that if they don't use their excess vacation time, they will lose it.[3] As a supervisor, you now face the unenviable choice of either allowing a bunch of people to take off from work, which will place a severe crimp in your capacity; or denying many of the requests, which will result in a group of unhappy employees. Either way you lose.

If you find yourself in this position, it is most likely a problem of your own making. You probably managed the employees' attendance in a haphazard manner without developing an overall leave plan.

The better approach is to require all employees to request their vacation periods at the beginning of the year. In this way, you can plan the year out in a holistic manner, ensuring that you have appropriate coverage throughout every week of the year. You can identify scheduling conflicts early on, and address them accordingly. Moreover, you can ensure that everyone takes enough leave so that nobody will have to forfeit any vacation time. Finally, employees will get the message that they need to plan their leave and that you expect emergency leave to be kept to a minimum.

Encouraging Employees to Save Leave. One of the sadder situations that can occur is where an employee has a personal emergency, yet has no leave to tide her over during that time. This usually happens because the employee was not judicious in the use of her leave throughout her career, so when she really needed it, it simply wasn't there. When this happens, the employee is truly in a bind, and can easily become a frustrated and embittered individual.

While saving leave is the responsibility of each employee, the supervisor also plays a role in this matter. Each supervisor should encourage employees to save their leave, because you never know when an emergency will occur. You may get sick, or you may be required to care for a family member. It is impossible to predict the future. However, you can prepare for the unknown, and saving leave is one of the single best ways to protect yourself.

As I began writing this book, for instance, I was hit with a series of health issues. I developed a herniated disk in my back that was so severe that I literally could not walk. Several weeks later, I underwent back surgery. Twelve days later, my wife was rushed to the hospital and underwent emergency surgery for a very serious chronic condition, and suddenly my physical problems went on the back burner (no pun intended). Shortly thereafter, my disk reherniated and I had to undergo a second back surgery. During this time and for the last 15 months of my government career, I was placed in the unexpected position of being both a caregiver and a care receiver. There was no way that I could go to work under these circumstances, but given the medical bills that I was suddenly facing, I also needed a steady income.

Fortunately, I had had the foresight to save my leave throughout my government career. As a result, when I was hit with so many medical and personal problems seemingly at once, I was able to cope. By saving enough sick leave and vacation time to cover me for those 15 months (although I did do some work for the government at home during that period, which reduced my leave usage), my income remained steady, which made my life a lot easier.

At the beginning of this section, I noted that there are three main types of leave: annual leave, sick leave, and leave without pay. Let's look at those in more detail.

Annual Leave

Virtually every government organization grants annual leave to employees who achieve permanent status, understanding that employees need some personal time off in order to be effective for the long term. Annual leave is generally considered to be an employee right, although the right to take it is subject to supervisory approval.

Many organizations encourage their employees to take at least one two-week period of annual leave per year for the purpose of rest and relaxation. These relatively lengthy periods of leave are rarely a problem from a leave administration standpoint, as long as they are scheduled in advance and coordinated with the leave of other employees.

When employees request leave for the same periods of time and not every request can be granted, objective criteria should be used to resolve such disputes. The criterion usually seems to be either length of service with the government or length of service with the local organization, and is generally negotiated with the local union. However, I would encourage you to carefully think this issue through before simply using length of service as the sole criterion.

We used length of service within our organization to resolve conflicts in leave requests. Although this worked well for the more experienced employees, it greatly frustrated our newer employees, who represented the future of our organization. Every time newer employees wanted time off during a major holiday (Christmas, Easter, Thanksgiving, etc.), employees with greater tenure seemed to bump them. We wanted to give due deference to the people who had worked for us the longest, but we also wanted to give our newer employees the opportunity to take time off during at least some of the major holidays.

We finally decided to give the more experienced employees priority for their most desirable holiday and then give the newer employees priority for the second choice. In this way, we were sending two distinct but important messages: (1) experience with our organization was important to us and would be rewarded; and (2) all employees, even the newest ones, were important to our organization.

Leaves for extended absences are relatively easy to administer because they are usually requested in advance. However, requests for shorter periods of annual leave are tougher to handle because they often occur with little or no advance notice. The best way to handle short-term annual leave is to follow five points:

1. Leave policy and procedures are clear and understandable.
2. Employees recognize that every unplanned absence diminishes the ability of the organization to achieve its goals.
3. Emergency leave is expected to be kept to a minimum.
4. Management is perceived to be reasonable, willing to make a good-faith effort to grant an occasional request for emergency leave where appropriate.

5. Employees are aware that if their leave request is denied, they must report for work.

If these five key points are applied in a reliable and consistent fashion, and periodically reinforced at team meetings, requests for emergency leave should go rather smoothly.

Employees also need to be aware that leave administration is a two-way street and that they have a major role in its success. Far too often, I've heard employees complain that events beyond their control prevented them from coming to work, when in fact they had far more control than they believed. While clearly, some events do occur that cannot be anticipated (a sudden illness, a traffic accident, etc.), these events are generally few and far between and are not a part of the normal course of events. Let's look at a few cases in point.

1. An employee suddenly notified us that he needed to take two weeks of annual leave during the Christmas holidays. He advised us that he had already booked his trip, and it was too late to cancel it. Since we had already approved all vacations for the Christmas holidays and since we were counting on this employee's services during that period, we denied his request.

He became very angry and argued that it was unfair to force him to cancel his vacation plans, since he had already paid for it. In essence, he blamed us for his own actions. From our perspective, since he did not request annual leave prior to booking his vacation plans, he was at fault, and we simply could not accommodate him.

Despite our denial of his leave request, the employee took the vacation anyway. We charged him AWOL for the entire two-week period, and his employment quickly ended with our organization.

2. One of our employees had difficulty coming to work on time because of the traffic. She often sat in traffic for long periods of time and frequently came to work late. When we sat down with her to discuss her attendance, she indicated that she was already getting up early to try and beat the traffic and couldn't possibly get up any earlier. Her position was clear: It was not her fault that the traffic was so bad, and she shouldn't be held accountable for something that was beyond her control.

Obviously, we saw the situation a little differently. We were not responsible for the traffic, either. It was a fact of life, and everyone had to deal with it. She was a government employee who was expected to come to work on time, just like all the other employees in our organization. The time she woke up was not our concern; the time she arrived at work was.

We suggested that she consider a different tour of duty (her position did not lend itself to an alternate workplace arrangement), as we wanted to see her succeed. We were more than willing to work with her, but one thing was not negotiable: She had to come to work on time. We also advised her of the consequences of continued absences. As soon as she realized that we were serious and that it was her responsibility to come to work, she got the message and immediately started coming to work on time.

3. A long-time, solid employee started missing work. His reasons varied from family problems to car troubles to health issues. Although we were initially sympathetic and granted leave, we began to see a disturbing pattern. He often came to work disheveled, exhausted, and/or a bit disoriented. We suspected that his leave problems were symptomatic of a larger problem—drugs and/or alcohol. When we confronted the employee with our suspicions, he simply denied them.

Given the situation, the only thing we could do was to focus on his behavior. In other words, every time he requested emergency leave, we treated him the same way we would any other individual in a similar situation—we granted leave when appropriate and denied leave whenever his presence was required. Several times he did not come to work, so we charged him AWOL. This led to a number of personnel actions, until the employee realized that his job was in serious jeopardy. At that point, he confessed that he had a substance abuse problem, got some professional help, and eventually started coming to work on a regular basis.

Annual leave is relatively easy to administer as long as everyone knows the rules and understands that unplanned absences hurt the organization, you are fair and consistent, emergency leave is kept to a minimum, and you keep the focus on the work.

Sick Leave

Sick leave can be used for many purposes, including illness, appointments with a doctor and/or dentist, maternity, or caring for a sick family member under the Family Medical Leave Act. Unlike annual leave, which is an employee right subject to supervisory approval, in many cases, sick leave is a right that does not require approval. The general rule of thumb is that an employee is entitled to take sick leave when sick, although under certain circumstances, management may request to see documentation that the employee is indeed incapacitated for duty.

Since management's rights with respect to sick leave are normally more restricted than they are with annual leave, this can be a more complicated area to oversee. However, if you follow the guidance contained in this section, you will find that it is not as complex as would first appear.

In my experience, most people request sick leave for legitimate purposes. As long as they know the rules and expectations with respect to notification and documentation, they almost always comply without difficulty.

Sick leave generally becomes a problem when dealing with the bottom 10 percent of the employees, who always seem to experience some sort of difficulty. These individuals frequently call in sick just as soon as they earn sick leave. On many occasions, they will call in sick for the period of time that the organization does not require a doctor's note (usually up to three days). Moreover, they often schedule doctor's appointments with little notice, which can cause disruption in the workflow. Lastly, these same individuals will occasionally request sick leave for extended periods of time, which will complicate matters even further.

Let's look at several examples of this type of behavior.

Conditions on Sick Leave. An employee has only seven hours of sick leave left. He typically calls in sick several times a month, particularly on Mondays and Fridays. He should be counseled that his balance is extremely low and that he is unprepared in the event that either he or another family member develops a major illness.

His supervisor should also consider giving this employee a sick leave restriction letter. This type of letter is used by many government organizations and places the employee on notice that: (1) his attendance is unsatisfactory and needs to improve; (2) based on his pattern of attendance, he appears to be abusing his entitlement to sick leave; (3) effective immediately, every time he is requesting leave due to illness, he will have to provide a doctor's note verifying that he was incapacitated—regardless of the length of the absence; and (4) in the event that he is unable to produce a satisfactory note, he may be charged AWOL, which could eventually lead to his removal. This type of letter ups the ante for people who appear to be misusing their sick leave and places management in a much stronger position to monitor the employee's use of sick leave.

Last-Minute Doctor Appointments. An employee frequently advises his supervisor at the last moment that he has a doctor's appointment and needs to take sick leave. This type of behavior places the supervisor in a bad position, since she is unable to plan for these last-minute absences. She should handle these requests by advising the employee that he needs to schedule medical appointments in advance, and to give her plenty of notice before she will approve leave. Unlike sick leave for illness, which is an employee right, sick leave for routine medical appointments is generally a right that is subject to management's approval. The supervisor should make sure that the employee is aware of this and must comply with the guidelines or the leave will be denied.

Here's a case in point: One of our employees was out of work for an extended period of time due to an injured wrist. While she was unable to perform all aspects of her job because it required some lifting (she was a nursing assistant), we had other tasks that only required light duty, which we felt she could perform. However, she kept providing us with doctor's statements indicating that she was unable to come to work, which placed us in a difficult position.

We therefore gave her a written order requiring her to provide us with a doctor's statement listing what work she could physically perform and what she could not. When we received this statement, it indicated that she could not do any lifting, typing, etc., but that she could do such light tasks as answering the phone and directing visitors.

Obviously, it was better for the government that she stay on the job performing light duty than it would be if she were home getting paid to do nothing. Accordingly, we ordered her to return to work for a light-duty assignment, and when she refused, we suspended her from duty for 30 days. The case eventually went to a third party, which sustained the suspension because we had sound medical documentation that the employee was able to return to work.

This case occurred early in my career. As I gained more experience, I began to question the value of suspending someone who did not come to work for a lengthy period of time. In essence, we were taking action against that person for not coming to work by forcing them to not come to work.

As time went by, I decided that (1) if the AWOL was bad enough to warrant a 30-day suspension, it probably justified a removal; and (2) if not, I would consider a 30-day paper suspension whereby the employee was suspended only on weekends. In this way, we established a pattern of progressive discipline that would easily justify a removal for one more offense, and we still had the services of the employee.

When dealing with sick leave issues, don't fall into the trap of deciding whether an employee is truly sick. You are not a medical professional, so fighting that battle is almost always a losing proposition. Moreover, if you claim that the employee's doctor's statement is unacceptable, be aware that the employee will eventually be able to find a doctor who will provide you with an acceptable note.

The better approach is to focus on what the employee can and can't do. In this way, you won't get involved in medical debates, and any action you take will be based on the needs of the job and the employee's physical ability to do the job.

Moreover, you will be far less vulnerable in the event that an employee alleges that you did not make a reasonable accommodation for his handicap.

Leave Without Pay (LWOP)

This should be the easiest of the three main types of leave to administer, but supervisors often seem to be unclear about how to handle this issue. The thing to keep in mind is that in most government organizations, LWOP is not a right except in a few, rare instances (e.g., a veteran receiving treatment for a service-connected medical condition). LWOP is analogous to annual leave in that it requires the supervisor's approval; however, unlike annual leave, the employee has no right to LWOP.

The best way to administer LWOP requests is through prevention. That is, if you constantly remind your employees that it is important to maintain high leave balances, they will hopefully think twice before wasting their leave on unimportant issues. That is another reason why, in Chapter 5, I recommended that you include employees' leave balances on their performance report cards. By periodically seeing their leave balance in writing (other than on a pay stub), and by knowing that their leave usage is being scrutinized by management, the goal is that employees will be judicious in their use of leave, which is to everybody's advantage.

On occasion, some very good employees will have low leave balances. Obviously, a pregnancy or a serious illness can quickly use up an enormous amount of leave. However, these individuals are simply using leave as it was intended to be used.

The bigger challenge involves requests for LWOP from people who do not manage their leave wisely. These are the same individuals that generally make the bulk of the requests for emergency annual and sick leave. They are the same people who seem to have a never-ending series of problems. They are also the same ones who frustrate the good employees, who wonder why management is so lenient with their requests for leave.

The best way to handle requests for LWOP from these employees is to put them on notice that their leave has been unacceptable and needs to improve. Earlier, in the section on sick leave, I discussed issuing a sick leave restriction letter. For those individuals who appear to be abusing their entitlement to sick leave and whose sick leave balances have been so low that they have begun requesting LWOP, I would issue them a similar letter and also advise them that (1) future requests for LWOP will be carefully scrutinized and will be denied, *even if they are legitimately sick,* should the workload require their attendance; and (2) if they are denied LWOP and charged AWOL, a personnel action may be taken against them, up to and including removal. You may be surprised to learn that you do not have to grant LWOP to a sick employee, but remember—unlike sick leave and annual leave, LWOP is not an employee right.

This approach places the employee on notice that continued absences will be carefully scrutinized and that the employee should think twice before continuing this pattern of attendance. While you do not have to issue this type of leave restriction letter in order to deny a request for LWOP, it is always better that the employee sees such a denial coming, particularly the employee who is absent so frequently.

Throughout my career, I have issued this type of restriction letter, and it has proven to be very effective. In most cases, employees have gotten the message that they need to come to work more often and on a more regular basis. Once employees recognize that they have no entitlement to LWOP and that management (1) is serious about dealing with their absences; (2) will not accept an unending series of excuses; and (3) is prepared to deny LWOP and charge them AWOL, which could potentially place their job in jeopardy, most of them come around and change their attendance patterns. If that happens, the leave restriction letter will eventually be withdrawn, usually after about six months.

On occasion, the employee does not get the message, or chooses to ignore it, at which point management needs to take action each time it denies the request for LWOP. These cases are relatively easy to handle and win if they go to a third party, because the restriction letter provides ample documentation of the employee's poor attendance pattern and shows that the employee had been placed on notice that continued absences could lead to management action.

Multiple instances of AWOL following the issuance of a leave restriction letter simply require you to follow the terms of the restriction letter and your leave policy. If you take that approach, you will be in a good position to take action. However, isolated requests for LWOP involving extended absences can be a bit trickier, since they generally don't involve the same obvious patterns of poor attendance. Let's look at a few cases involving these types of requests for LWOP.

1. An employee called in one day and informed us that he needed LWOP for at least six months. When we asked him why, he indicated that he had been arrested for spousal abuse and expected to be in jail for the foreseeable future. He argued that he wanted to come to work but was being held in jail against his will, and therefore, his absence was beyond his control.

As you might expect, we denied his request. We needed someone to do his job, since he obviously was not going to be able to do it. The fact that he was arrested and being held in jail was his fault, as he made a personal decision to abuse his spouse. We proposed his removal, and he ultimately resigned.

2. A senior management employee fell down and sustained a significant number of injuries. This was only one of several personal problems for this employee, who generally came to work on time but always seemed to have personal issues that distracted her. Her absence left us in quite a bind because her counterpart had recently left and we had not yet replaced him.

While we approved her remaining leave and some LWOP, we could not afford to have her absent from the job for an indefinite period. After a couple of months, we denied her request for LWOP and required her to come to work. While she was in some pain, she was no longer in any danger, and we desperately needed her presence. This was a difficult decision for us to make, but this employee needed to learn that she had to take responsibility for her actions.

Whether you are considering requests for annual leave, sick leave, or LWOP, the same basic principles described earlier in this chapter should apply. Make sure that your employees are aware of the leave policies and procedures, and that you reliably and consistently follow these policies, procedures, and principles. If you do this, you will have a strong and effective leave administration program that will help ensure you have the best possible attendance.

Key Points to Remember

- Work schedules need to be established in a manner that best meets the organization's needs.
- Each situation is different (schedule, workplace, etc.) and needs to be decided on its own merits.
- The leave policy should be frequently communicated to everyone and should be based on a clear set of principles.
- Administer your leave system in a reliable manner.

Labor Relations

Overview

Labor relations can be very difficult. However, the degree of difficulty can vary at certain levels of government because there is no right to strike at the federal level, while unions at the state and local levels sometimes have that right. Moreover, at times you deal with union officials who are members of the workforce, while at other times, you may deal with individuals who are actually employed by the union. Although this chapter cannot possibly cover every type of labor situation you may encounter, it is intended to provide you with an understanding of the key issues from both management's and the union's perspective.

Far too often, management tends to see the union as a minor annoyance or, in some cases, as a major impediment to getting the job done. Sometimes this is true, while other times it is not. In many cases, management's negative attitude toward the union often becomes a self-fulfilling prophecy.

Management needs to be aware that the union is a political organization and, as such, needs to answer to its constituency—the bargaining unit. As with all politicians, union officials need to retain the confidence of the people they serve, if they hope to win reelection. This constant pressure to stay in office often drives the behavior of union officials. From their perspective, if they are too cooperative with management, the bargaining unit will perceive them as being "in bed with management" and will conclude that they are not out to serve the unit's employees. They are also bound by the governing labor law, which usually requires them to represent all of the bargaining unit members, even if they do not agree with the employee's position.

Union officials come with all sorts of agendas, just like management officials. Some are driven by the desire to help their fellow employees, while others feel they've been mistreated by management and want to pay them back in kind. Certain union officials are reasonable people who want to do the right thing for the right reasons, while others use their position in the union to try and insulate them from management action in response to their poor performance and/or behavior.

The point is that as a manager you have to be prepared to deal with all types of union officials in the same way that you have to deal with all sorts of employees. The more skills you have, and the more tools you have in your toolbox, the better prepared you will be to address whatever labor situation confronts you.

In one of my earliest experiences with unions, I dealt with a union president who was a decent individual. He was occasionally loud and cantankerous in describing certain supervisors, but I always had the sense that he was a fair person who was trying to do the right thing.

He was also a part-time union president who spent a portion of his day as a nursing assistant, so he was not very knowledgeable from a technical perspective when it came to labor relations. In dealing with him, I simply tried to treat him with respect and promptly address the issues that he brought to my attention. When he was right, I attempted to quickly resolve the issue at hand so I would build some trust with him and establish a good working relationship.

In my second assignment, I encountered a union official who very angry with local management. Earlier in his career, he had applied for a job in a different organization. However, because his assistant division chief had given him a poor appraisal, he was unable to get that job. He blamed local management for this and was determined to get a measure of revenge by filing a wide variety of complaints.

In a given year, he would file more than 100 unfair labor practice charges (ULPs) against management. His true motivation was revenge, not helping the bargaining unit, so in this situation, I had to take a different approach. I decided to use the labor relations system to try and contain him. Otherwise, if I tried to resolve every single complaint that he filed, I would waste an enormous amount of management time and only encourage him to file more complaints. As a result, I scanned every ULP that was filed and, in most cases, allowed them to go forward to the Federal Labor Relations Authority (FLRA). I knew that the FLRA would dismiss the vast majority of these cases, as I had enough knowledge about labor relations that I was confident in my judgment. That was exactly what happened.

Meanwhile, for those few cases that had merit, I generally negotiated a settlement. In this way, I was able to prevent our managers from wasting their time on complaints that had no merit, while resolving cases that had merit before they ever resulted in third-party intervention. Eventually, that union official stopped filing so many ULPs because he was not accomplishing anything other than annoying the FLRA.

On occasion, I have also dealt with full-time national employees of the union. The government does not employ these individuals, so their perspective is quite different. They are less understanding of the local situation and have a greater appreciation of the big picture, particularly the union's broad goals. Also, because they are full-time union employees, they tend to be more professional and much more knowledgeable about labor law, including case law.

When dealing with these individuals, the relationship tends to be less emotional because they are not caught up in local politics. However, just like anyone else, they also bring their own personality and agenda into the equation, and need to be dealt with accordingly. Many of these individuals also bring a wide range of experience, expertise, and money to the table, and can be intimidating to relatively inexperienced members of management.

The best way to deal with these types of union officials is to be professional, be prepared, and not take things personally. If you are an HRM specialist, you need to learn as much as you can about labor law, strategy, and tactics. If you are not an HRM specialist, you need to remain cool, calm, and collected and make sure you have a good advisor. You also have to understand the national union's broad goals, so you will have a better idea as to where it is coming from.

Regardless of the type of union official(s) you are dealing with, it is important to develop an overall philosophy and strategy for dealing with unions. Let's examine these concepts in greater detail.

Overall Philosophy

Keep the Union Informed

In my experience, a large number of labor problems develop because the union lacks basic information. Far too often, it hears about a problem from a bargaining unit employee and winds up filing a complaint based on limited information. The best way to prevent this situation from happening is to maintain an open and upfront relationship with the union, whereby it is kept informed about key developments in the organization.

I have learned that if most people were sitting in my seat and had access to the same information that I had, the vast majority of the time, they would make the same decision that I made. The problem is that people rarely have access to that information, so they wind up making decisions that affect them based on a limited base of information, or, in many cases, misinformation.

From the union's perspective, every time it hears a complaint from a bargaining unit employee regarding an issue it is unfamiliar with, it looks bad. The union appears to be out of the loop, and insignificant because management has chosen not to share information. This, in turn, frustrates union representatives because they feel disrespected, so they often turn to the internal complaint system to get management's attention. As managers see the number of complaints begin to rise, they tend to get angry with the union, so in response, they start communicating even less. As you can see, this becomes a self-fulfilling prophecy where everyone winds up losing.

The better approach is to share information with the union as often as you can, in a variety of different ways (in writing, through one-on-one meetings, etc.). Through this approach, the union will feel valued and respected and will be in a much better position to address the complaints of its constituents. Moreover, as it starts to feel valued, it will begin to share information with you, which will help you address problems before they develop to a significant degree.

I used to meet with our union president at least twice a month in order to let her know what was going on. I would give her my sense of the national picture and then let her know what was on my mind and what we were planning to do locally. I also gave her the opportunity to challenge some of my long-term plans, since I wanted to hear her objections at that point, rather than waiting until we were in negotiations. By taking this approach, I developed a strong working relationship with the union president, and I found that she was often willing to share information with me that would help keep me out of trouble.

I also learned that she often spoke very highly about our management team to outsiders. This added bonus helped to positively shape the outside world's view of our organization's labor climate, which is always a good thing in a highly political environment.

One time the union president came to me in exasperation because one of our division chiefs had announced a major reorganization that affected many members of the bargaining unit. She had been caught off guard when the reorganization had been announced, which made her appear to be weak and incompetent in front of the unit. Moreover, we had not fulfilled our bargaining obligations prior to the announcement, so we had mishandled the situation from both a legal and a tactical perspective.

I immediately apologized to the union president, instructed the division chief to commence negotiations with her prior to implementing the reorganization, and ensured that in the future, she was aware of major changes well in advance of their implementation. While we mishandled the situation and hurt our relationship with the union in the short term, by admitting we were wrong and promptly resolving the issues in question, we were able to quickly repair our relationship.

In another example, I once visited an organization that had a terrible relationship with its union. There was absolutely no trust and virtually no communication other than what was legally required, and that was almost always done in writing. The leader of the organization had an imperial style that tended to turn people off. Moreover, she considered the union to be beneath her, so she saw no point in sharing information with union representatives.

The union officials felt marginalized by management, as they rarely knew what was going on and were never included in any substantive decisions. As a result, they felt that they had no choice but to strike back at management by filing complaints as often as possible. They concluded that this was the only way that they could get anything accomplished.

While both parties were at fault, upper management was largely responsible for the poor labor-management relationship, as it set the tone by refusing to share information or treat the union with respect. The relationship continued to flounder until the organization's senior leader retired, after which communication and the overall relationship finally began to improve.

Treat the Union Well

I'm always amazed how shabbily union officials seem to be treated by management. Their rights are often disregarded; they are frequently kept out of key decisions; and far too often, they are simply ignored. Sometimes this works just fine, especially where the union is weak or does not care. Under this scenario, the union is not a key player, and everything seems to work out. If you are in this situation, consider yourself lucky. However, on other occasions, when management treats the union poorly, the union will find ways to reciprocate.

I'm a firm believer in treating the union well, because in most cases, it will respond in kind. If you believe the union is important and treat it as a valued stakeholder, it will act the part and will deal with you on a higher plane. It will be far less interested in raising petty issues if it thinks it is a player. By contrast, if it feels unimportant, then every issue, no matter how trivial, will be important to the union, because it will provide union representatives with an opportunity to demonstrate their power. Under this scenario, the worse you treat them, the more powerful they will become, because they will use their inherent power to push you around with the tools provided them by law and contract. They will follow your lead, so it is up to you to choose.

At one point in my career, I became the leader of an organization that had a tenuous relationship with its union. The first thing that struck me was how poor the union's office was. It was virtually a cubbyhole, which almost screamed out that management thought the union was unimportant and unworthy of decent work space. This message was not lost on the union, and all of its officers felt slighted by management. I immediately offered the union better space, which sent a message that I valued its contribution to the organization.

Although giving the union more space certainly did not solve all of our labor–management problems, it did establish a level of respect and cooperation between management and the union that was not there before. In addition, it helped establish a healthier tone in the relationship, which made it easier to address the difficult issues that we faced down the road.

Whenever I held group employee meetings, I always made it my practice to call on the union president for comment. It let her know that her opinion was important to me, and it let others know that I truly valued what the union had to say. It elevated her status both within the organization and with the bargaining unit, and almost compelled her to respond in kind.

Whenever I called on her to speak, she generally spoke in a professional and dignified manner, befitting the status I bestowed upon her. Interestingly, during times when I did not pay as much attention to labor relations, and perhaps was not as respectful as I could have been, she tended to revert to a more traditional and confrontational manner.

On occasion, no matter how well you treat the union, nothing seems to work. A kindness is not returned, a respectful act is ignored, and so on. I've faced this situation several times during my career. The first time involved a new union president who was seeking more official time than his predecessor. We resisted giving him more official time because we were not required to by contract and because we wanted him to focus on his regular job. However, this angered him, and he began filing a series of complaints on almost any issue that arose.

I tried to treat him with respect and to explain to him why we were not in favor of granting more official time, but he ignored my efforts and continued to file complaints. This angered the management team, which was frustrated about all of the time required to respond to his complaints, and they started to treat him poorly. The net result was that things were spiraling out of control.

As time went by, I began to wonder if we were cutting off our collective noses to spite our faces. It began to dawn on me that we were sometimes spending many hours per week fighting over a bunch of issues that would probably not come up had we granted him a few more hours of official time.

Eventually, when we negotiated our local supplemental agreement, we agreed to increase his hours in exchange for virtually everything else we wanted as management. Not only did we wind up with an incredibly short labor agreement, but we also improved our relationship with the union president because he suddenly felt more valued and he now had more official time. The bottom line for us is that we gave him a few more hours of official time in exchange for far more time that could be devoted to our core work, and we had defused a very tense relationship with the union.

A new union official assumed power. She was an extremely cynical individual who was near the end of her career. She had had a checkered career, which was marked by performance and conduct-related problems.

Prior to her election, she had spent many years in various capacities with the union, and several of her mentors were among the most difficult individuals I had ever dealt with. Once she took over, it quickly became clear that she would be tough to deal with. She was unsure of herself, other than what appeared to be her contempt for management. She was not very knowledgeable about labor-relations law, reluctant to make commitments, and difficult to trust. We tried to treat her well and elevate her status, but she didn't bite. Apparently, she just had so many bad experiences in her career (and perhaps her life) that she was going to use this opportunity to get some payback and make things difficult for management.

The only thing I could do was to deal with her professionally and without emotion, and to try and address each issue that she raised. The goal in this situation was to ensure that she caused as little damage to the organization as possible, and to allow the supervisors to focus on their work, rather than on her complaints. I tried to resolve issues whenever possible, but stuck to my guns when cases were referred to third parties. Given the fact that I was much more knowledgeable about labor-relations law than she was, it was relatively easy for us to prevail in the vast majority of cases.

Since management did not overreact to her complaints, and since she almost always lost before third parties, she began to see that she was not achieving many of her goals. Moreover, after I left the organization, the same pattern continued, as my successors adopted a similar approach. Eventually, she realized that constantly attacking the organization with little apparent success was not particularly reward-ing, and she retired.

Let the Union Have Some Victories

Being in a political organization, union officials need to show some positive results if they are going to remain in office. If management tries to beat them down at every turn, and never acknowledges that the union can be right, it is taking a dan-gerous approach. Under this scenario, union officials are going to quickly become frustrated and will look for other ways to show the bargaining unit that they are protecting its interests. This may involve filing an increasing number of complaints, lead to a greater reluctance to resolve outstanding issues, or trigger a harder edge to the union's rhetoric. Whatever happens, managers need to clearly understand that for every action there is a reaction, and unless the union gets some victories, there will surely be a reaction that they won't like.

Earlier in my career, I did not see things that way. My view was much more narrow, and I used to brag about the fact that the union had never won a case. Eventually, I realized that we were winning all of the battles but losing the war, because our reluctance to give the union any victories was triggering more and more complaints, which was taking up a larger portion of our time. I finally figured out that maintaining good relations with the representatives of our employees was much more important than winning every time.

That's not to say that you have to compromise your values. Rather, you need to recognize that union officials are people, they have a role to play, and, just like everyone else, they want to succeed. If you take a practical approach to dealing with the union, don't take it personally, and understand where it is coming from, in most cases, you will do well. Consider the following true scenarios:

1. A few years ago, I wanted to implement a dress code within our office. It was important to me because it was part of my overall strategy to make our office more professional. The dress code banned jeans, tee shirts, sneakers, suggestive out-fits, baseball caps, and similar informal apparel. From my perspective, having the employees improve their appearance would make them feel like they were part of a class organization, make our customers feel that they were being served by profes-sionals, and shape the outside world's view of our organization by showing them that we were becoming more serious about our work.

The union understood where I was coming from but faced resistance from certain members of the workforce, who wanted to retain our more relaxed atmosphere. The most emotional issue seemed to be my insistence that all men wear ties. I thought that we could prevail should this case wind up at impasse, but that would take time to unfold, and I was concerned that hard feelings would also be created and the union could lose face. Eventually, I agreed that only male employees who greeted the public would be required to wear ties. I also agreed to a casual dress day on the last Friday of each month. I got 95 percent of what I wanted out of the dress code, yet the union had a victory as well.

2. In another related episode, the union missed the due date for filing a grievance and, after the fact, asked me to extend the deadline. It was obvious that it was embarrassed by this mistake and did not want to have to go back to the grievant and tell him that the union blew his grievance. I could easily have declined to extend the deadline because we had a contract, but in situations like this, the door swings both ways. I could tell that this was an important case to the union, so I agreed to extend the deadline.

By my taking this approach, union representatives did not lose face with the grievant, I built some goodwill with them, and we both knew that if I missed a deadline, they would cut me some slack. Moreover, I still had the opportunity to reject the grievance if I felt that it lacked merit.

3. At another juncture, we issued performance improvement plans to several of our employees. The union complained that these plans were technically deficient because we had not previously advised these employees that their performance had been under par. As relief, it requested that we withdraw the improvement plans.

I thought the union's argument was somewhat shaky. There was some evidence that the employees had been counseled, although perhaps not to the extent envisioned by the contract. After considering all of the facts, I decided to withdraw the performance improvement notices. The union had an arguable position, and there was no real harm in taking a bit more time to tighten up our case. The union had a small victory, while we formally counseled the employees. Within a month or so, we wound up reissuing the performance improvement plans to most of the affected employees.

In all three of these cases, I listened carefully to the union and gave ground where it was appropriate. That being said, in most cases, I normally decided against the union. However, because my decisions were well reasoned, and because I did not always decide against it, the union was at least able to accept the fact that I would always consider its position and sometimes agree with it. In essence, I gave union representatives enough victories to strengthen them politically, while preserving management's position on the key issues.

By contrast, when I was dealing with a union that was dead set on harassing management, I would still consider each issue on a case-by-case basis, and try and do the right thing. However, I did not look to give union officials any unnecessary victories, because I had no interest in giving them any political cover.

Negotiations

Negotiating with unions is an art unto itself. It requires considerable skill, a careful understanding of the issues at hand, knowledge of labor relations, a cool hand, and the ability to look down the road and see the ramifications of the agreements that you make. It also requires keen insight into human behavior, as you need to be able to read the people you are negotiating with and understand when to settle and when to stick to your guns.

I have been involved in all sorts of negotiations. Some have been relatively easy and straightforward, while others have been painful and exhausting. Some have been local in scope, while others have had national ramifications. From these negotiations, I have learned the following lessons, which have served me well throughout my career.

Be Prepared

Whenever I approached negotiations with the union, I always tried to prepare as much as possible. This meant trying to learn as much about the union's perspective in advance as possible, so I was totally prepared to address the issues. This also meant understanding management's position, so I knew the boundaries, as well as what we were trying to accomplish.

I tried to get copies of agreements pertaining to similar issues that had been negotiated by other offices, and a sense as to how those agreements were playing out. Also, I tried to read as much case law as possible, so I was aware of potential negotiability issues as well as cases that had been decided at impasse. Following is an example of these lessons in practice.

At the start of negotiations on a new local agreement, the union presented me with a 55-page, single-spaced series of proposals. At first blush, it appeared that we would be involved in a series of never-ending negotiations to deal with all of these proposals. However, I had already been engaged in many behind-the-scenes discussions with the union, so I knew that the 55-page proposal was just a ploy to pressure us into giving it what it really wanted, which was more official time for one official.

Moreover, having done my homework, I knew that many of its proposals were nonnegotiable in the federal sector.

I sat down with the management team (I was the personnel officer at the time), explained where I thought the negotiations were going, described the strategies that I intended to use, and got the go-ahead to move forward. I then sat down with the union representatives, advised them of management's positions, including its belief that many of the union's proposals were nonnegotiable, and explained to them that I was prepared to focus on the core issues, which were official time and employee breaks. Shortly thereafter, the union realized that it was dealing with a worthy adversary and began to negotiate in a professional manner.

The eventual agreement gave more official time to the one official, but reduced the total amount of official time for the union. We also agreed to raise employee breaks from 10 minutes to 15 minutes, which was the informal practice anyway. The final agreement was only three pages.

Stay Cool

Staying cool is one of the keys to being a good negotiator. Labor negotiations can be very emotional, because a lot is often at stake, so it is imperative that you stay relaxed. People who stay calm tend to see things clearly and exercise good judgment. People who get emotional tend to speak before they think, and once you say something stupid, it is too late to take it back.

One of my rules of thumb is to remember that labor negotiations never affect my personal life. They are part of my business life and are important, but they don't affect my family or my friends. This helps me keep the negotiations in perspective whenever things get emotional or seem to be out of control.

The first time I was involved in major negotiations, the union brought in a strong, savvy, and determined individual to represent it. He frequently tried to intimidate me by threatening to take certain actions (filing complaints, going to the media, contacting my headquarters, etc.) if I didn't comply with his demands. When I gave him management's proposals, he literally took a pair of scissors, cut them up, and threw the pieces on the table.

This individual was clearly attempting to throw me off my game and force me to act emotionally. He knew that if I let my emotions color my judgment, I would make mistakes that he could take advantage of. For example, if I made any anti-union remarks, he would be in a good position to file a ULP and claim that I was not negotiating in good faith.

Fortunately, by nature, I am not an overly emotional person. Every time he attacked me, I simply took a deep breath and stayed calm and composed, which tended to make him look silly. Moreover, I knew he was becoming frustrated, because his game plan was not working. Eventually, he changed his tactics and behaved more professionally. After that, we were able to complete negotiations.

Understand the Long-Term Impact of an Agreement

When you negotiate an agreement with the union, you are committing your organization to live by the terms of that agreement for years to come. That is a major responsibility, since if you make a mistake, the organization will pay for it in many ways. That is why it is so important to be prepared and to stay cool under pressure; you never want to agree to something that will later come back to haunt the government. You need to carefully consider each issue on the table, make sure you have the perspective of the people who will have to live with the agreement, recognize how the agreement affects your organization's ability to manage the workload, and then (and only then) agree to a proposal if it makes sense.

Naturally, you also need to be aware of the political ramifications of the negotiations and have a good feel as to the strength of your position(s) in the event you go to impasse. However, the bottom line is that when you are representing the government during negotiations, you need to do right by the government—both in the short term and in the long term. Two stories will illustrate the point.

1. I was involved in negotiations on a local contract. We reached agreement on all articles of our contract except for one clause that related to the manner in which we assigned our employees. The union wanted to place an overly restrictive clause in the contract that would have made us "jump through hoops" to dole out certain assignments to our employees, and I simply refused to agree to it. Although I had enough personnel knowledge that I probably could have gotten around that clause, I would have also been placing my successors in an uncomfortable position. As a result of my intransigence on that one clause, we never signed that contract. From my perspective, that was preferable to living with an agreement that I knew was not in the best interests of the government.

2. Many years ago, our administration negotiated a national labor agreement. The negotiations were very contentious, and were marked by ill feelings on both sides. What was striking about these negotiations was that the head of our administration had an unusually close relationship with the union, and often seemed to side with the national union president more than he did with his own negotiating team.

He made it clear that he did not want any outstanding issues going to impasse, which forced the team to agree to certain provisions of the contract that it was not particularly happy with. Performance-based actions required more steps and took additional time, disciplinary actions took longer, grievances became more difficult to deal with, and so on. The head of the administration left shortly after the contract became effective, but the supervisors below him had to live with the additional burdens of that contract.

Several years later, a new leader came in and initiated negotiations with the union to improve the terms of that agreement.

Frame the Issue

As negotiations proceed toward the end game, on occasion, the parties can be so far apart that they are unable to reach agreement on one or more of the remaining issues. When this happens, it is extremely important that you frame the issue to your best advantage. Otherwise, if the union frames the issue, or frames the issue better than you do, a mediator and/or an impasses panel will tend to see the issue from the union's perspective. This is somewhat analogous to a judge giving instructions to a jury. If the judge's instructions favor either side's position, that party starts off with a major advantage.

Framing an issue simply means clarifying exactly what issue is to be decided. If the issue is not clarified properly, the wrong issue may be decided, which can be to your disadvantage.

As discussed earlier, I entered negotiations with our local union to implement a dress code. It tried to frame the issue by asking, "Why do we need a dress code?" If that became the issue, I would be in the difficult position of having to explain how a dress code would help our organization improve its service to our customers. While there is plenty of literature available that states that a dress code helps organizations to improve, there is perhaps an equal amount of literature that takes the opposite point of view. Since I did not want to get into a debate about that point, I decided to frame the issue differently.

I found an old national policy statement that indicated that if local offices wanted to establish dress codes, they should be consistent with the business dress in the area surrounding the office. Accordingly, I framed the issue as being, "What is the local business dress?"

We put together a dress code team and sent it into the community to look into this further. Instead of debating the need for a dress code, the team's mission became one of fact-finding. Once it gathered the data, we used the information as the basis for our negotiations, which kept things less emotional and more professional, and, more importantly, focused everyone on the issue that was important to me.

A peer of mine decided to establish a similar dress code in another office. Rather than using the national policy statement as the basis for local negotiations, he simply tried to develop and implement a local dress code. As you might expect, the union fiercely resisted the code, arguing that there was no need for it. Contentious negotiations ensued, after which the issue was finally referred to the Federal Services Impasses Panel (FSIP) for resolution.

Management framed the issue by arguing that a dress code was needed to improve the office's productivity. It based its position on the belief that a more professionally dressed workforce tends to perform better. The union countered by arguing that a dress code was unnecessary, and pointed out that its office already had very high productivity. The FSIP bought the union's argument, and decided that a dress code for that particular office was not required.

In retrospect, had that office framed the issue differently, it would have been in a much better position to prevail. It might have framed the issue this way: "Will a dress code help present a more professional image of our office to both our customers and the public?"

Unfair Labor Practice (ULP) Charges

Federal, state, and local statutes create rights and obligations on the part of management, unions, and employees in a workplace represented by a union. If management or the union fails to live up to its obligations to the other, a ULP may be filed with the appropriate body. A ULP can also be filed if either management or the union interferes with the rights each has been given under the appropriate statute. Employees may also assert their rights under the governing statute by filing ULP charges against labor or management.

Examples of management ULPs include negotiating in bad faith, retaliating against employees for exercising their right to seek union representation, excluding unions from certain management meetings with bargaining unit employees, and refusing to provide a union with information that it needs to fulfill its representational responsibilities. Examples of union ULPs include negotiating in bad faith, refusing to represent bargaining unit employees because they are not members of the union, and attempting to influence management to discipline employees who did not join the union.

A ULP charge is a tool that can be used by both labor unions and management, although in the vast majority of cases, unions usually file it. This is because management holds the majority of the cards, so unions often file ULPs in order to get the attention of management.

ULPs typically involve the filing of a charge and an investigation by the body that handles these types of issues (the FLRA in the federal government, a state Labor Relations Board, etc.). If the investigation demonstrates that there is merit to the charge, a formal complaint is then issued, which is adjudicated by an administrative law judge of that same body. If the parties are unable to settle the matter, a decision is then rendered, either dismissing the complaint or finding that a violation has been committed and ordering appropriate relief. Appropriate relief can range from posting the violation notice wherein the agency agrees that it violated the law and pledges not to repeat the offense, to, in some cases, a much more severe penalty that could involve a return to the status quo.

As you can see, ULPs are not to be taken lightly. By the same token, because they take a long time to be adjudicated, there is plenty of opportunity to resolve the issue at hand before a violation is ever issued. The key in these matters is to (1) understand and try to follow the law; (2) ensure that the supervisors are aware of their labor-relations obligations; and (3) develop a good relationship with the union, so that if a violation occurs, you will work together to try to resolve the issue without the intervention of a third party.

However, if you are involved in an adverse relationship with the union that is not of your making, you may find yourself in the ULP arena far more often than you would like. Under these circumstances, you need to develop a strategy that will allow you to contest the ULPs without getting bogged down in a series of seemingly never-ending battles.

Let's look at a few cases to see how I dealt with ULPs that were filed by the union.

1. I took over an organization that had just undergone a change in the union's leadership. The new team was younger, more aggressive, and much less willing to work with management. Shortly before I arrived, the new team began filing a series of ULPs. The complaints alleged that management failed to negotiate with the union on changes in working conditions, and that the union was not given the opportunity to attend certain formal meetings with the bargaining unit.

The local management team resented this new approach to labor relations and took the ULPs very personally. It stopped talking to the union, communicated with the union almost exclusively in writing, and did nothing to address the issues described in the ULPs.

When I arrived, the FLRA was in the process of investigating seven ULPs. After examining the charges, I quickly concluded that the union was right and that management was likely to lose every case. I discussed the cases with the FLRA's investigator, who informed me that I was right and that he would soon be issuing formal complaints against our organization. At that point, I sat down with the union, discussed its concerns, and settled the cases by agreeing to (1) bargain where appropriate; (2) include the union at all meetings where it had a right to be present; and (3) conduct labor relations training for management so it would not continue to make the same mistakes.

Although I knew that this group was going to be difficult to deal with, I had at least gotten off to a good start with it by earning its respect through my knowledge of labor relations and my willingness to try and address its concerns.

Moreover, the local management team realized that I had saved it the pain and embarrassment of losing seven ULPs, so it deferred to me on future issues involving labor-management relations.

2. The union just described would periodically file ULPs whenever it wanted to pressure management into giving it what it desired. I addressed each complaint on a case-by-case basis, settling cases where we were wrong, while disputing those complaints where we were right. I did not want to settle every case, since that would only encourage the union to file more and more complaints. Perhaps the hardest thing to do was to not take things personally, as it was clearly frustrating to be constantly on the receiving end of a seemingly never-ending series of complaints.

Over time, it became clear to me that the union was abusing the federal labor relations system. It was simply filing complaints as a means to an end—that is, more power—instead of complaining about issues that it truly believed in. Eventually, we started pushing back. We filed several ULPs and grievances against the union, alleging that it was dealing with us in bad faith. This got the union's attention and the attention of its headquarters, and at least made the union more cautious in trying to use the system to harass us.

3. I was working with a different union that rarely filed complaints. After several years, it filed its first ULP against our organization, alleging that we were excluding the union from certain meetings, and it was right.

This was a wake-up call to me, because it let me know that while this union was much more reasonable than the last one, it wasn't a pushover, either. We had been taking the union for granted, and it had responded in kind. We quickly settled the complaint, conducted training for our supervisors on which meetings the union had the right to attend, and instituted more frequent meetings with the union so we would be aware of its concerns before they became formalized.

Grievances

Grievance Procedures

Grievances are complaints filed by employees expressing dissatisfaction with some aspect of their working conditions. Typically, there are two kinds of grievance procedures. The first, and most common, is the negotiated grievance procedure. This procedure is developed by both management and labor and covers all members of the bargaining unit. It establishes the issues that are subject to grievance,[1] as well as the procedures to be followed. This usually includes the time frames for both filing and responding to grievances, as well as the process for resolving them in the event that management is unable to satisfy the grievant.

The other procedure involves the government organization's internal process for resolving grievances. This procedure is often more restrictive than the negotiated one in terms of the issues that can be grieved, the time frames for filing and responding to the grievance, and so on. Moreover, unlike the negotiated procedure, which usually calls for arbitration as the final step, the final decision under the internal grievance procedure normally rests with the government.

How to Handle a Grievance

The best way to handle a grievance is to fully and fairly consider each issue on its own merits. Even if you find against the employee, if she believes you at least gave her her day in court, she is unlikely to come out of the process angry or embittered.

I always tried to meet with the employee (and her representative if she brought one), and listen carefully to her complaint. During the meeting, I usually took notes (or had an HR specialist take notes for me) and always asked a few questions. If you don't take notes or ask any questions, both the employee and her representative will quickly conclude that you had already made up your mind before the meeting and were not truly interested in considering the grievance and trying to do the right thing.

At the end of the meeting, I always tried to rephrase the employee's grievance in order to ensure that (1) I understood all of the issues at hand; and (2) the employee recognized that I was paying attention to what she was complaining about. I also tried to give her management's perspective so she would have a more three-dimensional view of the issue.

If the employee were a chronic complainer, the type that tried to abuse the system, I would still look at each issue on its own merits and try and do the right thing. I made sure that I did not act or respond emotionally, and that I was professional at all times. At the same time, I did not want to encourage this individual to continually file complaints (unless the complaints had merit), so I looked at his grievances in the context of his overall pattern of behavior, and made my decisions accordingly.

Every time you make a decision on a grievance, you are playing to several audiences. The employee, his representative, the entire union, and at least some members of the bargaining unit are closely watching your decision. At the same time, the supervisors are watching you, too, wondering if you are going to support their decision or side with the employee. Lastly, you also need to be sensitive to the fact that if the grievant is dissatisfied with your decision and wants to pursue it further, your decision will be subject to review by another person. That's a tough position to be in, and it's why you need to be aware of the message you are sending each time you make a decision.

In responding to grievances, I keep all these audiences in mind. As a result, I try to phrase my responses in a professional and sensitive manner, to make sure that anyone reading my response understands that I carefully considered the grievance and attempted to do the right thing. I also try and give enough information so that the reader understands the rationale behind my decision, while not writing so much that the information contained in my response could be used against me.

For example, the union filed a grievance over a number of performance improvement plans that we had issued to our employees. The grievance was based on its belief that we should not issue such plans to our employees until we had made a good-faith effort to train them. As part of the grievance, it pointed out a number of deficiencies in the training.

After looking into this issue, I concluded that the union was right. Our training had been rather skimpy and clearly needed to be improved. If we were to go forward with the performance improvement plans, and later took action against the employees, I believed we were likely to lose before a third party. More importantly, I thought withdrawing the improvement plans was the right thing to do, as our employees deserved to receive quality training. Accordingly, I sustained the grievance and sat down with our management team and crafted a strategy that ensured that our employees received the appropriate training. Later on, after the training had been completed, we were able to successfully take action against several individuals based on poor performance.

In another instance, an employee filed a grievance over the fact that he had not been allowed to work overtime. After looking into the matter, I learned that he had not been allowed to work overtime because his day-to-day output had been very low. In addition, we only had a limited amount of money available for overtime, and his division chief wanted to ensure that he was spending it wisely.

I met with the employee and carefully listened to his concerns. I then explained management's position and asked him what he would do if he were in the same position as his division chief. He stated that he probably would have done the same thing, but that he needed the money and really wanted to work overtime in the future. I told him that I believed he had been treated fairly, so I was likely to deny the grievance. However, I also stated that I would ask his division chief to meet with him and tell him exactly how much more work he needed to do on a daily basis to qualify for overtime. The employee felt this was fair and, after receiving my written denial, which restated the reasons I had verbally given him, did not pursue the grievance any further.

Another example occurred early in my career. An internal statistical quality review of the work of one of our employees resulted in his being charged with a total of 29 errors. This employee had been a long-term problem, and he tried to have these errors reversed by filing 29 separate grievances. He knew that his job would be in jeopardy if the errors were not reversed, so he did everything he could to make things difficult for management.

As personnel officer, I participated in the grievance meeting along with the grievant, his union representative, and the director, who was the deciding official. The employee attempted to make a farce out of the meeting by walking in and out of the meeting and arguing that each error was wrong, without providing any evidence to indicate why the error was incorrectly called. All along, he kept contending that he had 29 different grievances. Eventually, the director terminated the meeting, indicating that he had heard enough from this individual.

When I crafted the director's response, we decided to turn the tables on the employee. We agreed that there were 29 separate grievances, and denied them accordingly. By taking this approach, if the employee wanted to pursue these grievances further, the union would have had to agree to share in the cost of 29 separate arbitrations. We knew that this would never happen; the grievances ended at that point, and the employee was eventually demoted.

Lessons Learned

Build a Personal Relationship with the Union

I learned early on that if you constantly fight with the union, you may win most of the battles, but you will still lose the war. All of the time that you spend fighting the union is wasted time, since it is time that cannot be devoted to your core mission. While there may be occasions where you have no choice but to go down that path, most of the time you can avoid that ordeal by developing a personal relationship with the union.

I have found that the more you deal with union officials on a human level, and the more they see you as a thinking, feeling individual, the more difficult it becomes for them to attack you on a personal level. That is why I strongly advocate building a personal relationship with union officials. Try and find a common interest with them, go to lunch with them, do whatever it takes to build a relationship. The more work you put into such a relationship, the less work you'll have to put into fighting the union.

I once became involved in a very difficult situation wherein management and the union clearly despised each other. Both parties did not trust each other, which resulted in a never-ending series of grievances, complaints, and confrontations. Upon my arrival, I saw why management did not like its union counterparts. By and large, they were a group of angry, disenfranchised individuals whom I did not particularly care for either.

My initial reaction was to fight them tooth and nail on everything, but that only caused more trouble. I had to find a better way to deal with this situation. Eventually, I tried to get to know the union president better, since he was the driving force behind our labor problems.

I found out that he had a personal interest in professional wrestling. Since my son was also into wrestling at the time, I was familiar with many of the names and characters. I began to discuss wrestling with the president on a regular basis, which gave us something in common. As our relationship developed, he slowly began to open up to me, which gave me more insight into his thinking and enabled me to address many of the underlying issues.

Use Humor

Labor relations can often be a tense business, since it usually involves the union coming to management with complaints about the working conditions. As such, management often anticipates these meetings with trepidation, while the union knows that it will not be welcomed with open arms. The natural tension between these two parties often becomes a self-fulfilling prophecy, leading to posturing, mistrust, and outright anger.

I have found that humor works very well in a labor-relations setting. A little levity goes a long way toward keeping things on an even keel and preventing meetings from getting out of hand. Whenever things get tense to the point where someone is about to say something that he or she will regret, I often chime in with a wisecrack or a whimsical story in order to defuse the tension. The more often you can keep the discussion grounded, the more productive will be the meeting, and humor is simply a superb elixir for your short-term labor problems.

A union president once came to see me in an angry mood because she felt that a certain management official had treated her disrespectfully. While I disagreed with her interpretation of the official's behavior, I knew she was emotional and would not listen to reason at that point. Accordingly, I began the meeting by telling her the following story involving my young son Marc:

"Marc had to do a paper on someone whose job it is to help people. He decided that he was going to do it on me. He asked me what my job was. I told him that my job was to help veterans. He dutifully wrote that down. I asked him if he knew what a veteran is. He replied, 'Sure, a veteran is someone who takes care of sick animals.'"

The union president laughed at my story and almost immediately relaxed. While she was still upset about the management official's behavior, a little humor had helped to deplete some of her anger, and we proceeded to pleasantly and professionally discuss the incident in question and resolved it shortly thereafter.

Be Wary of Union Factoids

As managers, we not only have to deal with the union, but we also have to deal with our employees and our supervisors as well. These groups, particularly the supervisors, often interact with the unions on a daily basis and frequently hear the union say things that sound right.

For example, the union might say, "You can't have that workload meeting without the union being present because it involves members of the bargaining unit." On first blush, that might make sense to many supervisors who are inexperienced in labor relations, since in certain segments of government, the union has the right to be present at formal meetings. However, formal meetings normally mean meetings where working conditions are discussed, not simple workload meetings. Unfortunately, because the supervisor heard a union official say this in a firm and decisive manner, he believed him and acted accordingly.

I refer to these types of statements as union factoids, because in most cases the union official is espousing what he believes to be true, and not necessarily what the law or union contract requires. Union officials can often be wrong because they are typically full-time government employees who spend part of their time working for the union and therefore are not technical experts with respect to labor relations. Other times, union officials hold a *legitimate* point of view on an issue that is different from management's perspective. The problem here is that in many cases, the supervisor is even less knowledgeable on labor law than the union official, and therefore acts according to the law and/or contract in a way defined by the union's pronouncement of factoids.

Obviously, as managers we want to prevent such a situation from either developing or continuing. The best way to handle this situation is to (1) give frequent training on labor relations to your supervisors; and (2) ensure that they have access to an HR specialist who is highly knowledgeable about labor relations. In addition, they should be taught that in the event the union tells them that they are doing something wrong, they should reply, "Okay, let me look into this issue and I'll get back to you," rather than conceding defeat on an issue where they may be absolutely correct. Consider this situation, which actually happened.

The union told one of our supervisors that he was required to invite a union official to a meeting where we gave our employees a disciplinary or adverse action. In fact, the union has no such legal right. However, the supervisor believed the union official and began inviting him to every meeting in which he gave out an admonishment, a reprimand, or other disciplinary action.

As a result, whenever this union official attended such a meeting, he prolonged it by arguing about the personnel action. Moreover, instead of being at his desk working, he was attending a meeting that he had no legal right to be at. This all occurred because the supervisor believed the union official's factoid instead of first checking with an HR advisor.

Learn to Think Like the Union

The more you understand where the union is coming from, the better you will be able to deal with it. When union officials come to you with an issue, it is generally either driven by one or more complaints from the bargaining unit, or based on one of the unit's hot-button issues (i.e., those it is very sensitive about).

Complaints from the bargaining unit may be broad-based, although in most cases they involve only a limited number of people. That is because many of today's government unions have a relatively limited base of support, since the newer and more educated employees do not see them as adding much value.[2] Their base is generally the older employees and the marginal and disaffected employees, who feel that they need the union to protect them.

In these situations, the union often focuses on the perception that the top employees are treated better than the bottom ones. From their perspective, the top employees get the plum assignments, they receive the largest awards, and so on. Over time, the union begins to believe that management is rewarding its favorites, while from management's point of view, it is simply rewarding its best employees. Since the core constituency feels that they also deserve to be treated well, a natural tension develops between labor and management.

The best way to deal with this situation is to follow the principles described earlier in the book. That is, make sure your systems are applied as reliably as possible. In this way you will be able to demonstrate that everyone is being treated equally, and that people are being rewarded based on performance, not favoritism. The second thing you need to do is to try and pull up as many people as possible. If you do this, you'll develop more stars and reduce the number of people who feel that they have been treated poorly. Moreover, the union will be able to demonstrate to its core constituency that it is doing its job because management is treating everyone fairly.

Hot-button issues are situations that the union has seen happen over and over again that have frustrated it to the point where it has become overly sensitive to them. They generally involve a practice or practices that reek of favoritism, reflect a lack of concern for the union and/or the bargaining unit, or give the impression that management is making a series of secret decisions that will ultimately harm people. The more you understand these issues and try to keep them from developing, the better will be your relationship with the union. Here's an instance.

Every year, a group of predominantly white senior management officials would get together and go motorcycling in the desert. African-American employees were not invited, nor did they participate in this annual event. Over time, African-American employees began to refer to this event as an example of racism, and it became a hot-button issue with the union, which was comprised mainly of African-American employees.

Although I did not personally believe that there was anything sinister going on in this social activity, I could see the symbolism and understand why the African-American employees were upset. Accordingly, I suggested to the organizers of this event that they either make it more inclusive or try some other activity.

In a similar scenario, prior to my arrival, many of our management officials used to keep their doors closed for hours at a time. It made the employees nervous and gave them the impression that secret decisions were being made by a few people in smoke-filled rooms. When people asked the union what was going on, it had no answers, which made it look weak and ineffective.

In reality, the doors were closed because the management officials were looking for some private time to get their work done, but this was lost on everyone. As time went by, it became a hot button for our employees and the union. I addressed this situation by announcing that my door would stay open except when I was involved in a sensitive personnel issue, and I expected our supervisors to take the same approach. By opening up our doors, we gave the employees the sense that we were becoming a more open and inclusive organization.

The other issue that seems to drive union officials is respect. If they feel respected, they will be much more willing to work with you than if they feel as though they are an afterthought. Unfortunately, far too often, they feel disrespected by management, and that seems to set the tone for the relationship. This perception is often fueled by events happening that they are unaware of, by management discussing changes with them after the fact, and so on.

Imagine if you were the union president and constantly felt like you were behind the eight ball. Every time a bargaining unit member came to you to discuss a particular issue and you were unaware of it, you would look silly, and you would begin to feel resentful. In short, you would think that management doesn't respect you, and you would treat managers accordingly.

Treating the union with respect is not difficult; in fact, it is easy and is the right thing to do. If you learn to think like the union, you will understand just how important it is to treat the union with respect and will do just that.

Here's one more story to illustrate the point: I always tried to make it a point to acknowledge our union president's position and accomplishments and to treat her with respect. Whenever we had an awards breakfast, I would always introduce her to the group, and emphasize her importance to the organization. Whenever a VIP came to our office, I made sure I introduced her to the VIP. Whenever I wrote an article for our all-employee newsletter, I tried to acknowledge the union and our employees in some way. Because I knew that the union officials craved respect, I made sure that I tried to give it to them, while, of course, expecting them to respond in kind.

Key Points to Remember

- Treat the union well; recognize that there are all types of union officials, and adjust your strategy accordingly.
- Don't take things personally.
- Understand the ramifications of any labor agreement you may sign.
- When responding to a labor issue, always remember that several potential audiences may read your response.

Equal Employment Opportunity

Overview

Equal employment opportunity (EEO) is a principle that has become accepted throughout our country. This principle was codified into law in Title VII of the Civil Rights Act of 1964, which bans employment discrimination based on race, color, religion, sex, or national origin. Other acts that followed along the same lines include the Age Discrimination in Employment Act of 1967, Title I and Title V of the Americans with Disabilities Act of 1990, and the Civil Rights Act of 1991. Simply put, EEO is the law of the land, and allegations of discimination should be treated very seriously.

That being said, anyone who has ever been charged with discrimination knows how frustrating, emotional, and personal such complaints can be. Once you've been charged with discrimination, it is extremely difficult to deal with the complainant on a personal basis. Your natural tendency is to want to strike back, because in your heart you probably believe that you have been unfairly charged as an alleged discriminating official. Of course, the worst thing you can possibly do in this situation is to retaliate against an EEO complainant. If you do, the case will quickly spiral out of control, and you will surely pay a much heavier price for the retaliation than you would for the alleged act of discrimination. That is why the first thing you need to do in these cases is to take a deep breath, sit down with a knowledgeable advisor, and look at the facts in a dispassionate manner.

You need to be able to distinguish between those who legitimately feel they are victims of discrimination and those who simply seek to abuse the system. It is likely that you will come across both types of individuals in your career, and the better you are able to distinguish between the two, the better you will be able to respond to each complaint.

The person who sincerely feels he is a victim of discrimination is trying to get management's attention and advise it that he believes he has been wronged. This individual is less interested in winning his case than he is in ensuring that the alleged act(s) of discrimination will be addressed and not repeated. He is motivated by core values; his primary interest is in doing the right thing, and he is relatively easy to deal with. If you sit down with him at the informal stage, listen carefully to his concerns, and treat him with respect and dignity, in most cases you can probably resolve his complaint with relatively little pain.

EEO Claim—Model Scenario. A solid, successful employee felt that his supervisor was giving him a hard time. From his perspective, the supervisor was constantly interfering in his work and making it difficult for him to succeed. He eventually concluded that he needed to get management's attention, so he filed an informal complaint of discrimination, based on age, sex, and handicap (he was a 55-year-old white male with a variety of physical problems).

After the complaint was filed, the supervisor sat down with him in an informal setting, listened to his concerns, and explained the reasons behind her actions. They discussed the issues as professionals, eventually arrived at a meeting of the minds, and the complaint was withdrawn.

In this situation, the employee was not looking to take advantage of the EEO system. He was simply trying to address a situation where he believed that he had been wronged, and his supervisor's quick intervention resolved the complaint rather quickly.

By contrast, the person who tries to use the EEO complaint system as a tool to get what she wants is an entirely different breed of animal. This person is less interested in doing the right thing than she is in getting a promotion, getting a financial settlement, or getting back at a particular supervisor. She is a dangerous person because she is prepared to make you jump through all sorts of hoops in order to achieve her goals. Most likely, she has learned throughout her career that the EEO system is so costly and time consuming that many management officials are willing to settle with EEO complainants in order to make their complaints go away.

EEO Claim—Problem Scenario. A nurse filed 47 discrimination complaints against a VA medical center's chief nurse over a wide variety of issues. It was clear to us that she was more interested in pursuing her case, seeing the chief nurse fired, and receiving a large monetary settlement than she was in helping patients. Under the circumstances, we decided to aggressively defend ourselves against her complaints.

The 47 complaints eventually went before an EEO administrative law judge (ALJ), who supported our organization on every charge. Shortly thereafter, the employee filed a new series of EEO complaints, in part to continue to pressure the organization into giving her a large monetary settlement, and in part to insulate herself from her poor performance and misconduct (she had been insubordinate on a number of occasions).

Eventually, we fired her for her unacceptable performance/misconduct, and, as you might expect, she alleged that her removal was retaliation for her prior and current EEO complaints. Before the next EEO hearing began, we settled her case by allowing her to resign and by paying her attorney fees (by this point, it would have been much more expensive for us to continue fighting the first 47 complaints, which were still moving through the system, and the new set of complaints, than it would have been to settle). However, I insisted that the agreement contain a clause wherein she agreed never to apply to another VA medical center for the rest of her life. My fear was that if I settled that day, tomorrow she would simply apply to a different VA medical center, not be selected, and begin a new round of discrimination complaints. While she was not happy with this clause, she reluctantly agreed to it.

Within a few months, I learned that she had, in fact, applied to another VA medical center, had not been selected, and had filed a new discrimination complaint. She alleged that she had been coerced into signing the agreement, and therefore it was not binding. Her complaint was administratively dismissed based on the clause I discussed earlier. However, it eventually worked its way through the courts, where, years later, the Court of Appeals finally dismissed it, based on the terms of the settlement agreement.

Obviously the strategy in dealing with these two types of individual complainants is going to be very different. The better you become at distinguishing between these two types, the more successful you will be at handling discrimination complaints.

Philosophy

Be Honest

The best way to deal with discrimination complaints is to try to prevent them from being filed in the first place. Although you cannot prevent all complaints from being filed, you can foster a culture where people at least feel that you are fair and are trying to do the right thing. If you do that, most people will give you the benefit of the doubt, and that alone will prevent at least some complaints from being filed.

Many times, when people feel angry or frustrated about a particular action, they file EEO complaints. They do so because management has not been open and up front with them, which causes them to suspect that there must be a hidden reason for the action. When management gives employees the unvarnished truth, they almost invariably appreciate hearing it, even if it is not what they really wanted to hear. This is because people are so accustomed to hearing obfuscations, half-truths, or outright lies that when someone tells them the truth, they find it refreshing and are much more willing to work with that person, rather than using the EEO system to seek relief.

EEO Claim Averted—Honesty Scenario. An employee was not selected for a promotion. He asked his first- and second-level supervisors what he needed to do to get promoted in the future, and they were either evasive or nonresponsive. He began to wonder why no one would give him a straight answer, and considered filing a discrimination complaint. However, because I had a reputation for honesty, he came to see me before filing a complaint.

Prior to the meeting, I met with his supervisor and learned why he had not been selected. As a result, at our meeting, I was able to tell him that he needed to improve his attendance and increase his output. While I could not promise him that improving in those two areas would automatically get him the next promotion, since other employees were likely to compete for the same position, I was able to tell him that improving in those two areas would definitely increase his chances. He thanked me for my honesty and stated that it would have been very helpful if someone had told him this earlier. He left the meeting satisfied and did not file a complaint.

In another example of the benefits of being "up front" with employees, the work of one of our largest divisions (over 100 people) was going to be transferred to another office as part of a national consolidation. We were one of the last offices to be affected because of our size and location. Obviously, the transfer of so much work was going to have a significant impact on the careers and lives of many of the employees in that division. Moreover, most of these employees were minorities, and they were very suspicious of the motives behind the consolidation.

I met with the entire group on a frequent basis to let them know what was going on. I told them the rationale for the consolidation, why we were losing the work (the cost of living in our area was a major factor), and why the work was being transferred to a specific office (the cost of doing business there was much lower and that office had a strong record of high performance). Although the employees were not happy with the decision, they at least felt that I was being up front with them. From their perspective, if they were being told the truth, they would at least be able to make important career decisions based on solid information.

Moreover, I did not sugarcoat anything for them, nor did I blame anyone for decisions that I made. For example, at my insistence, the effective date of the transfer was moved up by about six months, because I knew that a long delay in the workload transfer would only prolong the agony and would result in increasingly poor service to our customers. I told the employees that it was my decision to push up the effective date, and explained to them my rationale. Again, while they were not happy with the decision, they at least knew who was making the decisions and why they were being made.

I also told them that no one would lose a job as a result of the workload transfer. While I could not promise that everyone would retain their pay grade, I was least able to assure them that no one would be out on the street. Since I was honest with them about the bad news, they were more likely to believe me when it came to good news. We completed the workload transfer much more quickly than most people anticipated, and not one discrimination complaint was filed.

Look at Things from the Other Person's Perspective

When you become a supervisor, you tend to view things from a management perspective, which can quickly make you out of touch with the way your employees see things. Suddenly, you start looking at the bigger picture and begin to focus on achieving your organization's goals. Before you know it, you no longer see things the way the troops do.

Oftentimes, whenever a selection is to be made, the employees engage in seemingly endless speculation as to who will get the job and why. They review the pool of potential candidates and try and anticipate management's decision, while frequently coming up with insidious reasons as to why certain people might get selected (everyone knows he is one of management's favorites, she is probably sleeping with the boss, etc.).

From management's perspective, it is simply trying to select the best person for the job, while keeping its collective head above water. Many of the issues that the employees are looking at and are sensitive to, management may not be aware of. This means that when a selection is finally made, management may not anticipate the fallout from its decision, and a complaint could be filed.

Obviously, whenever you make a selection decision, the selectee is going to be happy while the nonselectees will be unhappy. However, their reaction will be muted if they perceive the decision as being fair. If you are sensitive to the way people perceive things, and address these issues before they ferment, people will give you the benefit of the doubt. Ultimately, employees will make their assessments based on the way everyone is being treated before, during, and after the process, and not based on the selection alone. Here's an example from my own experience.

One of our long-term clerks was usually asked to train newly hired claims examiners, which was a higher position than hers. She became increasingly frustrated that she was being asked to train people who were destined to rise higher in the organization than she. She wanted to know why she was good enough to train these new people, who brought no experience to the table, but was not good enough to be selected for their position.

From management's perspective, she was training the new employees on one narrow aspect of claims examining. Management believed that while she was a good clerk, she lacked the education and ability to be a good claims examiner, so they continually nonselected her whenever a vacancy arose.

This frustrated the employee, and she started telling everyone how unfair management was. Eventually, she got fed up and filed a discrimination complaint. Had management been more sensitive to this good employee's growing frustration, it could have (1) given her opportunities to boost her skills in order to become a stronger candidate for future claims examiner vacancies or to demonstrate that she was incapable of performing the duties of that position; or (2) allowed other clerks to train future classes of claims examiners. Either approach (or perhaps both) would have been perceived as being fairer, would have reduced her frustration level, and most likely would have prevented a complaint from being filed.

In this second example, an assistant division chief went to lunch every day with a subordinate female employee. This raised many eyebrows, as it gave everyone the impression that she was his favorite employee and triggered a fair amount of gossip that they may also have been sleeping together.

When we confronted the assistant division chief about this, he argued that it was his right to go to lunch with anyone of his choosing. From a narrow point of view, he was correct. However, we pointed out that on the one hand, if this woman were to apply for a promotion and get selected, others would perceive it as outright favoritism and were likely to file discrimination complaints. Moreover, they could easily allege that the assistant division chief had created a hostile atmosphere by creating the impression that you had to grant him sexual favors in order to get promoted.

On the other hand, if she applied for a promotion and was not selected, she could infer that she was not selected *because* of her relationship with the assistant division chief. In other words, she might conclude that she was not selected in order to insulate management from potential complaints from other female employees. Under these circumstances, she might be inclined to file a complaint.

The assistant division chief finally got the message and stopped going to lunch with her. Other employees immediately noticed this and were pleased to see that management dealt with this situation. Shortly thereafter, the issue disappeared.

Know Your Statistics

If you know your EEO statistics, you will be in a much better position to manage your EEO program. Knowledge is power, and in the field of EEO that is certainly true. At a minimum, you need to know the following statistics for your team, division, or organization as applicable to be successful in this area:

- The current distribution of employees by race, sex, and national origin relative to the standard metropolitan statistical area (SMSA)[1]
- The current distribution of supervisors using the same criteria relative to the SMSA (assuming the entity contains multiple supervisors)
- The distribution of both new hires and promotions using the same criteria relative to the SMSA
- The distribution of disciplinary/adverse actions relative to the SMSA

You need to know this information for two primary reasons: (1) so you can identify and address any conscious or unconscious biases within your organization that may be contributing to acts of discrimination; and (2) so you can defend yourself in the event that you are charged with discrimination.

When people consider filing EEO complaints, they first look at the organization's statistics to see if they will buttress their cases. If the statistics are consistent with their perceptions, people are more likely to file complaints. By the same token, once a complaint is filed, the first place that an EEO counselor, investigator, and ALJ will turn to is the organization's statistics, since they will paint a broad picture of the organization's success at EEO. Although statistics in and of themselves are usually not enough to sustain a discrimination charge, they often go a long way toward painting the picture of the local EEO climate for a neutral third party.

For instance, for years, our local union believed that we discriminated against African-Americans. Part of that perception was fostered by the fact that almost every union official was African-American. Knowing that perception, I periodically reviewed our statistics in all of the SMSA categories in order to make sure that we were handling everyone in an even-handed manner. I made sure to bring these statistics to the attention of our division chiefs so they were on the same page as I was. Whenever we took an action against an employee(s) or hired en masse, I first reviewed our statistics before allowing the process to go forward.

By keeping abreast of such actions that I knew could be emotional for some, I was able to defend our practices whenever challenged. In fact, on several occasions, our union wrote to me contending that it believed our practices were discriminatory and requested several of the described statistics. I was always happy to provide this information because I knew that it would undercut the union's argument. Despite receiving several inflammatory letters, the union never took the issue further because the statistics were inconsistent with these beliefs.

Let's look at another similar case. Early in my career, I worked for a government organization that was heavily represented with minority employees. Despite this distribution, we had no minorities represented in our most important and highest-paying unit. A newly hired director recognized this disparity and changed the way we normally recruited for these positions in order to increase the pool of minority candidates.

This action caused several white employees to protest vehemently, arguing that this was just a form of reverse discrimination. The director responded by stating that it was hard to see how whites were being discriminated against, since this elite unit was composed entirely of white people, and stuck to his guns. Eventually, other white people came forward and stated how ashamed they were of the actions of the people who were protesting the change in the recruitment pool.

A potential EEO problem was averted, and today, that elite unit is well represented with minorities.

The Most Common EEO Issues

People generally seem to be sensitive to, and file complaints about, two primary issues: (1) disparate treatment, which involves allegations of favoritism; and (2) in response to a management-initiated action. Complaints regarding the second issue are more difficult to avoid, especially if you are taking action when appropriate. To some extent, they are the cost of doing business. The best way to handle these types of complaints is to make sure that you have a solid rationale for your actions, and that you apply your systems reliably and have good documentation, in the manner described earlier in this book.

Complaints involving disparate treatment/favoritism are more far-reaching, as they are not as individualized as complaints involving management-initiated actions. They tend to involve more employees and to be more destructive, since they go to the very heart of the way management conducts itself. When employees believe that management is treating one or more people differently from others, their antennas immediately go up, and they tend to view future management actions through the prisms of race, sex, national origin, and so on.

That is why it is so important to treat people in a fair and consistent manner. If you don't, people will not trust you, and they will conclude that there are ulterior motives for your actions. At that point, they will believe you are discriminating against them and will simply go underground with their complaints, or, in some cases, formally file EEO complaints against you. Either way, you lose, as these instances illustrate.

1. A newly hired white male division chief convinced a young, attractive white female from his former office to come and work for him at his new office. Roughly two-thirds of the employees at the new office were minorities. Upon her arrival, the division chief treated her differently from the other employees by frequently conferring with her and by giving her a series of special assignments. As time went by, she began spending more and more time with him in his office.

Everyone noticed their relationship, and people clearly resented it. His supervisors noticed it, too, and warned him to be careful. Although no one filed a formal complaint, it was a frequent topic of the gossip mill, and their relationship became well known across the country. By treating this employee so differently, the division chief lost some credibility with his employees, his supervisors, and within the entire organization. Moreover, every time that female employee was up for a promotion, the organization was in a precarious position, because it would have been difficult to defend a discrimination complaint had she been selected and a minority and/or a male been nonselected.

2. Someone I knew was out of work and was looking for a job. Since we were recruiting for more than 40 people, I told him about our vacancies and encouraged him to apply through the normal channels. Eventually he was selected and began working for our organization.

Quickly, word got out that we knew each other. People assumed that because I knew him and he was a white male like me, I would push him ahead of others. The fact that we both took the same vanpool, along with two other employees, probably contributed to that perception.

I advised him that for both of our sakes, as well as for the sake of the office, I was not going to talk to him unless I had a legitimate business reason to do so. Even on the van pool, I did not talk to him. (I rarely talked to the other employees van pool, either.) Although he was upset that I seemed to cut him off, I knew that it was extremely important that there be no appearance of favoritism or impropriety. He needed to stand on his own two feet, and I wanted everyone to see that I would treat each employee in the same manner, whether I had a personal relationship with him or not.

Very quickly, employees could see that this individual was not receiving special treatment. In fact, sometimes he actually complained to his co-workers that I was not speaking to him enough. The point was made, our relationship ceased being a topic of interest, and I had defused a potentially difficult issue that could have ultimately led to one or more EEO complaints being filed.

EEO Issues Involving the Disabled

Another somewhat more narrow EEO issue that often develops involves reasonable accommodation of the handicapped. In general, the Americans with Disabilities Act requires employers to provide reasonable accommodation to qualified individuals with disabilities so that they can enjoy the benefits and privileges of employment equal to those enjoyed by similarly situated employees without disabilities.

Organizations are required to provide reasonable accommodation for known physical or mental limitations of qualified employees and applicants, unless to do so would cause undue hardship. Since government organizations usually have extensive affirmative action plans, which include the handicapped, they usually have quite a few handicapped individuals on the rolls, and this can cause some interesting challenges.

I have worked with blind employees, the hearing impaired, people in wheelchairs, and people with serious diseases such as AIDS or multiple sclerosis. We worked closely with these individuals, identified their needs, and usually came up with a solution that was satisfactory to all. To illustrate some of the issues, here are some occurrences from my own experience.

1. Our organization was employing two blind people: One served as a customer contact representative, while the other one was a typist. We gave the contact representative a voice-activated computer that provided him with enough oral information to answer telephonic questions from the public. The typist simply transcribed dictated information using a customized word processor. Both of them have been productive employees for many years.

2. Due to the cost of living in southern California, one of my predecessors hired about 20 hearing-impaired clerks. The rationale was that these individuals were more likely to be satisfied with clerical positions and would stay with the organization for the long term.

However, communicating with these individuals is not easy, because they seem to process information and instructions differently from other employees. Accordingly, the organization hired a full-time translator to address this issue. Moreover, a number of individuals received extensive training in sign language, which helped foster communication with this group. Although communication will always be a challenge, most of these individuals remained with the organization for at least 10 years and were considered to be at least fully satisfactory.

3. An experienced and highly skilled employee developed a disease that made it impossible for her to come to work. We were able to reengineer her job and allow her to work at home on a full-time basis. As part of the arrangement, we had an employee who lived nearby both deliver and pick up her work on a weekly basis. This arrangement has worked well for many years.

Dealing with people who have employment handicaps has not been particularly difficult, especially when they bring it to your attention when they are first employed or at the onset of their condition. Under these circumstances, the employee is usually up front with you, and you know exactly what you are dealing with. At that point, the best thing to do is to (1) ask for medical information that documents the employee's condition, including a statement of the employee's limitations, if any; and (2) determine if the employee is requesting reasonable accommodation. Once you have this information, in most cases you can reach a meeting of the minds and accommodate the employee's condition.

Problems usually develop in this area when people try to use reasonable accommodation as a crutch, in order to insulate themselves from a prospective personnel action. It's amazing how often people suddenly claim that they have an employment handicap *after* management initiates action in response to misconduct or poor performance. At that point, it seems that almost every employee is handicapped.

In these situations, you still need to take the same approach described earlier (ask for written medical evidence articulating the condition, the employee's limitations, and the request for reasonable accommodation). However, under these circumstances, you need to examine the request with a more jaundiced eye.

The first thing you need to determine is if the employee is truly handicapped. Under the law,[2] an individual with a disability has (1) a physical or mental impairment that substantially limits one or more of the person's major life activities; (2)

has a record of such an impairment; or (3) is regarded as having such an impairment. A major life activity is a function that the average person in the general
population can perform with little or no difficulty. Major life activities include activities such as caring for oneself, seeing, hearing, walking, breathing, speaking,
learning, sitting, standing, lifting, reaching, and working.

In many cases, I have found that an individual claiming to be handicapped
does not meet this definition. If she does not, you have no legal obligation to accommodate her. However, I would urge you to consider what the person is requesting,
since it may still be reasonable and appropriate to grant the request. Moreover, if it
makes sense and you do grant the request, if you have to take action against that
individual at a later date, a third party is more likely to conclude that you are a fair
person and sustain your action.

If you conclude that the person is indeed handicapped, you should next consider the person's limitations, along with any requests for reasonable accommodation. However, understand that being handicapped is no excuse for misconduct.
Moreover, being handicapped does not require you to lower the performance standards of an employee's position, since an individual with a disability must be able
to perform the essential functions of a position with or without reasonable accommodation.

By asking the employee to submit written medical evidence and to place her
request for reasonable accommodation in writing, you will pin down the issues and
prevent the ground from constantly shifting under your feet. Moreover, you will
know what you are dealing with and will be able to react accordingly. In many
cases, you will find that while the employee may technically have a handicap, she
will not be able to articulate any reasonable accommodation. For example, we once
disciplined a high-level supervisor for misconduct. Basically, he had been negligent
in dealing with certain key issues, and we needed to send him a strong message. He
reacted very emotionally to the disciplinary action, and for the first time in his
career, he took several weeks of sick leave.

When he returned from leave, he produced a doctor's statement that indicated
he was under a great deal of stress as a result of management's alleged harassment.
His doctor indicated that he needed to work in a less stressful environment, and he
requested as a reasonable accommodation that we withdraw the disciplinary action.

The first thing I noticed was that the doctor's statement was signed by the same
doctor that other employees went to whenever they wanted a sick leave note to help
their work situation. Unfortunately, it is a fact of life that you can always find a
doctor willing to help you out at work.

Anyway, it did not appear that the doctor's statement demonstrated that this individual was indeed handicapped. Moreover, even if he were handicapped, it would not be reasonable to guarantee a high-level supervisor a low-stress environment. Finally, since the disciplinary action apparently created the stress, and since the Disabilities Act and the Rehabilitation Act did not insulate him from management action due to misconduct, I concluded that it would not be reasonable to withdraw the disciplinary action. Eventually, we assigned this individual to a nonsupervisory position, which he held until his retirement.

In another instance, we discovered that one of our employees had been engaging in misconduct both with our employees and with outside individuals. We therefore suspended him for two weeks.

As a result of these actions, he became seriously depressed, and he provided a doctor's statement to support his contention. He also filed an EEO complaint against management, alleging, in part, that he was being discriminated against based on several handicaps, one of which was depression.

There was no doubt that he had become depressed, so I detailed him to another job in our organization. That did not work, as he remained depressed and was unable to concentrate on his job. I then decided that the right thing to do was to detail him to another agency that needed the help. This would give him a change of scenery and place him in a low-grade, low-stress job, giving him the chance to recover. He remained on the rolls of my agency at his previous grade pay.

After several months, we instructed him to return to duty with our organization, as we needed someone to do the work of his regular position. He refused, and submitted a doctor's note stating that the only way he could work was if he remained in the job to which he was detailed in a stress-free environment. Obviously, I could not in good conscience allow him to continue on my rolls for an indefinite period, working for another agency at a much lower grade, while receiving the same pay. Therefore, I denied his request and again ordered him to return to duty. At that point, I was confident that I could withstand an EEO complaint because I could clearly demonstrate that I had treated him in a fair and reasonable manner, and he was unable to perform the duties of his position with or without accommodation. Eventually, this individual retired and his complaint was dismissed.

Sexual Harassment

Sexual harassment is one of the ugliest and most destructive forms of discrimination, both to the victim and to the organization. It needs to be dealt with promptly and firmly, in order to let everyone know that sexual harassment will not be tolerated.

The most effective approach, of course, is avoidance, and this is best accomplished through training and a strong policy of zero tolerance. However, if a complaint is filed, you need to deal with it quickly by gathering the facts and taking appropriate action. If the facts are unclear, which is often the case, you are always better off erring on the side of caution and protecting the complainant, rather than simply preserving the status quo until more information becomes available. This may entail a detail, reassignment, leave, or other action.

As in all personnel decisions, the key is to do the right thing for the right reasons, as the facts dictate. Although each situation is different, if you follow this approach, you will generally resolve the situation in a satisfactory manner. Let's look at a few real-life cases in point.

1. A counselor was supposed to be assisting a female client who had been sexually abused by others. However, he took advantage of the situation and sent her a sexually offensive photograph, which greatly upset her.

Management immediately transferred her to another counselor, gathered the facts, and then proposed the employee's removal. He eventually resigned.

2. A supervisor was charged with sexual harassment by one of his employees. She alleged that he had made some inappropriate remarks to her, while he denied making them. Since there were no witnesses to the incident, it was a classic "he said, she said" situation.

However, because two other women later came forward and verified that this supervisor had previously made inappropriate comments, we had no choice but to take appropriate action. We assigned the female employee to another supervisor, gave the original supervisor a written counseling, and provided him with remedial training on avoiding sexual harassment. We later decided that the organization would be better served if he were assigned to a nonsupervisory position.

3. We had another "he said, she said" situation. A female employee accused a male employee of an inappropriate action. It seemed out of character for the male employee to do this, but since he admitted to briefly doing it (he said it was to express his sympathy for her personal problems), I reluctantly disciplined him. Others pressured me to take stronger action, but I believed that this was the right thing to do under the circumstances.

Shortly thereafter, a different male employee presented evidence that the same female employee had sexually harassed him. We disciplined her for harassing him. Since that placed the earlier incident in a different light, I agreed to withdraw the disciplinary action from the male employee's permanent record if there were no more incidents of inappropriate action for the next year.

Strategies and Tactics

Rally the Workforce Around the Mission and the Metrics

In my experience, the more employees are focused on achieving the organization's goals and objectives, the less focused they will be on EEO issues. When people feel that the organization cares about its mission, and that its leaders are trying to do the right thing, the employees will tend to fall in line. They will give the organization the benefit of the doubt on many EEO issues, because they see that the organization is trying to accomplish something important, and that it is serious about living up to its core values. In short, when they feel they are part of a team, they will frequently place the team ahead of their own complaints and grievances.

That is why I try to rally the employees around the mission and the metrics. After all, government employees have a mission that is inherently noble. As long as we can leverage that mission by reminding the employees how important it is, and by providing them with real-life examples of how their efforts have made a difference, the vast majority of them will stay focused on what is important. That is not to say that we don't need to address any EEO issues that develop; we still have to. However, if the employees feel that you are doing the right thing, most of them will reciprocate in kind.

Besides reminding employees of the mission, we need to also let them know how the organization is actually doing. That is where the metrics come in. If the employees see tangible proof of how the organization is doing, and are told what is going well and what needs to improve, they will be in a good position to know where to direct their efforts. More importantly, they will be able to understand what the organization is doing and why, and will be less suspicious of acts that may harm them. Here's a story to illustrate the point.

I inherited an organization that many people believed was full of EEO problems. This perception was fostered in part by the fact that there were many discrimination complaints pending. My view was that the organization was not focused on its mission, resulting in terrible customer satisfaction. Moreover, it was unwilling to deal with personnel issues, leaving almost everyone frustrated on some level. The net result was that many discrimination complaints were being filed to express that frustration.

We adopted a strategy of plastering the walls with pictures, posters, flat-screen TVs with videos, and other media that celebrated our mission. We also posted information that tracked all of our key performance metrics, and trained our supervisors on how to deal with poor performers. Over time, people once again became proud of the mission, and our performance improved significantly. Visitors came to learn from us instead of to beat us up. As employee pride increased, employee dissatisfaction decreased, and our pending EEO complaints declined by 80 percent.

By contrast, if employees see that management is acting in its own best interests, instead of doing what is best for the government, people will conclude that it is every man for himself. They will quickly see that what counts is self-interest, and not the organization's interests. They will realize that personal agendas are valued more highly than the organization's agenda. When this happens, people do not trust management, and they look to protect themselves, with EEO complaints being one of the first tools that they turn to.

When I was a management trainee, for example, I was detailed to an organization that was having all sorts of problems. The organization was rudderless, and people were focused neither on the mission nor on the results. Headquarters was clearly unhappy with the way this organization was being managed, and the employees were miserable. Quickly, it became clear to me that the leader of this organization was more interested in his own well-being than in the welfare of the organization. More importantly, the employees saw things the same way.

For example, everyone believed that this individual was having an affair with his very attractive special assistant. They would spend hours together behind closed doors, after which she would leave his office with her clothes rumpled and her face flushed. The employees concluded that management was not serious about accomplishing its very important mission. Several people left, while others started complaining, and the situation continued to deteriorate until the leader was finally replaced.

Be Careful What You Say

When you are in management, every word you say takes on added meaning. You are in a position of power and have the ability to influence the lives of many people. Moreover, the very nature of your position will require you to make certain decisions that will cause some people to be unhappy (nonselections, disciplinary actions, denying incentive awards, etc.).

Given your responsibility, people will listen carefully to everything you have to say and will remember anything you say that could be interpreted as being discriminatory. That is why you have to take your time before speaking and must watch everything you say. After all, as a supervisor, you are representing the government. Everything you say can and will be used against you.

You can spend your entire career having one triumph after another, and it can all be forgotten after one slip of the tongue. The experience of Al Campanis may be familiar to many readers.

Al Campanis, an executive for the Los Angeles Dodgers baseball team, was appearing on the ABC News program *Nightline,* in a show coinciding with the 40th anniversary of Jackie Robinson's Major League Baseball debut. *Nightline* anchorman Ted Koppel asked him why, at the time, there had been few black managers and no black general managers in Major League Baseball. Campanis replied that blacks "may not have some of the necessities to be, let's say, a field manager, or, perhaps, a general manager" for these positions; later in the interview, he said that blacks are often poor swimmers "because they don't have the buoyancy." Two days later, he was fired.

The best advice I can give you is to learn to think before you speak. Although most government managers will not be fired for one slip of the tongue like Al Campanis was, an ill-considered or poorly phrased remark can come back to haunt you in many different ways. That is why you have to be extremely cautious in what you say. Avoid metaphors that could be interpreted in more than one way, and be extremely cautious before you tell any jokes that could be deemed offensive by someone else.

An Unfortunate Miscommunication. A recently hired division chief selected a new section chief. It was a difficult decision, as there were many candidates to choose from. He knew that the selection would probably be controversial, since several of the applicants had previously filed discrimination complaints and were likely to complain again if they were not selected.

After he made his selection, one of the people who were not selected asked to speak with him. This individual was about 60 years old and an African-American female. She wanted to know why she had not been selected, since she had more experience than the person who was selected. The division chief, knowing that this individual had a relatively poor record as a first-level supervisor, replied that he did not select her in part, "because of (her) old baggage." In his mind he was referring to her poor work history, but she interpreted his remark to mean that he did not select her because of her age.

She immediately filed a discrimination complaint, alleging that her nonselection was due to age discrimination. The complaint worked its way through the system, and she eventually prevailed. The primary justification for the decision was the division chief's use of the phrase "old baggage."

Don't Act in a Vacuum

Walking in an EEO minefield can be very lonely. You feel like you are under attack by both people who work for you and people from outside your immediate organization (EEO counselors, EEO investigators, etc.). That is why it is essential that whenever you take action that could lead to an EEO complaint, you first discuss it with an HR expert and upper management. While no one can anticipate which actions will lead to complaints and which ones will not, you should get into the habit of always bringing these key players into the mix.

First of all, you will get an unemotional perspective on the action you are planning to take, so you will have a better sense as to how the case will be viewed in the event that it goes to a third party. More importantly, if these people support your approach and a complaint is later filed, it no longer becomes your problem alone; it becomes their problem, too.

Developing political support in the EEO arena is extremely important, because the more support you have up front, the more the organization is likely to support you along the way. Conversely, if upper management feels blindsided by a complaint, it is more likely to feel slighted. If that happens, they may quickly undercut you, reverse the action you've taken, and settle the case. Once that happens, the employee will feel emboldened, other employees will feel that you do not have the support of upper management, and your position will be substantially weaker. Consider the following:

We suspended a female employee for insubordination. She filed an EEO complaint alleging that her supervisor took this action because she was an Asian American. She also turned up the political heat by writing letters of complaint to the highest officials in our organization as well as to several congressmen.

Since I was well aware of this case before the employee had been disciplined, and supported the action, I told her supervisor that she had my full support, she should stay the course, and she should let me handle the outside world. Naturally, this made her feel a lot better.

I kept my boss in the loop at every step and carefully responded to inquiries from the officials the employee had written to, and shortly thereafter, the hullabaloo died down. The employee continued to be a problem. We proposed her removal and eventually settled her EEO complaint by allowing her to resign.

To illustrate further, over a period of several years, many people complained about a fellow director, alleging that he was abusing his power, but he always denied everything. Over time, the people in Washington began to lose confidence in him, because they felt that he was not being honest with them.

Eventually, a female employee filed a sexual harassment complaint against him, alleging that he had made inappropriate remarks to her. Since the powers that be no longer trusted this individual, they immediately placed him on administrative leave. I was detailed to his position as acting director and quickly concluded that (1) he had been abusing his power for quite some time; and (2) the sexual harassment charge was somewhat questionable, since it involved a "he said, she said" situation, and his version seemed plausible. However, because this individual had lost political support within the organization, a decision was made that he had to go. His supervisor proposed his removal, and he eventually retired.

Make Sure Your Supervisors Are Sensitive to Their EEO Responsibilities

Although you may occasionally deal with an EEO complaint involving two nonsupervisors, especially when it comes to allegations of sexual harassment, most complaints are filed against management. This is because they are generally filed in response to a management action (e.g., disciplinary action) or nonaction (e.g., nonselection).

One of the keys to establishing a good EEO climate and to avoiding discrimination complaints is to ensure that your supervisors are well trained in EEO and are sensitive to their responsibilities. Training doesn't simply mean one EEO class for each supervisor. That simply won't cut it. The supervisors need periodic training from a variety of sources in order to ensure that they can successfully deal with the wide variety of issues that they are likely to encounter.

In my experience, this means classes, videos, and reading materials, as well as periodic one-on-one mentoring from an expert in the field. While this may seem like a painfully expensive investment, in urban areas of the country and in other locations where people are more likely to file complaints, this investment will clearly pay off through complaint avoidance and resolution.

Given my background, I also personally gave a wide variety of training classes to my subordinate supervisors. I wanted them to understand the underlying HRM strategies for dealing with EEO issues, and to have the opportunity to apply these strategies in the classroom using down-to-earth, real-world examples. I also wanted them to discuss these issues with their fellow supervisors so they could not only learn from me, but also learn from each other's experiences. I would then supplement this training by periodically walking around and trying to address their day-to-day questions, so they would have a good understanding as to how everything fit together. Lastly, I spent a lot of time developing my HRM staff so they would provide a consistent message to the supervisors.

However, sometimes all of the training in the world is not enough. Sometimes, you simply don't have the right supervisor in the position. If that happens, you need to replace that supervisor.

An African-American female once came up to my office and complained to me that she was "sick and tired of seeing an African-American accused of stealing every time something is missing." I asked her what she was talking about, and she told me that her assistant division chief told her that someone had seen her stealing some old carpet tiles from the work area.

This seemed like an odd accusation to me, since I couldn't imagine why someone would want to steal a few old carpet tiles. Anyway, when the assistant division chief arrived, he told me that another employee had told the African-American female's supervisor that he had seen her steal the carpet tiles. When I asked for the name of the witness, the assistant division chief was unable to provide it to me, since the witness had allegedly shared this information with the supervisor under a strict pledge of confidence. I then asked why the supervisor, who was white, had not confronted the African-American female with the allegation of theft. She replied that she felt uncomfortable because the employee had previously charged her with discrimination.

At this point, I became highly suspicious and instructed the assistant division chief to bring the supervisor up to see me. She repeated the same story to me and refused to give me the name of the alleged witness, arguing that she had given him a pledge of confidentiality. I advised her that she had placed the organization in a bad position by having her supervisor accuse a former EEO complainant of theft without supplying the witness's name to upper management. Accordingly, I told her that she had 24 hours to give me the name of the witness, or I would personally propose her removal for failure to cooperate in an official investigation.

The next day she came up to see me and confessed that there was no eyewitness and no theft. She had grown increasingly frustrated with the complaints of the African-American female, and she saw this as an opportunity to get back at her. Needless to say, we immediately removed her from her supervisory position.

How to Handle Filed Complaints

Stay Calm

When someone files a complaint against you, you need to remain calm. That is easier said than done, because an EEO complaint tends to be very personal. No one likes being accused of discrimination, and the natural tendency is to get mad and get even. However, that is a formula for disaster, because if you start acting from your heart instead of your head, you are bound to dig yourself a hole that you may not be able to climb out of. Simply relax, take a deep breath, and then plan your next move.

If it is any comfort to you, the vast majority of seasoned managers have probably had one or more complaints filed against them. Again, when you are willing to make the difficult decisions, the odds are that some people are going to respond with EEO complaints. You simply have to treat such complaints as the cost of doing business.

After you have collected yourself, consult with your HR advisor and senior management and analyze the complaint. Make sure you gather all of your records so they can give you a sense of how your case looks on paper. Also, make sure you never destroy any records, even if they could hurt your case. It's much better to lose a case than it is to be caught destroying records. In my experience, you are much more likely to lose your job for destroying records than you will be if you do not win an EEO case.

An employee filed an EEO complaint alleging that he was removed from his position with our medical center because he used to be enrolled in its drug rehabilitation program, and that we held this against him. He argued that since no else who had gone through that program had ever been hired by the medical center, it proved that we were biased against people who had gone through the program.

We felt that his removal was for good cause, but we also felt that we should look into his allegation. Since we learned that another participant had been hired by our organization, we confidently went forward, defended our actions, and ultimately prevailed.

By staying calm, gathering the facts, and dispassionately analyzing his arguments, we were able to make the right choice regarding this case.

Settle Cases Where Appropriate

You may be surprised to learn that sometimes the complainant is right. If you come to this conclusion, sit down with the complainant, discuss the issues, and try to resolve them right then and there. There is no shame in granting relief where relief should be granted. That is simply the right thing to do. Moreover, you'll save the government a heck of a lot of time, energy, and money by resolving the inevitable at this stage of the game.

One complaint I encountered involved an Asian-American female who threatened to file a discrimination complaint about a display we had regarding the history

of America's wars. Specifically, it involved an identification card that had been re-
covered from the Vietnam War. The card showed a picture of a young Vietnamese
female and was accompanied by a placard which indicated, "She may have been a
prostitute."

The employee was offended because she felt the placard stereotyped all Asian
females as being prostitutes. I did not see it that way, nor did others, but I decided
that this was not a battle worth fighting. After all, the person who wrote the placard
had no firsthand knowledge that the Vietnamese woman portrayed in the picture
had been a prostitute; it was mere speculation on his part. Accordingly, we changed
the placard to indicate that she was simply a young Vietnamese female, and this
resolved the complaint. The government saved a lot of money by not having to
process the complaint, and the revised placard was actually more accurate than the
original.

When a complaint is first filed, that may also be a good time to try alternate
dispute resolution (ADR). ADR is a group of processes that provide alternative ways
for resolving disputes.

Perhaps the most popular approach is to use a mediator. A mediator is a
trained neutral third party that assists the disputing parties to find an acceptable
solution. Mediation focuses on the future, not on the past, and does not assess any
blame. It tries to get the parties to talk to each other in a constructive manner and
to uncover any hidden agendas. If there is a meeting of the minds, a settlement
agreement is usually crafted.

In my experience, ADR is far less painful than the normal complaints process,
and is certainly cheaper for the government, as long as it is not abused.[3] If used
wisely, it is an excellent approach to resolving complaints.

Here's an actual ADR scenario. We employed a rehabilitation counselor who
spent a great deal of time in the field. He was a talented individual whose actions
came under increasing scrutiny. Over time, questions began to arise about his relationship with a contractor. As we looked into the matter, we felt there was at least
an appearance of impropriety in his actions. Moreover, this was not the first time
we had had concerns about this individual.

From our perspective, his documentation was poor, and he didn't follow the
procedures that had been set up to govern the payment of contracts. While we
didn't believe he was stealing any money, his division chief decided to propose the
counselor's removal because (1) there was an appearance of impropriety; (2) he had
failed to follow the proper procedures; and (3) a substantial amount of money was
involved. Even though the division chief knew he did not have a strong case on

paper, he issued the proposed removal because he thought it was the right thing to do and he wanted to bring the case to a head.

The employee immediately filed a complaint, and the parties agreed to try ADR. The employee, his representative, and several members of management sat down with a mediator to discuss the case. All the players were forced to lay their cards on the table, and the counselor admitted that he had made some serious mistakes. We eventually resolved the complaint by assigning him to a different position where he would be under much tighter supervision.

Pick Your Battles

Although settling is a good thing, you don't want to settle too much, or you will encourage more discrimination complaints. You need to weigh each case on its own merits, conduct a cost-benefit analysis, and make your decision accordingly. However, you also need to periodically take a step back and ask yourself, "What message am I sending to everyone else?"

If you never resolve a case, you may be too inflexible, which could mean that others will conclude that you are not interested in listening to their concerns. Under this scenario, people will use the discrimination complaints system as a means to get your attention, while recognizing that they may have to go through the entire process before you actually listen to them. This approach generally costs the government a lot of time and money, since each case involves many different steps before it is finally adjudicated.

Conversely, if you always resolve complaints, people may take the message that if they want something, all they need to do is file a complaint. That is because you have taught them that they will eventually get what they want because you do not have the strength to stand by your convictions.

I believe the best approach is a balanced one, whereby you settle cases that should be settled, but resist cases that should not be. Under this approach, people will see you as being fair but principled: willing to stand up for what you believe in, but also willing to admit when the organization is wrong. This approach will, at least to some extent, discourage the fence sitters from filing complaints, while at the same token encourage the people who have legitimate complaints to come forward and give you the opportunity to resolve their complaints before they become formalized. Since I've already discussed several cases that were settled, let's look at a couple of cases that I did not settle.

1. I took over an office where EEO complaints were a part of the culture. In fact, several people were frequent filers, but as time went by, others started to file,

too. For example, a male employee was not selected for a promotion, so he filed a discrimination complaint, alleging that he was not selected because of his age and race. As relief, he asked for a promotion and back pay.

From my perspective, he had competed with other people for this position and was not selected for legitimate, nondiscriminatory reasons. I could see that he was looking to make a fast buck based on the way that other complainants had been treated before I arrived. I therefore decided not to settle and allowed the case to go forward.

Later on, he made it known that he would be willing to settle his complaint for $1,000, but I refused. I didn't want to set a precedent and encourage even more complaints. Eventually, the case was dismissed, and this employee did not file any more complaints.

2. We removed an employee for multiple acts of misconduct, including insubordination. He was a strange individual who, before working for the government, had been convicted of a felony. Apparently, the selecting official at the time was aware of this information, but, for some unknown reason, had hired him anyway.

He apparently started off as a good employee, but as time went by, his behavior deteriorated, and we were forced to remove him. He responded with a lengthy discrimination complaint, alleging in part that we discriminated against him because of a mental condition that influenced his behavior, and demanding that he be reinstated to his former job. However, having a mental impairment is no excuse for bad behavior, since an organization cannot tolerate misconduct on the part of its employees. Moreover, we were extremely leery of rehiring him, given his criminal history.

We decided to resist his determined efforts to get his job back. The case went through the normal EEO process, and then went to court, where it was eventually dismissed.

Final Thoughts

Discrimination complaints can be painful to deal with, but they can also be managed effectively. The more you apply the principles, strategies, and tactics described earlier in this book, the fewer complaints you are likely to receive.

That being said, if you are doing your job properly, you will probably receive an EEO complaint from time to time. When that happens, take your time, don't overreact, gather your records, and consult with both your supervisor(s) and your HR advisor. However, don't be afraid of a complaint. The complainant is exercising the right to file a complaint, and your job at that point is to participate in the complaint process and try and resolve the complaint, if possible and appropriate.

On the one hand, if you treat a complaint as simply another part of the job—do not take it personally or react emotionally—you will be fine. Simply follow the process, try to do the right thing, and the outcome will take care of itself.

On the other hand, do not allow a complainant to intimidate you by continually filing discrimination complaints. You need to be very careful and separate any complaints that are filed from any action you plan to take. If you would have taken a specific performance or conduct-based action had a complaint not been filed, then take it. If you would not have taken the action but for the fact that the employee filed an EEO complaint, then by all means resist the temptation to retaliate against the employee and do not take the action. If you remember this simple rule, you will avoid the land mines that have ruined the careers of far too many management officials.

Key Points to Remember

- Learn to distinguish between those who feel they are victims of discrimination and those who merely seek to abuse the system.
- Look at things from the other person's perspective.
- Know your statistics.
- The best approach in discrimination, particularly sexual harassment, is prevention.

Notes

Chapter 1

1 Remarks by Vice President Al Gore, opening session of International Reinventing Government (REGO) Conference, Thursday, January 14, 1999.

2 The Freedom of Information Act, 5 U.S.C. § 552, as Amended by Public Law No. 104-231, 110 Stat. 3048. State and local governments are usually covered by a state version of the Freedom of Information Act.

3 *Measuring Difference Between Federal and Private Pay,* A Congressional Budget Office paper, November 2002.

4 *Comparing the Federal Employee Benefits with Those in the Private Sector,* A Congressional Budget Office Paper, August 1998.

5 Steven Malanga, "Government Pay, Benefits Soar," *Budget and Tax News* (February 1, 2006).

6 John L. Guerra, "Alternate Pay Systems Must Accompany Mission Redefinition," *Government Leader* (October 18, 2005).

7 "Feds Favor Easier Removal of Poor Performers," www.FedSmith.com.

8 Michael H. Cimini, "1982–97 State and Local Government Work Stoppages and Their Legal Background," *Compensation and Working Conditions* (Fall 1998).

9 www.kentlaw.edu/classes/mmalin/Public%20Sector%20Employment/chapter9.htm.

10 Hart-Teeter Research for the Partnership for Public Service, *Survey of Nonfederal Workers' Attitudes Toward Government Employment,* October 2002.

11 Paul Nowack, quoted by John Rossheim in *Working for the Government,* Monster.com.

12 It is much easier to move around within a particular segment of government (federal, state, or local) than it is between segments, because the promotion rules generally apply only to people working for that particular segment.

13 "Backgrounder on the Pendleton Act," *Basic Readings in U.S. Democracy,* http:// usinfo.state.gov/usa/infousa/facts/democrac/28.htm.

14 Ibid.

15 www.Governing.com, "Grading States," Congressional Quarterly, Inc.

16 David Osborne and Peter Plastrik, "Civil Action," *The Washington Post Magazine* (June 8, 1997), pp. 8–14.

17 Conducted under the direction of the Princeton Survey Research Group and led by Mary McIntosh between February 7 and June 1, 2001.

18 "Feds Favor Easier Removal of Poor Performers," FedSmith.com.

19 *Federal Supervisors and Strategic Human Resources Management,* U.S. Merit Systems Protection Board, June 1998.

Chapter 2

1 Dean Smith, D. Gerald, John Kilgo, and Roy Williams, *The Carolina Way: Leadership Lessons From a Life in Coaching* (New York: Penguin Books, 2004).

2 Paul Gustavson, "Designing Effective Work Systems for Greenfield Sites" (November/December 1988).

3 The management systems are (a) the technical systems (tasks, technology, and physical arrangements); (b) structural systems (how people are organized and what they are organized around); (c) decision-making and information systems (What decisions need to be made? What information is needed? How are decisions made?); (d) people systems (how you select, train, and promote people); (e) rewards systems (intrinsic and extrinsic rewards); and (f) renewal systems (How will the organization renew itself?). Gustavson, "Designing Effective Work Systems for Greenfield Sites."

4 Jack Welch and J. A. Byrne, *Jack: Straight from the Gut* (New York: Warner Books, 2001).

5 Ibid.

Chapter 3

1 The Ned Herrmann Brain Dominance Instrument was developed by Ned Herrmann while the manager of management education at GE's Crotonville Office.

2 Stewart Liff and Pamela A. Posey, D.B.A., *Seeing Is Believing: How the New Art of Visual Management Can Boost Performance Throughout Your Organization* (New York: AMACOM Books, 2004).

3 Tom Peters, *In Search of Excellence: Lessons from America's Best Run Companies* (New York: Warner Books, 1982).

4 Jennifer Newman and Darryl Grigg, "Saying Thanks at Work," *Vancouver Sun,* (March 22, 2004).

Chapter 4

1 In the federal government, a disciplinary action is an admonishment, reprimand, or suspension of 14 days or less. An adverse action is suspension of more than 14 days, a demotion, or a removal.

Chapter 6

1 For example, see Gerald H. Graham and Jeanne Unruh, "The Motivational Impact of Nonfinancial Employee Appreciation Practices on Medical Technologists," *Health Care Supervisor*, 8(3) (1990), pp. 9–17.

2 A business line division provides a service that is directly related to a government organization's mission (e.g., patient care, processing claims, investigating security clearances, collecting taxes, etc.).

Chapter 7

1 In May 2006, a VA employee took home a laptop computer that compromised the privacy of 26,000,000 veterans and over 1,000,000 active duty service members. The laptop has subsequently been found, and personal information apparently was not compromised.

2 Other factors also contributed to VHA's success, including a state-of-the-art medical records system, consolidation of operations, and so on.

3 Many government organizations have a "use or lose" policy. That is, you can carry over only a certain amount of vacation time from year to year. If you don't use the excess vacation time, you simply forfeit it.

Chapter 8

1 In many cases, certain issues are excluded from the grievance procedure. For example, selections for promotion may be excluded, as well as any other issues that the parties agree upon.

2 This statement is particularly applicable to the federal government, where unions cannot negotiate pay. However, the teachers' union, the police officers' union, and others are still strong because they can negotiate on far more issues, including pay, which makes the employees want to support them.

Chapter 9

1 The SMSA is composed of a core area containing a substantial population nucleus, together with adjacent communities having a high degree of economic and social

integration with that core. *U.S. Census Bureau, Population Division, Population Distribution Branch.* Last revised: June 7, 2005.

2   The Americans with Disabilities Act and similar state laws prohibit employers from discriminating against qualified individuals with disabilities. In 1992, the substantive employment standards of the Americans with Disabilities Act, 42 U.S.C. Section 12111, et seq., were made applicable to the federal government through the Rehabilitation Act.

3   I have seen instances where someone constantly wants to refer every issue to mediation. This can be very time consuming, since ADR involves a fair amount of preparation time and may require several long-drawn-out meetings. Under these circumstances, I would be reluctant to refer every issue to ADR.

Index